IMAGES of America

WHITE PLAINS IN THE 20TH CENTURY

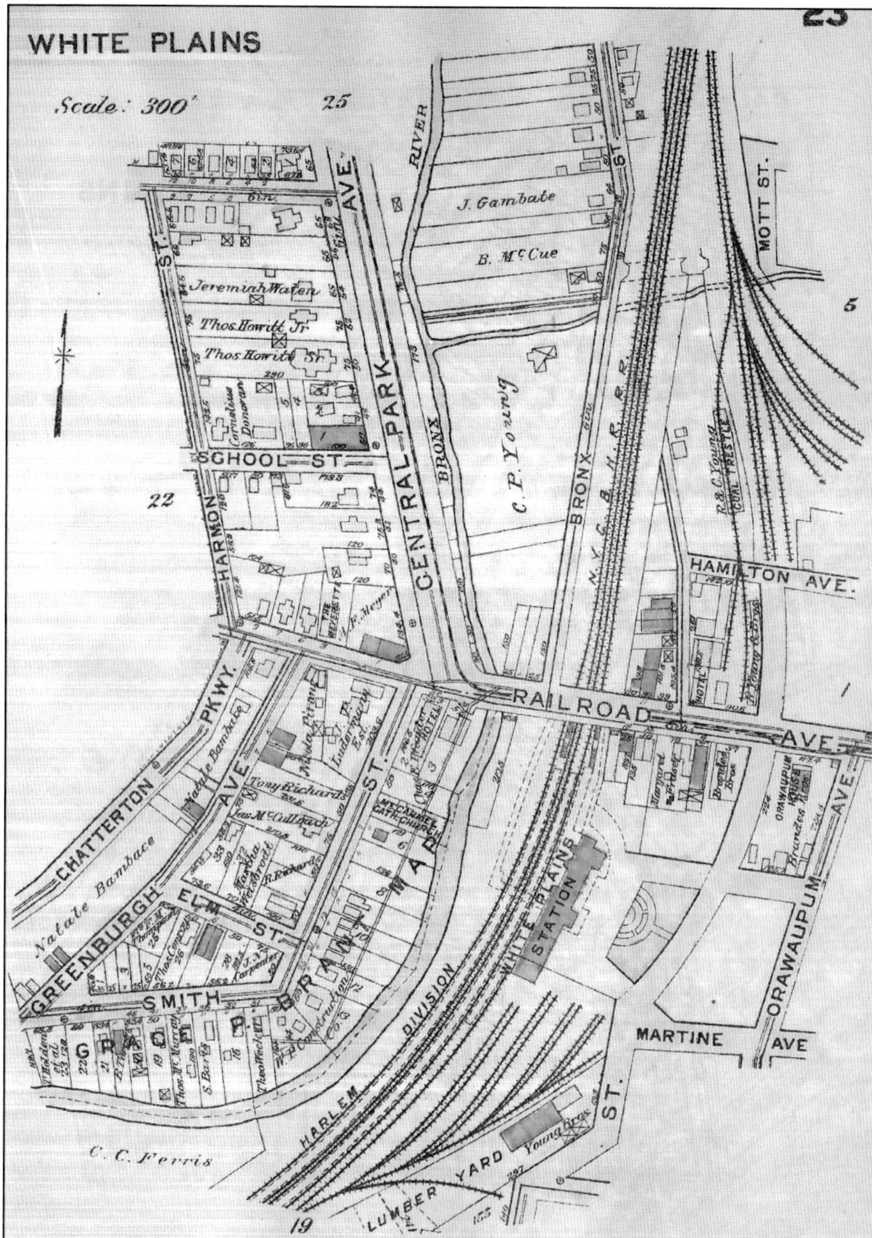

By the start of the 20th century, the Harlem Division of the New York Central Railroad was at the center of business life in White Plains, as seen in this 1914 "driving map" from G.W. Bromley and Company. Railroad Avenue would soon be renamed Main Street, and the Smith Street neighborhood would be eliminated to make way for the Bronx River Parkway. (WPCA.)

On the Cover: After World War II, White Plains hosted a victory parade on April 28, 1946. John Rosch was honorary chairman of the celebration at age 92 and was also the designer of the victory float. He created a scrapbook that included this photograph of city Girl Scouts marching near the White Plains Municipal Building and the Memorial Methodist Church on Main Street. (WPCA.)

IMAGES
of America

WHITE PLAINS IN THE 20TH CENTURY

Ben Himmelfarb and Elaine Massena

ARCADIA PUBLISHING

ISBN 978-1-4671-0383-1

Published by Arcadia Publishing
Charleston, South Carolina

Printed in the United States of America

Library of Congress Control Number: 2019932321

For all general information, please contact Arcadia Publishing:
Telephone 843-853-2070
Fax 843-853-0044
E-mail sales@arcadiapublishing.com
For customer service and orders:
Toll-Free 1-888-313-2665

Visit us on the Internet at www.arcadiapublishing.com

This book is dedicated to two people whose lives and work created the collections and knowledge from which we drew to create White Plains in the 20th Century: *John Rosch (1854–1949) and Renoda Hoffman (1909–2005). Each was passionate about collecting and preserving the history of White Plains, authored books on its history, and served as city historian.*

Contents

Acknowledgments

So many have contributed their help and expertise to the production of this book, but Elaine and Ben would especially like to recognize the following people: Brian Kenney, the director of the White Plains Public Library; Anne McPherson, clerk of the City of White Plains; archivists Jackie Graziano and Courtney Fallon from the Westchester County Archives; Patrick Raftery, the librarian for the Westchester County Historical Society; Tim Baird, the head of Adult Services, White Plains Public Library; Peter Kanze; and, of course, their spouses, Ralph Massena and Carolyn Fisher.

Elaine and Ben would also like to recognize all the patrons, researchers, historians, authors, genealogists, and community members whose use of the collections contributed to their knowledge base. Through assisting others with research, new stories were uncovered and a greater awareness of the depth of their collections was developed, for which they are grateful.

The images in this volume appear courtesy of various collections within the White Plains City Archives (WPCA) and the White Plains Public Library (WPPL), unless otherwise noted.

INTRODUCTION

White Plains, New York, is a medium-sized suburban city, located about 25 miles north of New York City, and it is the county seat of affluent Westchester County. White Plains is a center for shopping, education, health, business, and legal affairs with a daytime population estimated at 250,000. The official US census resident population for 2010 was 56,853.

On November 22, 1683, a group of New Englanders who had recently settled in Rye, New York, purchased 4,435 acres of land from the Weckquaskeck Indians. The Weckquaskeck called the land Quarropas, or "white marshes," because of the heavy fogs that enveloped the lowlands; for the settlers, the name became White Plains.

King George II granted a royal patent to 18 settlers in 1721. Houses were built along the Commons, which today we know as Tibbits Park. The Commons provided a recreational area, grazing for some animals, and was later a training ground for the militia.

White Plains became the seat of the Colonial government for the County of Westchester in 1759 when it replaced Westchester Town, which is located in the modern-day Bronx. Dr. Robert Graham donated land near the Commons in White Plains, and a new courthouse was built on the site of today's White Plains Armory.

On July 9, 1776, the New York Provincial Congress was meeting in the White Plains Courthouse, having left New York City because of advancing British troops. A messenger arrived from Philadelphia to deliver a copy of the Declaration of Independence that had been approved a few days earlier by the Continental Congress. The local body studied the document on the same day and adopted a resolution approving the Declaration of Independence and changing the name of their congress to the "Convention of Representatives of the STATE of New York," thus making White Plains the birthplace of New York State.

More revolutionary history took place on October 28, 1776, at the Battle of White Plains. The British, coming from the south, confronted the American troops at Chatterton Hill and forced their retreat across the Bronx River to Purdy or Dusenbury Hill. Gen. George Washington and his men held off the British in skirmishes for the next seven days, and finally the British returned to New York, denied a victory over the Americans. A British victory over the Americans at White Plains might have resulted in a very different ending to the war.

Having survived the Battle of White Plains, most of the village of White Plains, including the 1759 courthouse, was burned a few days later in a fire set by an American patriot. A new courthouse, reportedly in the same style as the incinerated one, was put up in 1787.

The population of White Plains grew slowly in the early days of the 19th century. Life was centered around the Commons, the "Village Street." With the coming of the railroad to White Plains in 1844, a period of growth began. The center of the village quickly shifted from the Village Street to the area near the railroad depot and close to the Bronx River. A new courthouse was built on the road to the depot, Railroad Avenue, in 1856, and in 1866, White Plains became incorporated as a village.

Early in the 20th century, the suburbanization of White Plains began. Real estate developers advertised the benefits of "healthy country living" for those who worked in New York City. By 1912, White Plains boasted two railroad lines as well as trolley service to other Westchester destinations. Railroad Avenue was renamed Main Street in 1914 at the time the streetlights were electrified, and the village celebrated the new "great white way." The following year, the governor approved the incorporation of White Plains as a city. The boundaries were expanded to include the Battle Hill section, which had previously been in the town of Greenburgh.

Residential and commercial construction was brisk in the 1920s. The latest county courthouse attracted new businesses to Main Street, and office buildings were needed to accommodate them. White Plains flourished. New schools were built as the population increased.

In the 1930s and 1940s, the business district began to shift again. B. Altman and Company opened its first suburban branch store at the corner of Mamaroneck Avenue and East Post Road in 1930. By the 1950s, part of nearby East Post Road was dubbed "Little Fifth Avenue" as other fashionable department and specialty stores located there. Back on Main Street, the Depression forced many smaller businesses to close. The housing in the downtown was aging, and in many cases, it was unsafe and prone to fires. This set the stage for the creation of the Housing Authority, building of the Winbrook complex, and eventually for urban renewal in the 1960s.

In the years following World War II, many sought homes in White Plains, and this included some large corporations. The Nestle Company was the first to relocate to the county seat in 1952. General Foods was welcomed to White Plains in 1954 when they moved from their New York City offices.

The ability to attract retail and corporate businesses to White Plains was due in large part to the construction of the Cross Westchester Expressway (Route I-287) in the late 1950s. Historian Marilyn E. Weigold called it "that six-lane ribbon of concrete linking the New York State and New England thruways."

Urban renewal changed the face of the downtown area between 1966 and 1980; 130 acres was redeveloped to facilitate growth of a modern central business district. Controversy surrounded the fate of the 1917 courthouse, which eventually fell to the wrecking ball in 1977. The 1980s saw growth out of the downtown onto what became known as the "Platinum Mile," to the east along Route I-287. The gleaming modern office buildings attracted major corporate offices.

White Plains was fortunate to have been the adopted home of artist and photographer John Rosch (1854–1949), who came to the village of White Plains in 1874. In 1928, Rosch donated to the city a series of 16 panels that he drew depicting the buildings that stood on Railroad Avenue in 1876. They still hang in the White Plains Municipal Building today.

Before his death, Rosch donated his collection of photographs and scrapbooks to the White Plains Public Library, and many pictures in the first half of the book are his. He also served as city historian from 1935 to 1942, was celebration chairman for the 1933 parade, designed all the historical floats and the souvenir program for that parade, and in 1946 designed the victory float for the celebration at the end of World War II.

Special mention should be made of the other person whose collection contributed greatly to the creation of this volume. Renoda Brown Hoffman (1909–2005) came to White Plains at an early age and became one of its strongest advocates for historic preservation and education. Hoffman served as city historian from 1970 until her death in 2005. She was a talented photographer who took thousands of pictures around White Plains beginning in the late 1950s. She created 49 volumes of newspaper clippings, thousands of index cards, and authored three books on the history of White Plains. The White Plains City Archives was born of her persistence to properly preserve and share the city's history. Together, the collections of the library and archives represent the largest, richest set of materials about White Plains history.

One

The 1900s

White Plains in the first decade of the 20th century was technically a village but well on its way to becoming a city. The population doubled in 10 years, with many new residents coming as part of immigration from Europe. The school system expanded, social services organizations grew, and the seeds of modern American society were planted. Immigrants—especially Italian immigrants, many who came to work as masons and laborers on large public works projects like the Kensico Dam—expanded the urban parts of White Plains.

The *Eastern State Journal* and *Daily Argus* were staples of Westchester's newspaper scene, with each representing a different political group. The YMCA had been founded in 1897 at old First Baptist Church on Mamaroneck Avenue and rapidly became the largest social service organization in the city, with operations in the rented Martine Homestead building by 1903. The Keeley Institute occupied a chunk of downtown real estate and brought people from all over the country who sought a cure for alcoholism and addiction. Established in 1893, White Plains Hospital moved to a large building on West Post Road, introduced a horse-drawn ambulance to the city, and opened a nursing school. In 1908, the White Plains Public Library moved to a Carnegie-funded building at the corner of Grand Street and Quarropas Street.

In 1903, there were just 746 telephones in a city of 8,500 people—that is one telephone for every 11 people. Even though White Plains was not a big city, it still had a varied commercial sector, with large stores like White's Shoe Store, that attracted business from across the county. The Hygeia Ice Plant near Silver Lake and Cushman's Bakery on Westmoreland Avenue were medium-sized industrial enterprises that provided products people no longer made at home. People who were driving north from New York in "motor parties" could stop at Tiffin Tea Shop on Main Street and enjoy an experience that people from White Plains now drive to places like Cold Spring and Millerton for. By the end of the first decade of the 20th century, White Plains was bursting at the seams, ready to transform into a city.

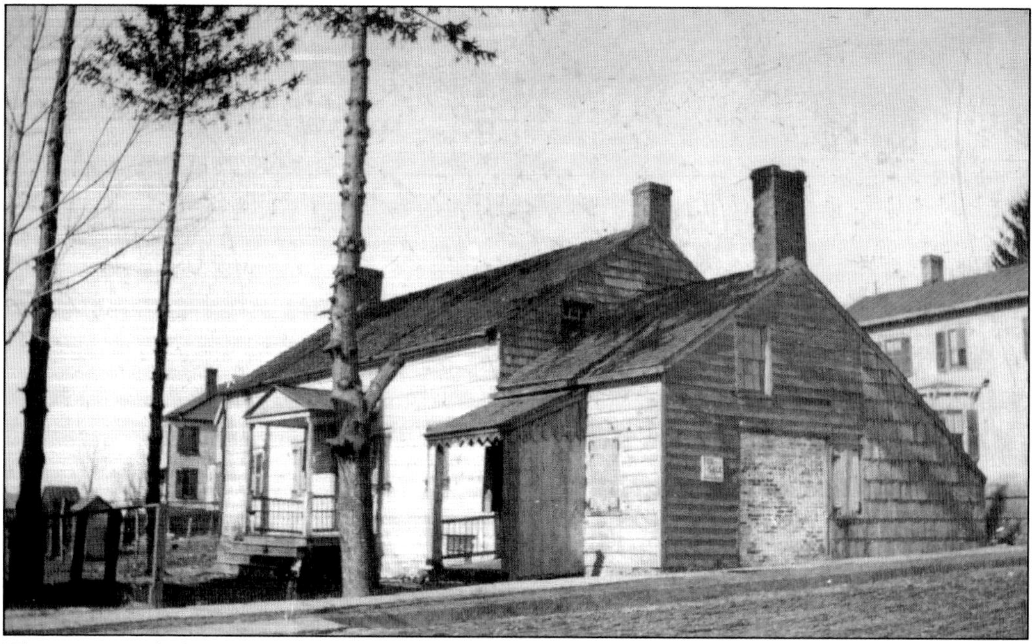

This picture of a home on Spring Street is from around 1900, labeled "My old homestead where I was born and married" and signed by Permelia Purdy Ferris. Now the home is known as the Jacob Purdy House, named for the third owner who served in the militia beginning in 1775. It has been shown through historical records to have been headquarters for Gen. George Washington during the Battle of White Plains in 1776 and again for a period of time in 1778. (WPCA.)

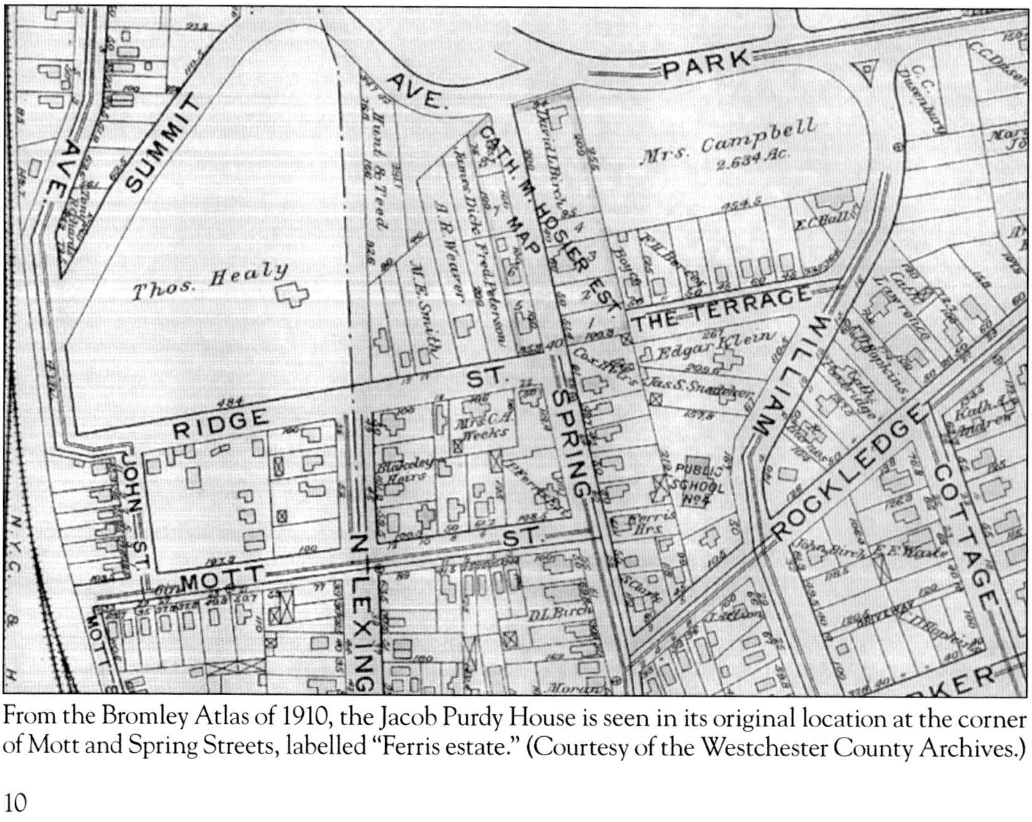

From the Bromley Atlas of 1910, the Jacob Purdy House is seen in its original location at the corner of Mott and Spring Streets, labelled "Ferris estate." (Courtesy of the Westchester County Archives.)

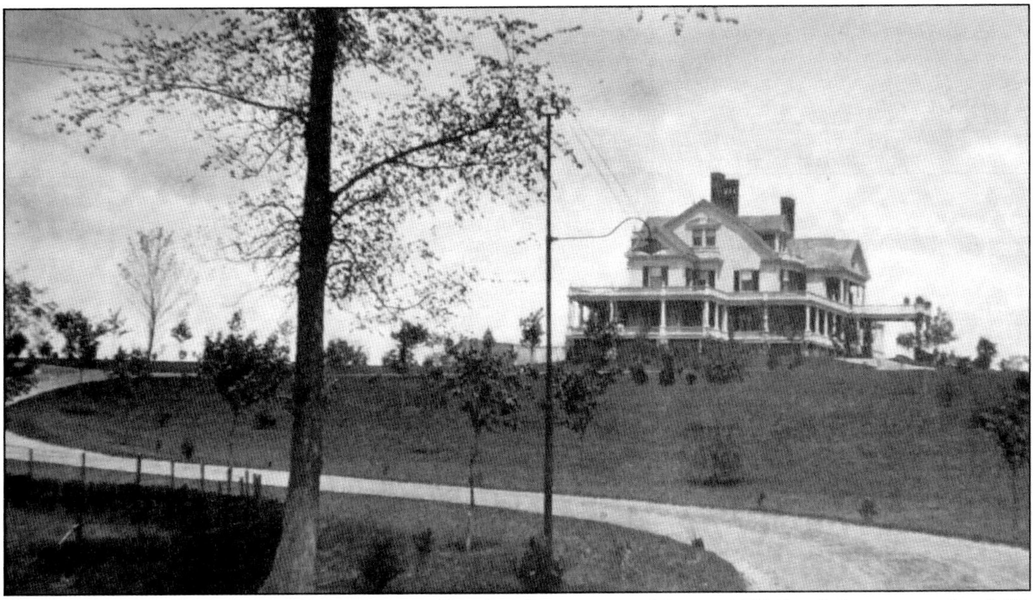

Today's Heatherbloom Road was originally the driveway to Howard Willets's home on the hill, built in 1902. From his home he could see both Long Island Sound and the Hudson River. Willets named his 300 acres of land Gedney Farm, in honor of the early owners, and he raised prize-winning cattle, dalmatians, and racehorses, including Heatherbloom, the jumper. In 1909, following a fire that destroyed his home, Willets made plans to subdivide his property and have a luxury hotel at the center of the residential development. This would become the Gedney Farm Hotel. (WPCA.)

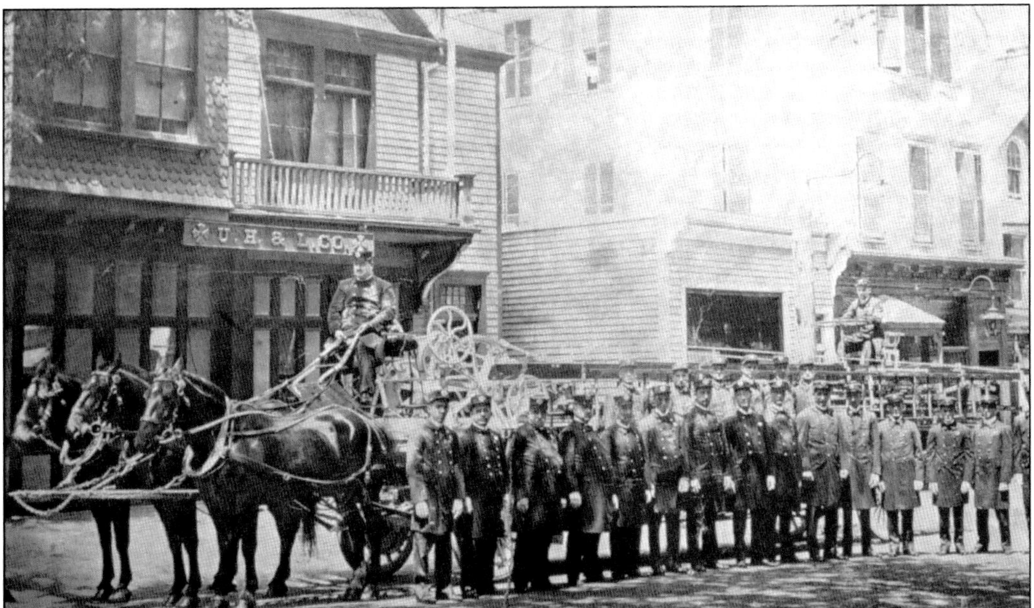

Until White Plains became a city in 1916, fire protection was entirely volunteer. Union Hook and Ladder Company was first founded in 1861. In 1908, the village bought a $5,500 American La France truck for the "Hooks." It was a white and gold aerial truck with a tiller that was pulled by three black horses. The company is posed here in front of its Grand Street firehouse, which was also the meeting place for the village board of trustees. (WPCA.)

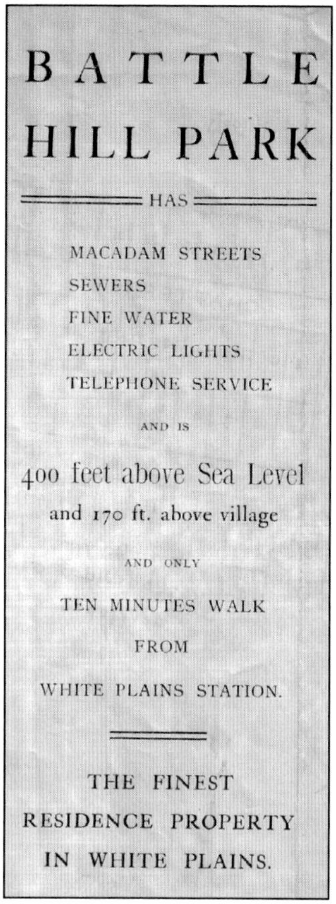

Before 1900, few homes dotted the historic hill that had been the site of the Revolutionary battle in White Plains. By 1905, however, developers were promoting several different sections of Battle Hill, and the "suburbanization" of White Plains had begun. The developers of the section known as Battle Hill Park pointed to the coming electrification of the Harlem railroad that served White Plains with 98 trains a day from Grand Central Station. (WPCA.)

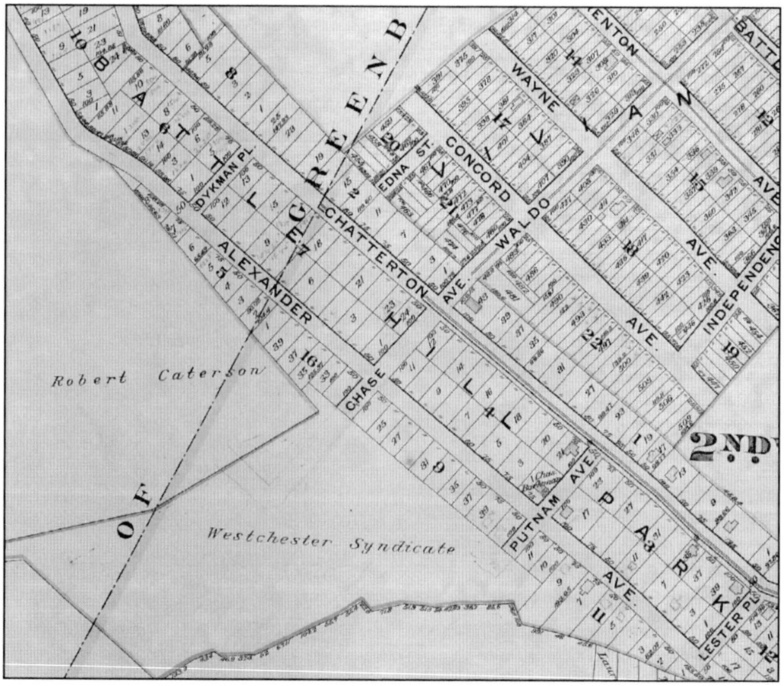

Maps like this 1910–1911 atlas were used by realtors. Try to find the area labeled "Battle Hill Park." Even though the neighborhood is shown with subdivisions and streets indicated, when the map was published in 1910–1911, Battle Hill Park had only a few houses in it—and most of the streets would not have been laid out yet, let alone paved! (Courtesy of the Westchester County Archives.)

During the Revolutionary War, George Washington's entrenchments in White Plains went over Purdy Hill, and where they crossed Broadway, commemorative events were held as early as 1844. A mortar was unearthed nearby, presumably left behind by retreating patriot forces in 1776. The Village Park Association and the Daughters of the American Revolution had the mortar mounted on a granite base with a bronze tablet. Dedication ceremonies took place on the 130th anniversary of the Battle of White Plains, October 30, 1906, at the North Broadway site. (WPCA.)

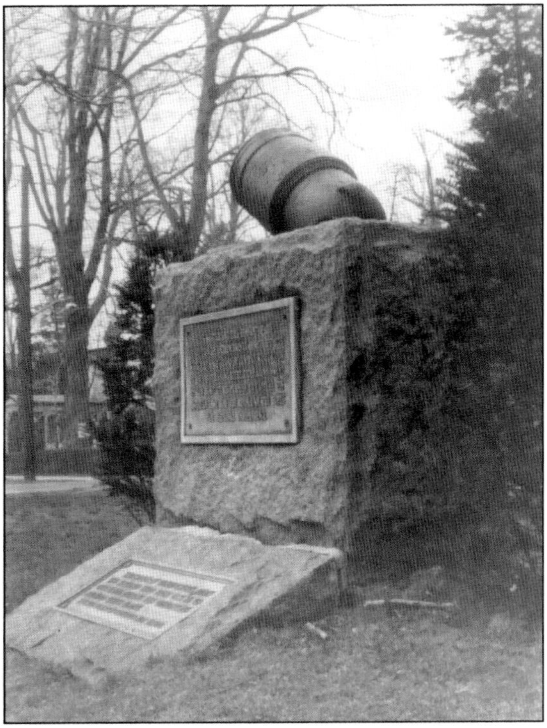

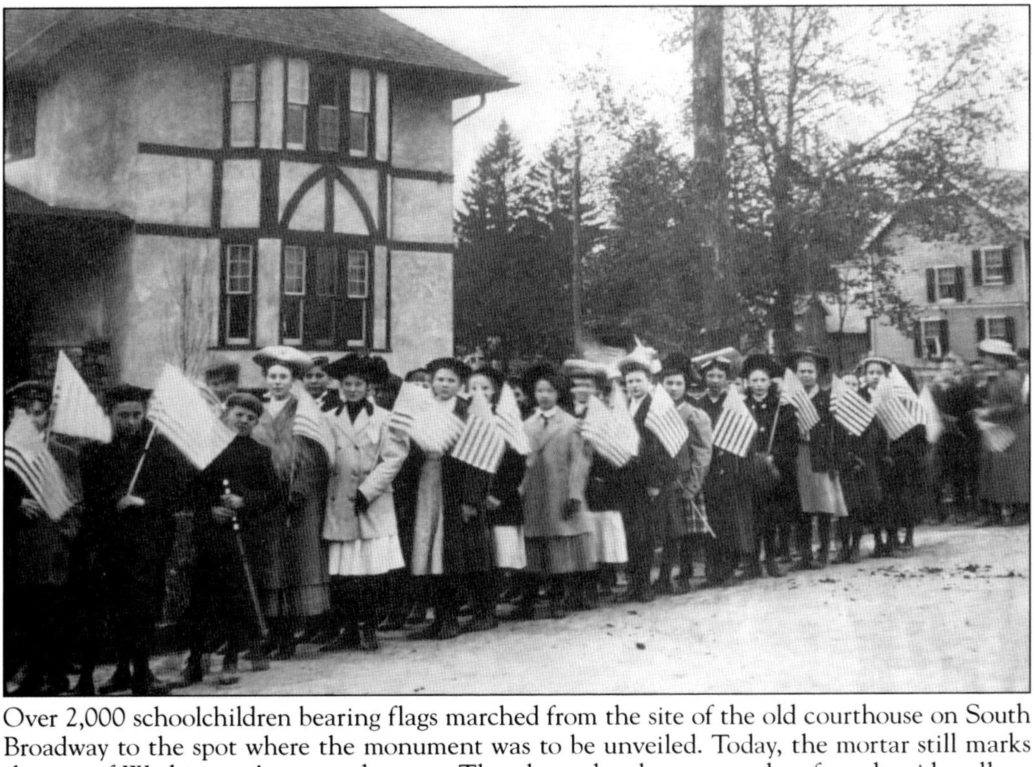

Over 2,000 schoolchildren bearing flags marched from the site of the old courthouse on South Broadway to the spot where the monument was to be unveiled. Today, the mortar still marks the site of Washington's entrenchments. The plaque has been moved to face the sidewalk so pedestrians can view it when passing by. (WPCA.)

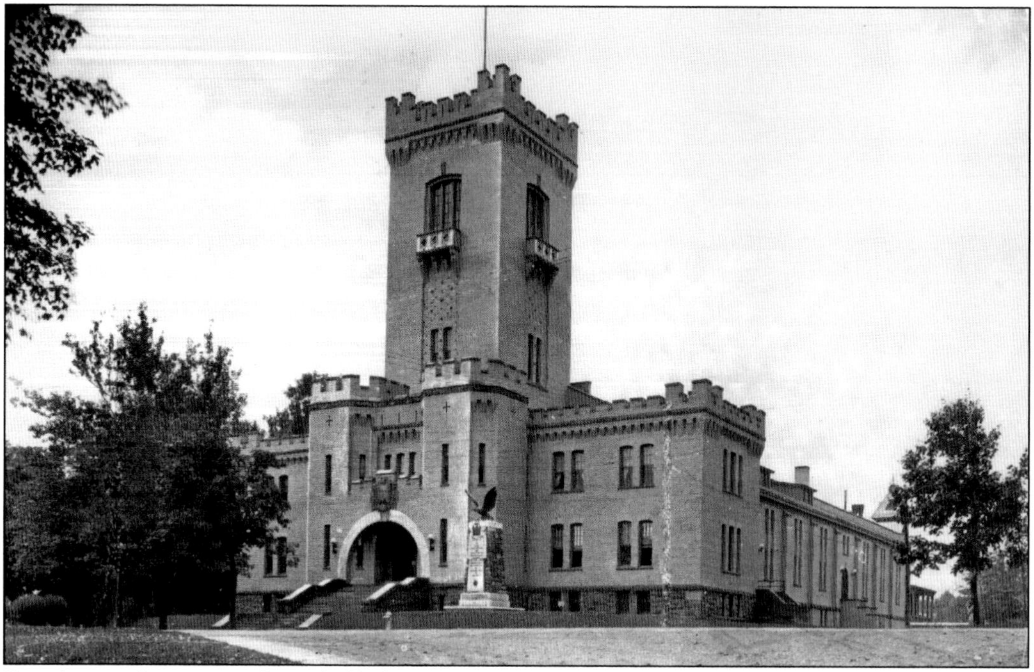

Standing at the corner of Mitchell Place and South Broadway, the White Plains Armory was built at a cost of $87,000 in 1909. Visible for several miles, the medieval tower was adapted for signaling. The famed Company L of the 11th Infantry Division was the first unit to make its home at the White Plains Armory. In 1985, after being added to the National Register of Historic Places, the White Plains Armory was converted to housing for seniors. (WPCA.)

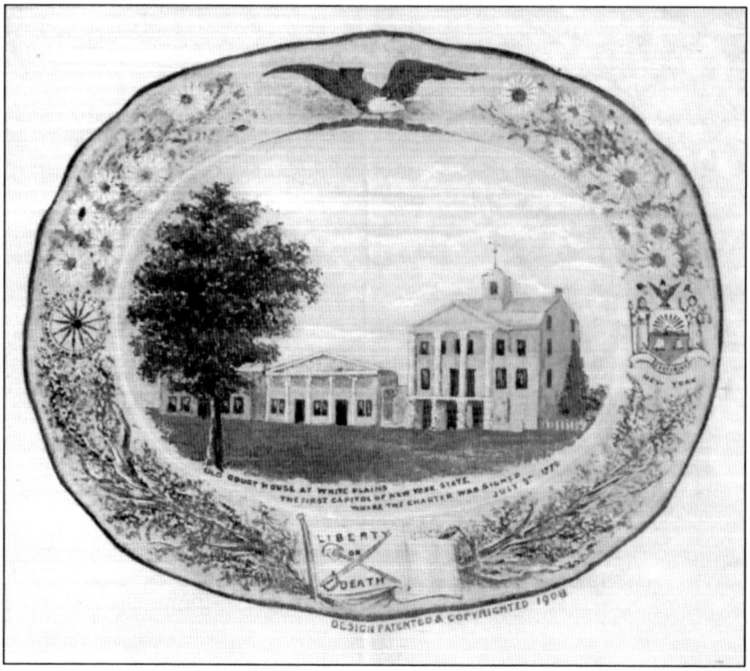

This platter was designed and produced by the newly formed White Plains Chapter of the Daughters of the American Revolution in 1908 as a means of raising funds. The chapter's goal was to place a memorial on the site of the birthplace of New York State, the first courthouse in White Plains. Platters were 10 inches by 14 inches, manufactured in England by Geo. F. Bassett and Co., and sold for $1.50. The DAR sold 500 platters. (WPCA.)

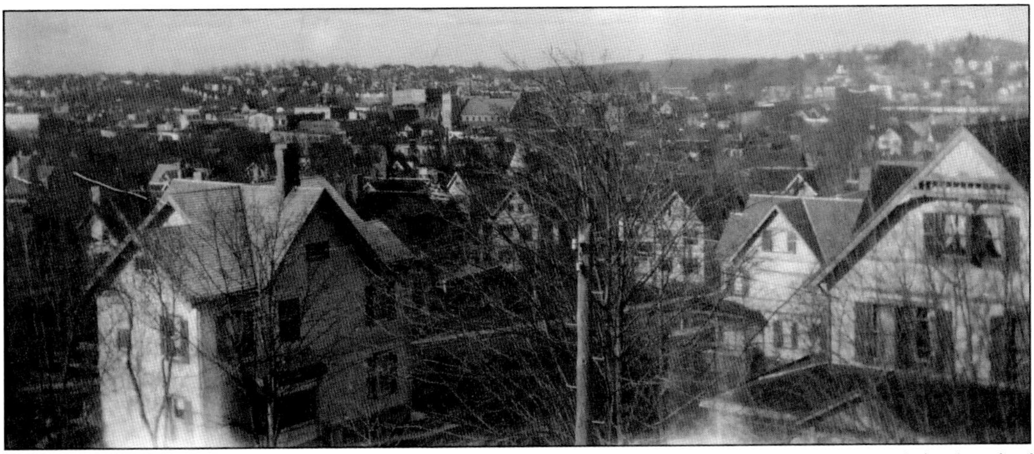

This view of White Plains in the first years of the 20th century gives a good sense of the level of development in White Plains at the time. The city was still a village, and even though there are a fair amount of industrial and commercial buildings in the downtown area, it was still years away from the tall structures and bustling traffic of the 1920s. The best way to orient the perspective of this picture, which was taken from the Park Avenue area of Purdy Hill, is to find St. John's Church near the middle. The hill on the right is Battle Hill, and the gentle rise in the distance on the left is Fisher Hill. (WPPL.)

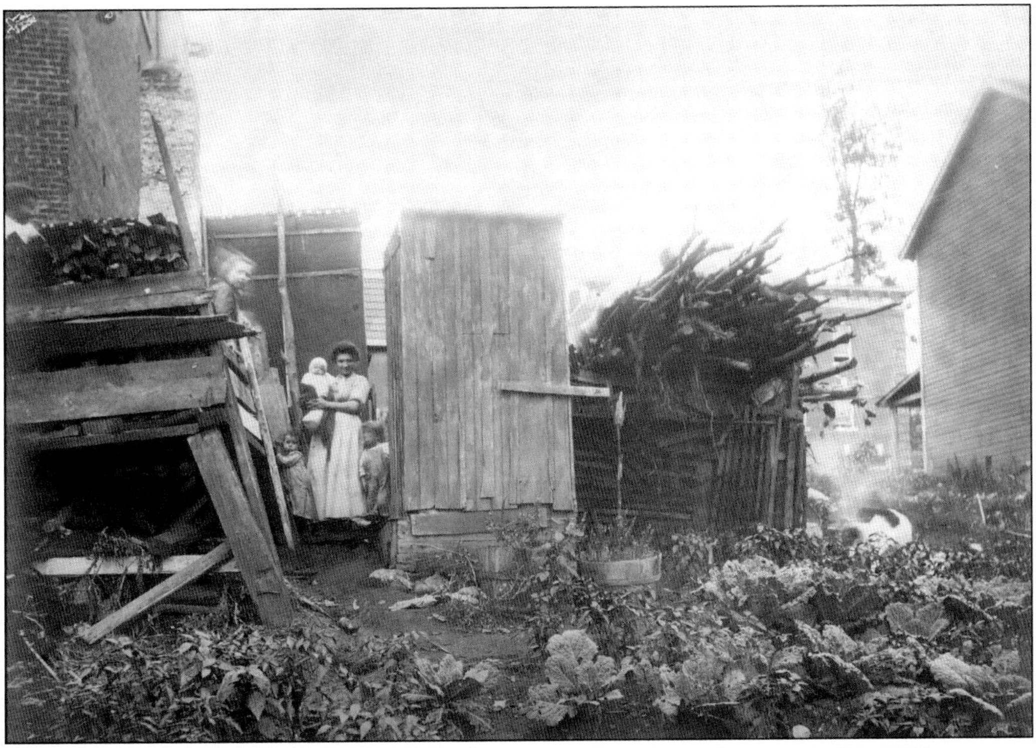

The YMCA in White Plains produced "Italians in an American Community" in 1913 to report on the status of the thousands of new immigrants who came to the city in the 1900s. There was concern about the conditions people lived in and anxiety about a new cultural and political element in the city. The YMCA hoped that the church and the school, along with the YMCA itself, would function as "a trinity of constructive forces in this community." (WPPL.)

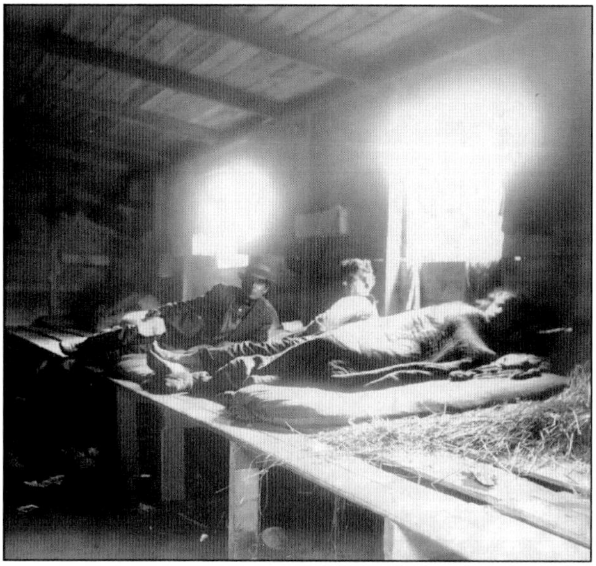

Charles Towson, the YMCA official who authored the report on "Italians in an American Community," worried that the harsh working and living conditions the recent immigrants faced would cause them to reject certain parts of American society. It was in bunkhouses like this one and work sites at places like Kensico Dam that workers would organize against their bosses, and this was what Towson feared. He felt that "ignorance of the true conditions leads them into a socialistic and even anarchistic spirit," and that it was the duty of organizations like the YMCA and churches to encourage them to embrace capitalism and the prevailing political systems in America. (WPPL.)

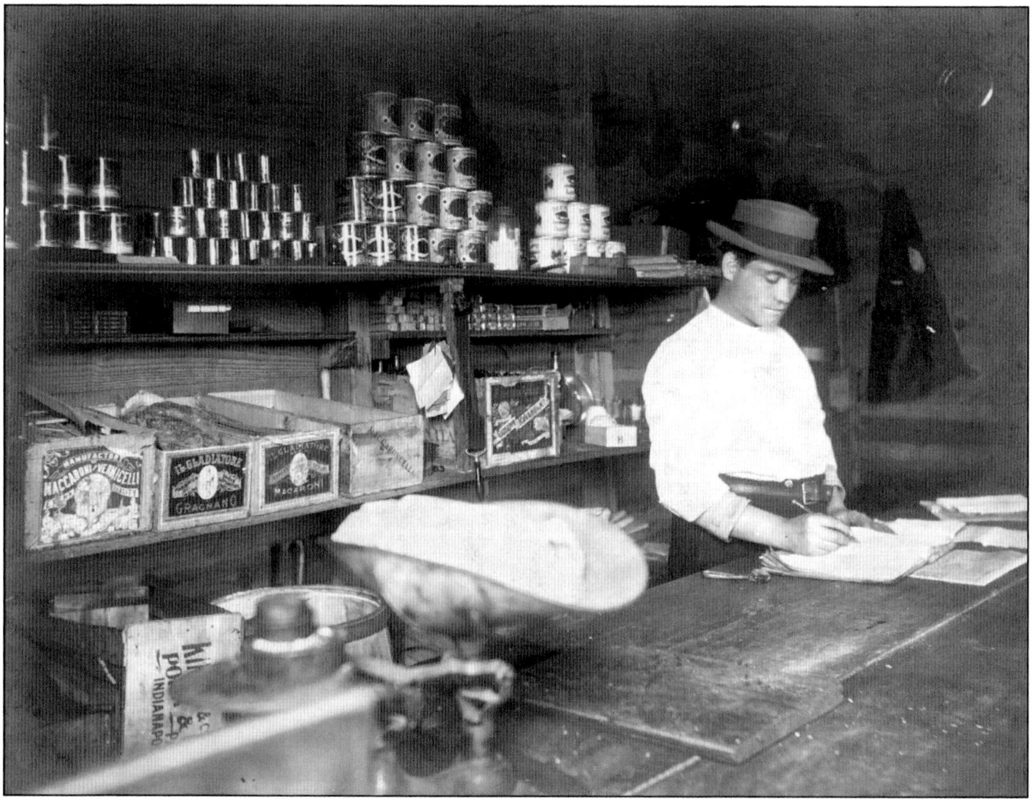

In a tone that would be recognizable to contemporary critics of immigration, the YMCA report said that the immigrants' "success and our safety requires that THEY BE AMERICANIZED." The commissary pictured above was located in North White Plains and probably served people who were working on construction projects in the area as masons, carpenters, and laborers. It is likely that working people gave some of their wages back to the boss, buying products at the commissary attached to the work site, regardless of the prices. (WPPL.)

Madison Avenue was changed to Ferris Avenue in 1907, and most of it remained unpaved until the 1910s. In 1907, around the time of this photograph, there were four grocers, three saloons, and one contractor listed in the city directory as operating out of Madison Avenue. On the right is Domenico Sestio's Choice Vegetables store. The flag hanging at left probably represents the site of a fraternal organization or club, which proliferated in the first years of the 20th century. (WPPL.)

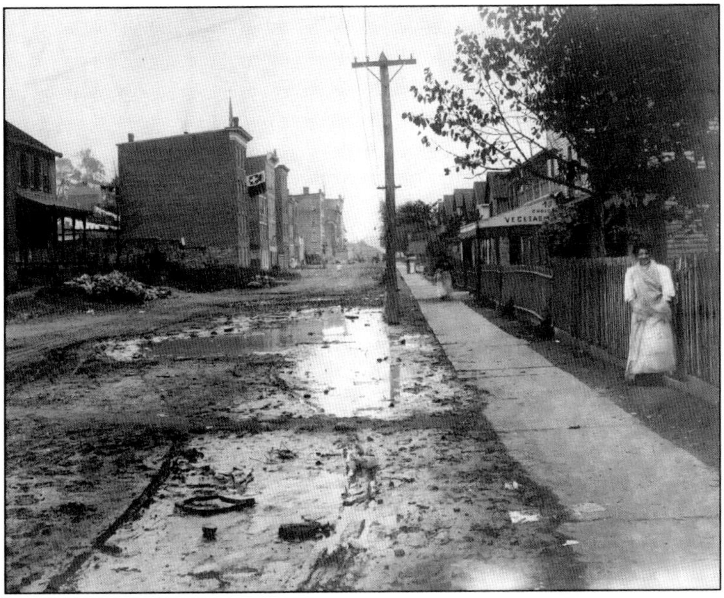

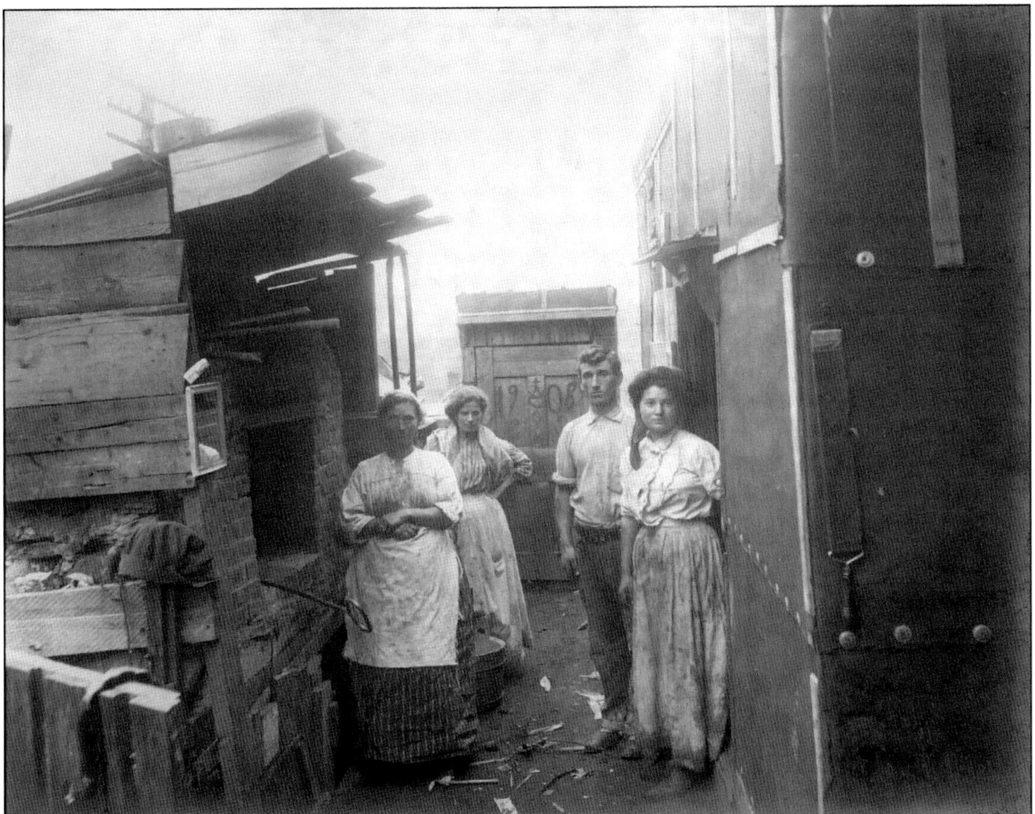

This image of people in a bakery along Madison/Ferris Avenue shows the ramshackle nature of development in the neighborhood. The people pictured may have been among the families described as living "in 3 rooms" in a building that housed as many as eight other families of various backgrounds—"Italians, Greeks, Negroes," according to the YMCA's report. (WPPL.)

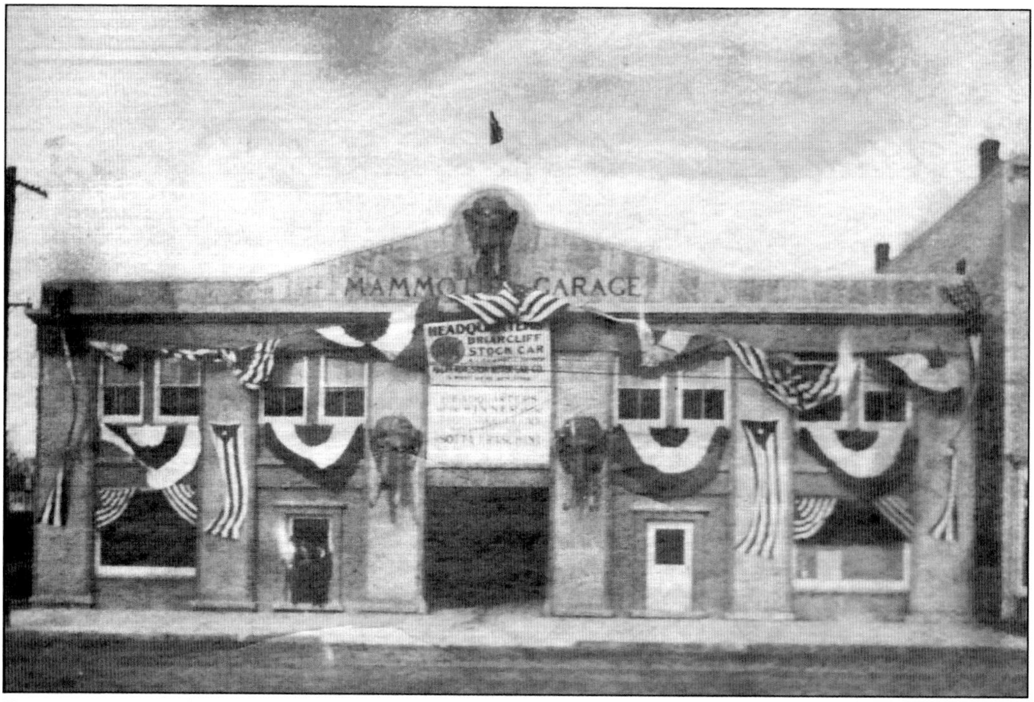

Between 1909 and 1913, over 100 automobiles were manufactured in White Plains on Mamaroneck Avenue. The G.J.G. Motor Car Company was founded by George Jacob Grossman, and autos were assembled in his 80-by-270-foot Mammoth Garage at 39 Mamaroneck Avenue. The facade was adorned with three cement wooly mammoth heads. Shown here, possibly decorated for its grand opening, the signs announce that the new garage was headquarters for the winning team in the Briarcliff Stock Car Race of April 1908. Production of the G.J.G. cars continued until mid-1913, when the facility was rented to a publishing firm. (Courtesy of the Grossman family.)

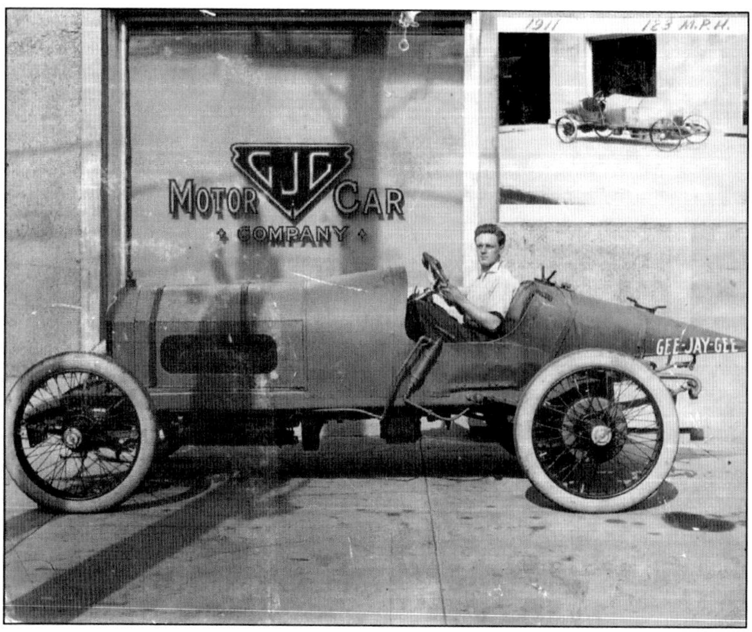

In addition to making touring cars and runabouts for the public, the Grossmans had an interest in race cars as well. Shown here is Wallace G. Grossman in 1911 in a car that he built at the Mammoth Garage. It reached a speed of 123 miles per hour at the Sheepshead Bay racetrack and may have been the same car that was driven by Paul Thebaud Jr. at the White Plains Fairgrounds in October 1912. (Courtesy of the Grossman family.)

Two

The 1910s

The second decade of the 20th century was when White Plains officially became a city. Prior, White Plains had actually been a village with a lot of unincorporated territory. The charter that divided the village into wards dated from 1878 and was outmoded for a place that had the distinction of being the biggest village in New York State. For the next 40 years, a series of lively and less-than-fair-and-free elections divided the leadership of the city between Republicans and Democrats. Its role as the center of the county was cemented with an increasingly modern transportation network of electrified trains, trolleys, and automobiles. In 1912, the New York, Westchester & Boston Railroad heralded a new identity for the county as a place of permanent residence for people whose business took them to the bigger cities of the East Coast. For all of the advancement, there were still about as many manufacturers and repairers of carriages as there were automobile garages during the 1910s.

The Business and Professional Men's Association of White Plains wrote that "no better argument for a community can be offered than the increase in population," and by the time they wrote that in 1914, the population had more than doubled since 1900. Electricity and gas utilities were developed throughout the village and city, with twice as many telephones present in homes and businesses as in the 1900s. A profusion of civic organizations took over the social life of the city, with at least one chapter of nearly every type of fraternal, professional, labor, athletic, and hobbyist organization.

The Red Cross organized in September 1914 and sent nearly one million surgical dressings to the war effort. The city was also extremely successful in raising millions of dollars for the war effort through liberty loan drives, thrift and war savings campaigns, and individual drives led by various community groups. After the war, a serious movement to create a memorial to soldiers and sailors banked on the continuation of public enthusiasm for collective enterprise. By 1920, White Plains was no longer an isolated village in a mostly rural county. Instead, it was a city that served as county seat and conduit between New York City and the Hudson Valley.

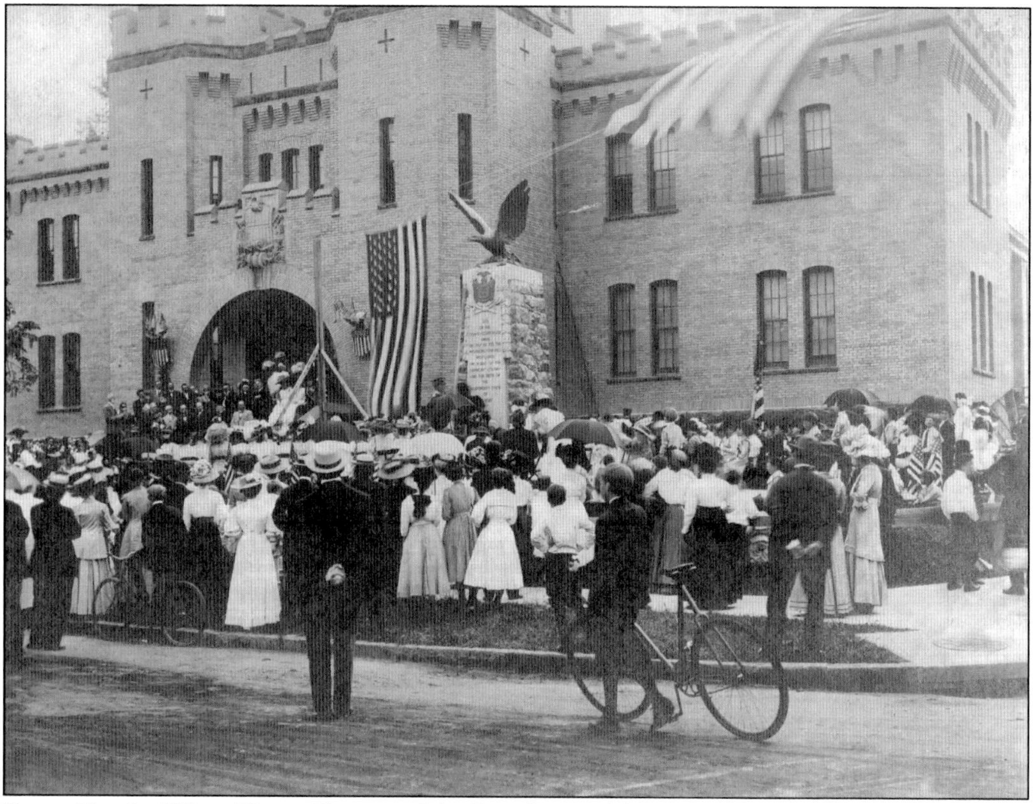

Erected by the White Plains Chapter of the Daughters of the American Revolution in 1910, this monument was unveiled on June 14 in front of the White Plains Armory. It commemorates the site of the original courthouse in White Plains, where the Declaration of Independence was read aloud for the first time in New York State. Here also, the Provincial Congress, on July 9, 1776, proclaimed the passing of the colony of New York and the birth of the independent state of New York, thus making White Plains the birthplace of New York State. (Courtesy of the Westchester County Historical Society.)

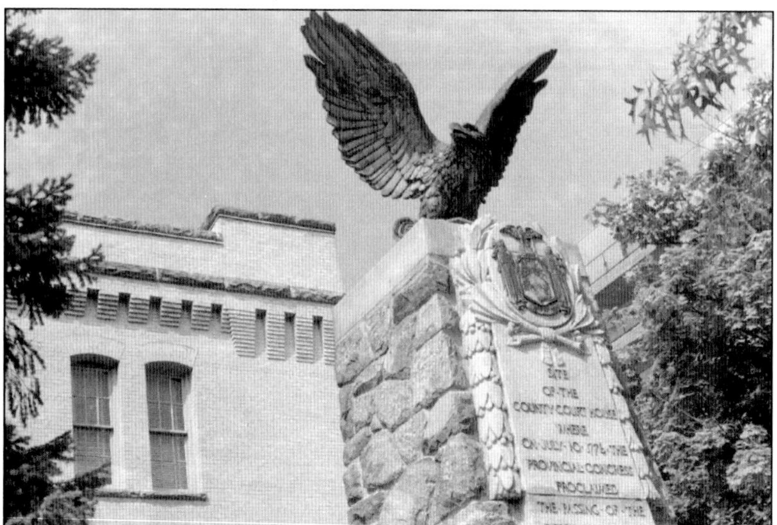

Stones used in the shaft of the 14-foot-high monument were taken from the foundation of the original courthouse, and stones forming the walk around the monument were from prison cells that were under the courthouse. (WPCA.)

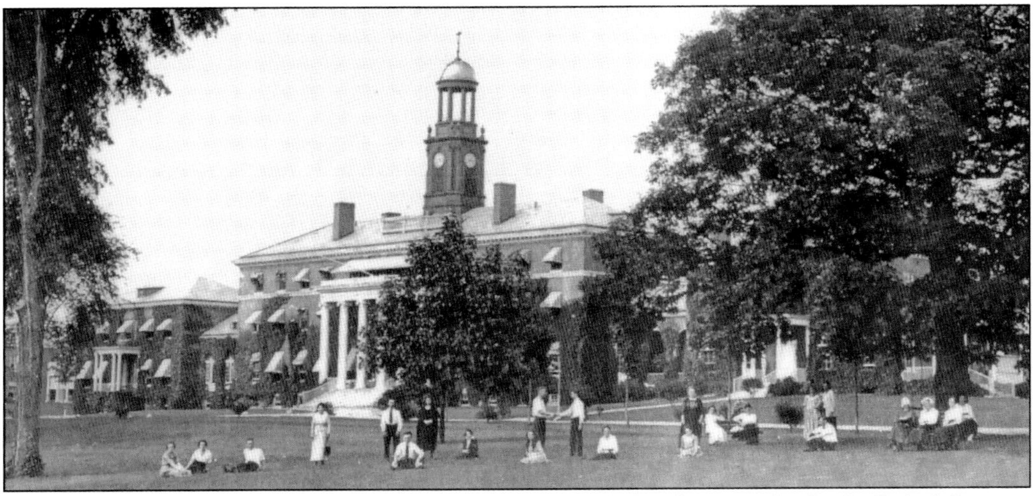

Ground was broken in July 1912 for the establishment of what became the Burke Rehabilitation Center, named after the benefactor's mother, Winifred Masterson Burke. When the center opened on April 7, 1915, there were 180 beds, one doctor, and five nurses. Patients came by bus from the admissions office on East Fifty-seventh Street in New York City. During World War I, Burke served as a naval hospital and cared for 2,000 sailors. A garden was planted yielding enough vegetables to supply all patient and staff needs and help feed hungry neighbors as well. (WPCA.)

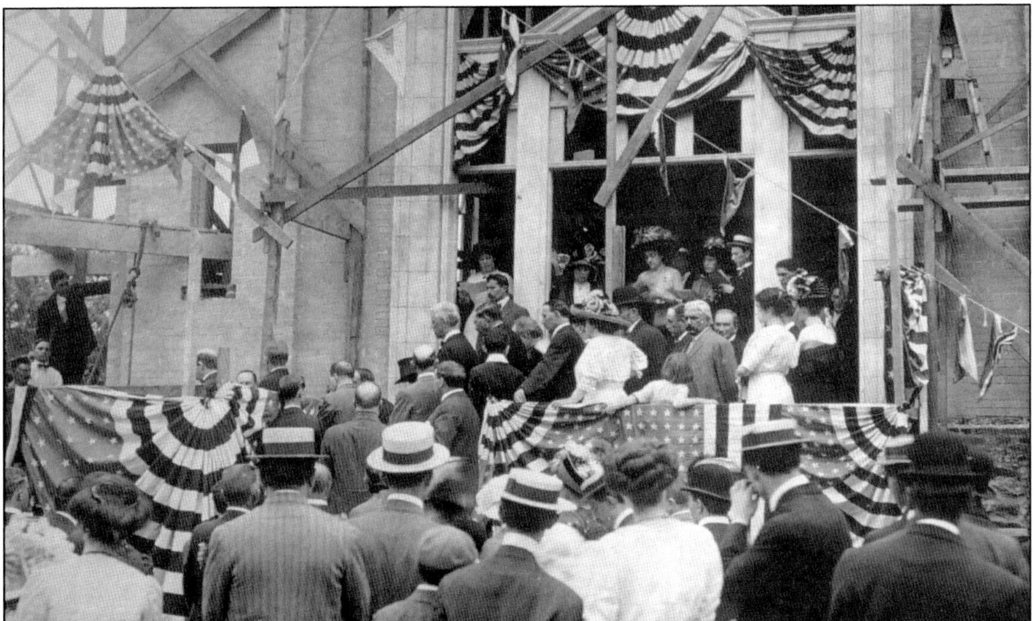

Rocco Briante was the contractor chosen by Congregation Sons of Israel to erect its original house of worship, the first synagogue in White Plains. Incorporated in 1907, the founding members included Paul Pincus, Hyman Gordon, Samuel Ellis, Harry Hecht, and "Admiral Dot," Leopold Kahn. Pictured here are the ceremonies marking the laying of the cornerstone in May 1911; opening ceremonies for Temple Israel were held on September 17, 1911. The congregation occupied the 65 Fisher Avenue location until a new Temple Israel Center was dedicated on Old Mamaroneck Road in 1948. The Fisher Avenue site later became home to the Allen African Methodist Episcopal Church. (WPCA.)

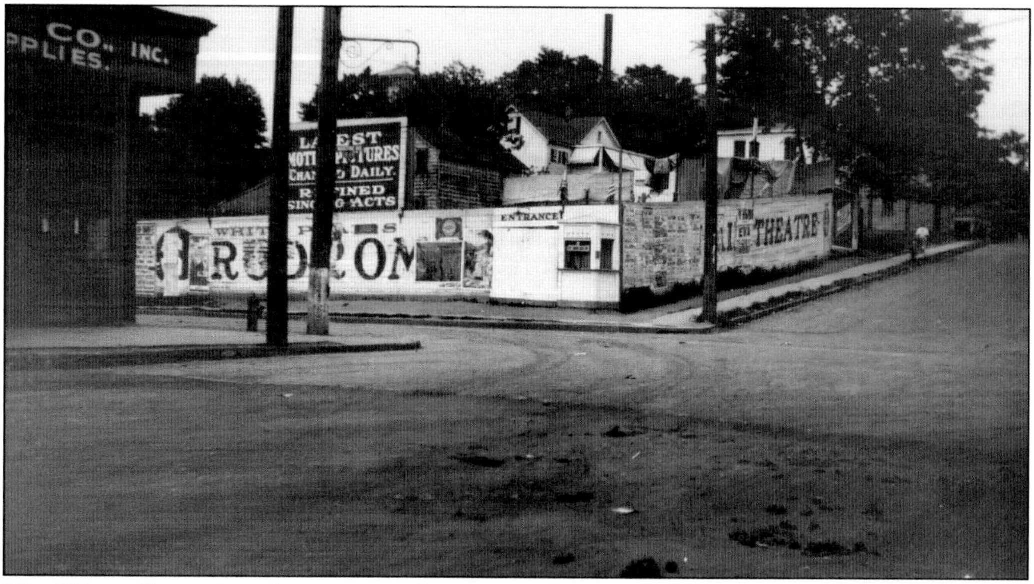

The White Plains Aerodrome sat at the corner of Martine Avenue and Grove Street. It was an open-air theater that showed the "latest motion pictures" and hosted "refined singing acts," according to its billboard marquee. This image of the theater appeared on a postcard that was mailed in 1912. (WPPL.)

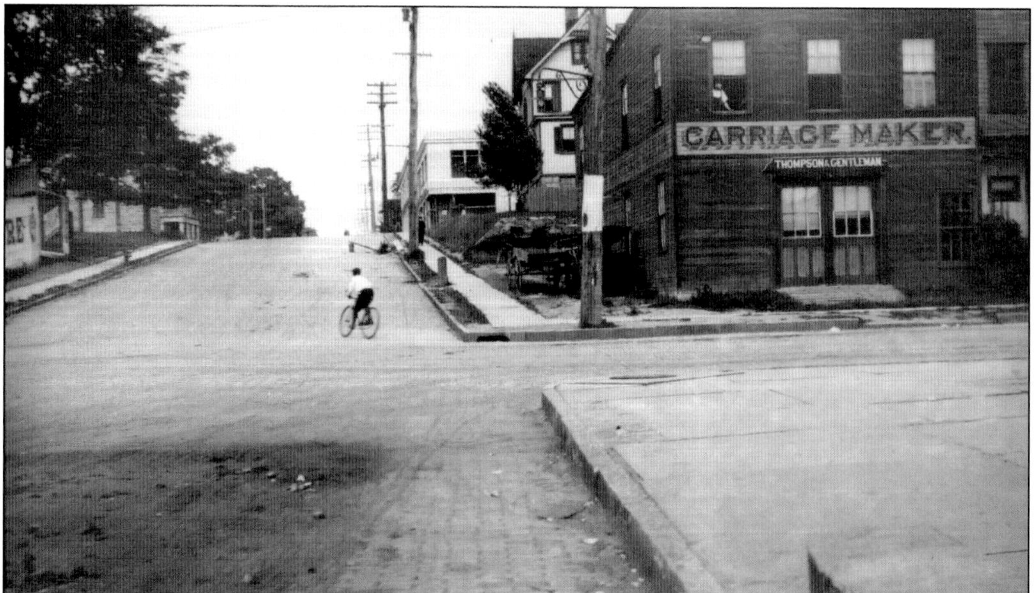

In 1907, Herbert F. Thompson purchased the carriage factory building at 23 Grove Street from John Philips, who had fallen ill but lived until his death in 1913 at 25 Grove Street. Thompson was a well-known carriage maker and blacksmith, having worked for Philips for over 20 years before taking over one of "the oldest and best established businesses in town," per the *Eastern State Journal.* William H. Gentleman was his partner in the business and a resident of Battle Hill. The bicyclist is heading up Martine Avenue toward Mamaroneck Avenue, with the Marion Building visible behind the telephone poles at right, the current site of the Westchester County Office Building. (WPPL.)

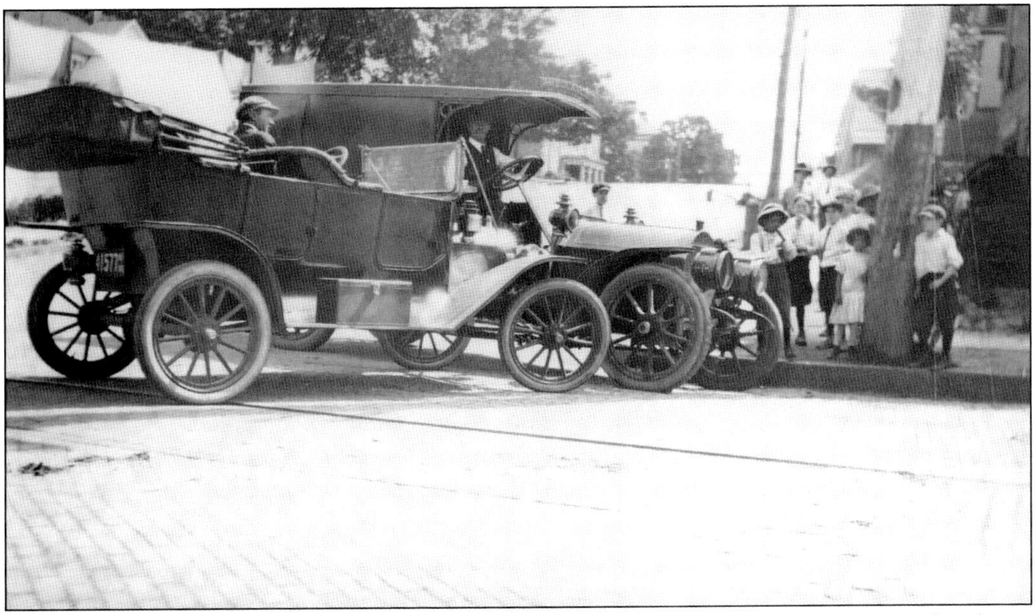

White Plains Hospital got its first ambulance in 1906. That horse-drawn carriage was refitted into an automobile by 1912. How soon after that it got in this accident with another car is unknown. It is possible this is at the corner of Martine Avenue and Grove Street, with the white walls of the White Plains Aerodrome in the background. (WPPL.)

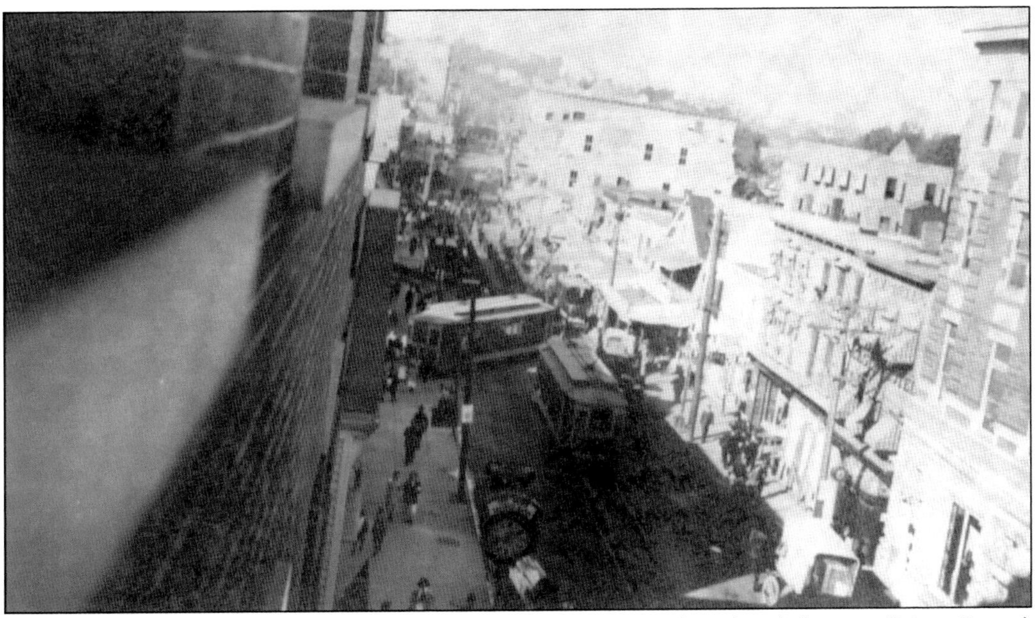

The streetcars passing at the intersection of Grand Street and Railroad Avenue (Main Street) were operated by the Westchester Street Railway. In 1916, the railway built a waiting room on Main Street, walking distance from the railroad station. Trolley cars ran all over the county, from Mount Vernon to Peekskill and from Tarrytown to Port Chester. As automobiles and buses began to dominate the roadways of the county, trolleys faded away, finally replaced by buses in November 1929. Buses were deemed more time efficient and cheaper. (WPPL.)

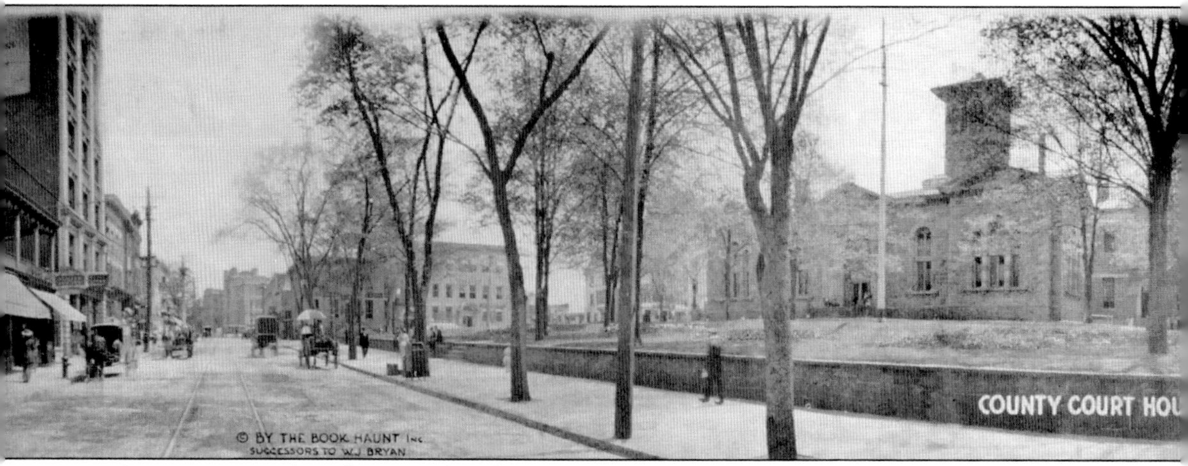

This panoramic shot shows Railroad Avenue (Main Street) just before the debut of the "great white way" and its renaming as Main Street. The Business and Professional Men's Association was behind the drive to illuminate the street with electric lights and give "First Aid" to the city's "principal business street," a reform effort that also saw the institution of ordinances about signage and building character. In this photograph alone, there are many examples of how the city was growing before the outbreak of World War I. At left is the Eastern State Journal Building (tallest on left), Realty Building, Newell Theater (later RKO), and across the street is the Central Bank, the

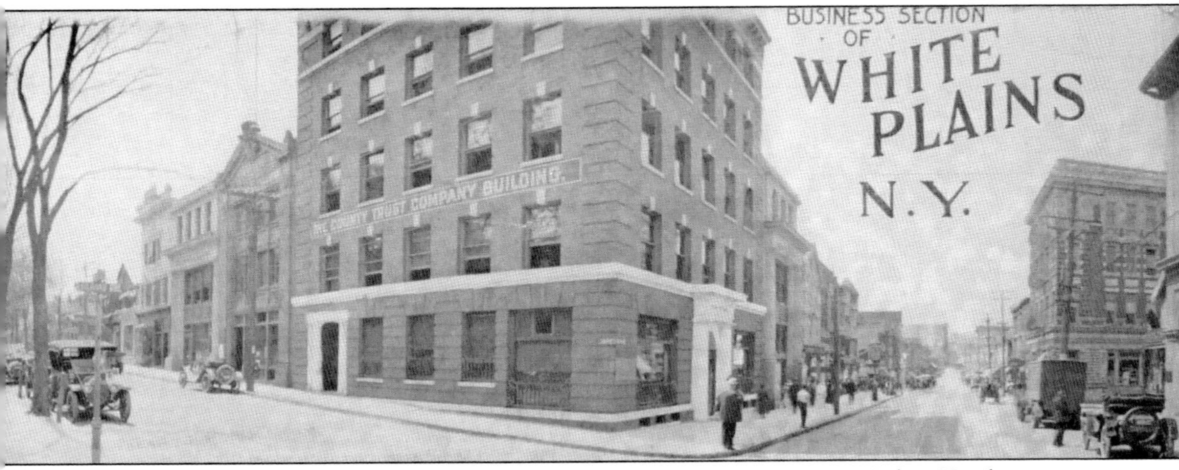

Barnum Building, and the Court House. To the right of the Court House are Police Headquarters, the Sutherland Building, and the Barrett Building, which contained the County Trust. Next are the Home Savings Bank, First National Bank, and Title Insurance Company. Directly behind the photographer was Birch's Restaurant, where "the twenty-five cent dinner served . . . will not suffer a bit by comparison with fifty-cent dinners elsewhere," such as the ones at the Maloney Building Hotel and Rathskellar, which had "high-grade music and cabaret every evening. (WPPL.)

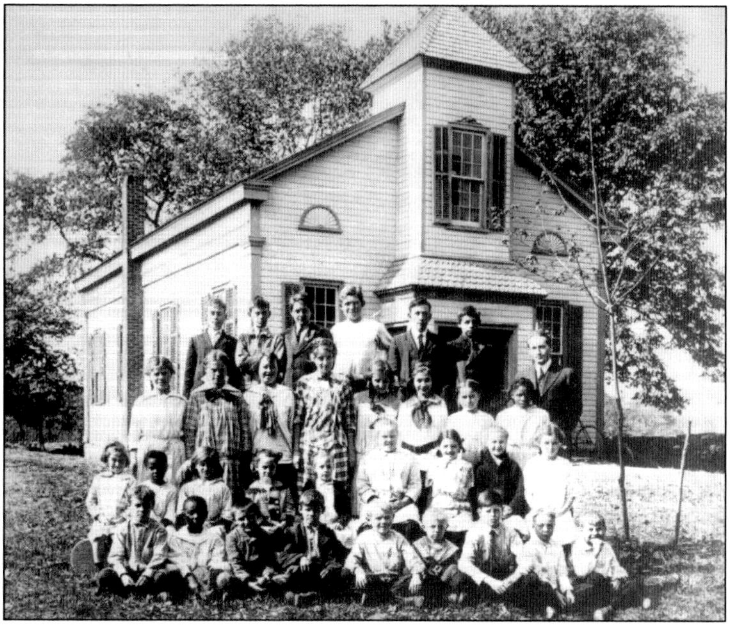

The members of the Methodist Church in White Plains built a mission church on West Street in 1844. Around 1890, it was converted to a one-room schoolhouse, serving the children of the Rosedale neighborhood in the south end of the village. The teacher in this 1914 photograph is Ivan Cheney. When the new Ridgeway School opened in 1953, a total of 21 children were transferred there from the Rosedale School. It is now a private residence. (WPCA.)

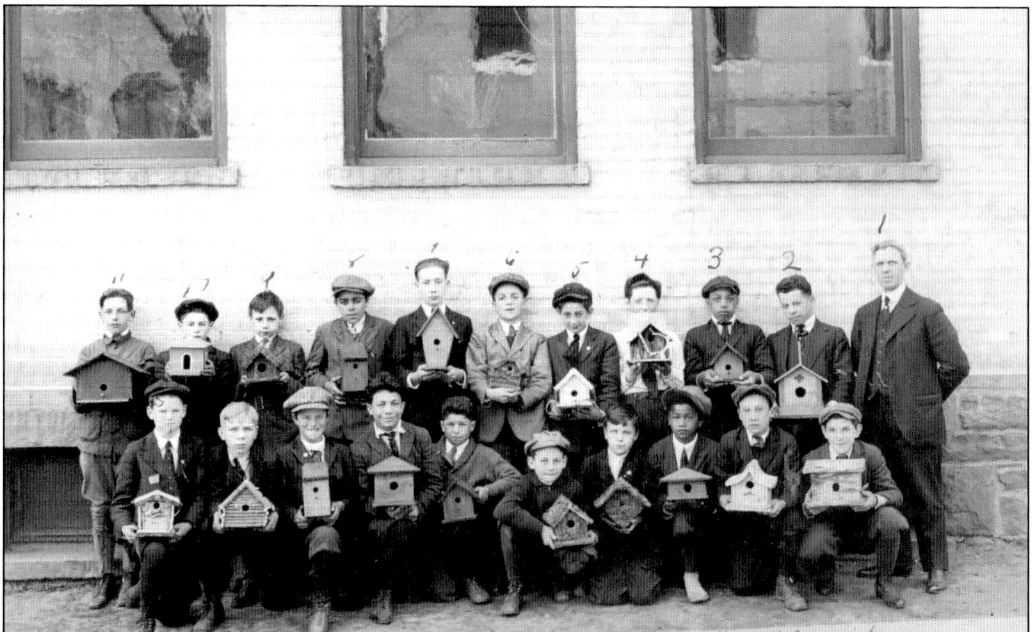

This shows students from the Court Street School in 1918 with the principal, William S. Maxson (No. 1), with birdhouses that were built to attract birds to the in-progress Bronx River Parkway Reservation. When a high school on Main Street was completed in 1909, only elementary grades remained in the Court Street School, which had been built in 1856 with rooms added in 1895. During the 1910s, the White Plains School District was expanded, and new primary schools were built from Battle Hill to West Harrison. In 1907, one reason for constructing schools at other locations was the growth of the business district and increased trolley traffic, which created noise. (WPPL.)

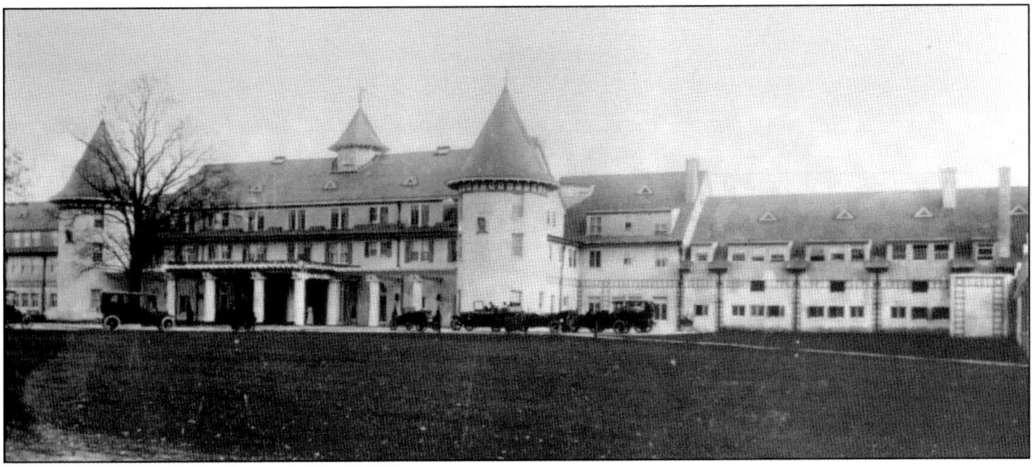

Architect Kenneth Murchison made plans to use Howard Willets's cattle barn, built of reinforced concrete, for the planned Gedney Farm Hotel. White Plains contractor Frank Goble began work on the project in 1913. Two great silos that stood at either end of the barn were transformed into towers, giving the appearance of a French chateau. The sheep run became the bowling alley, and the deep recess used for refuse was changed into a swimming pool. In April 1914, the Gedney Farm Hotel, which accommodated about 300 guests, opened for business, dubbed "New York's Suburban Hotel Deluxe." (WPCA.)

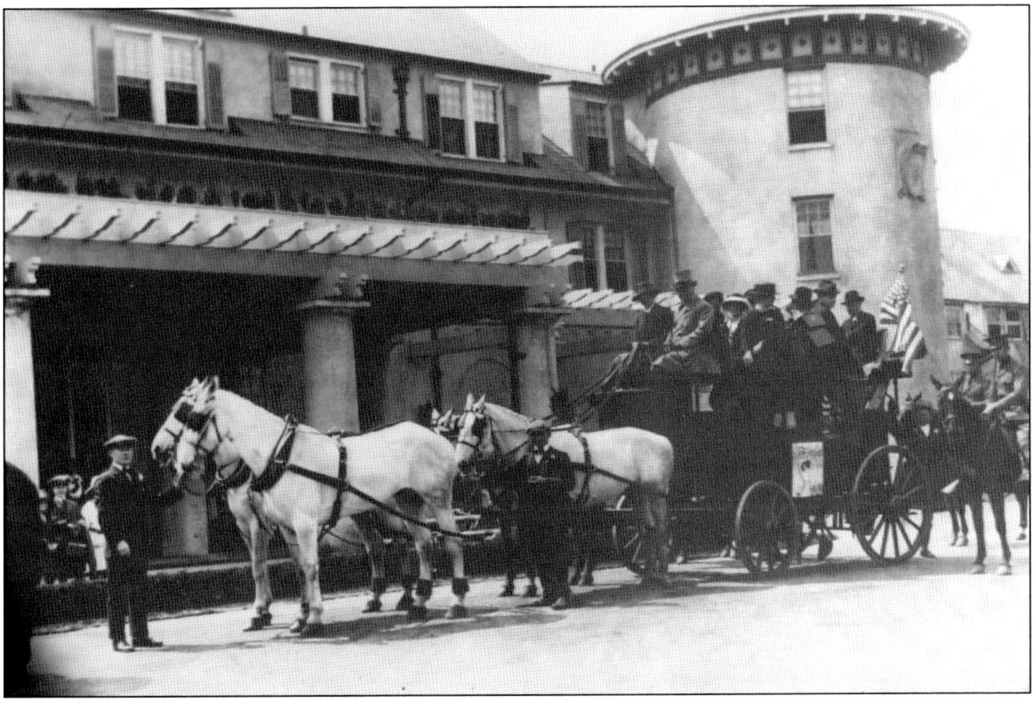

Guests at the Gedney Farm Hotel were offered indoor and outdoor recreations of many types, such as trapshooting, horseback riding, roller skating, squash, and golf. In the winter, the resort offered tobogganing, sleigh riding, and winter tennis. Another favorite activity was coaching, with the famous Liberty Coach, pictured here. On September 20, 1924, fire ravaged the hotel, leaving little but the two towers and six chimneys, thus ending a brief but enchanting era at Gedney Farms. (WPCA.)

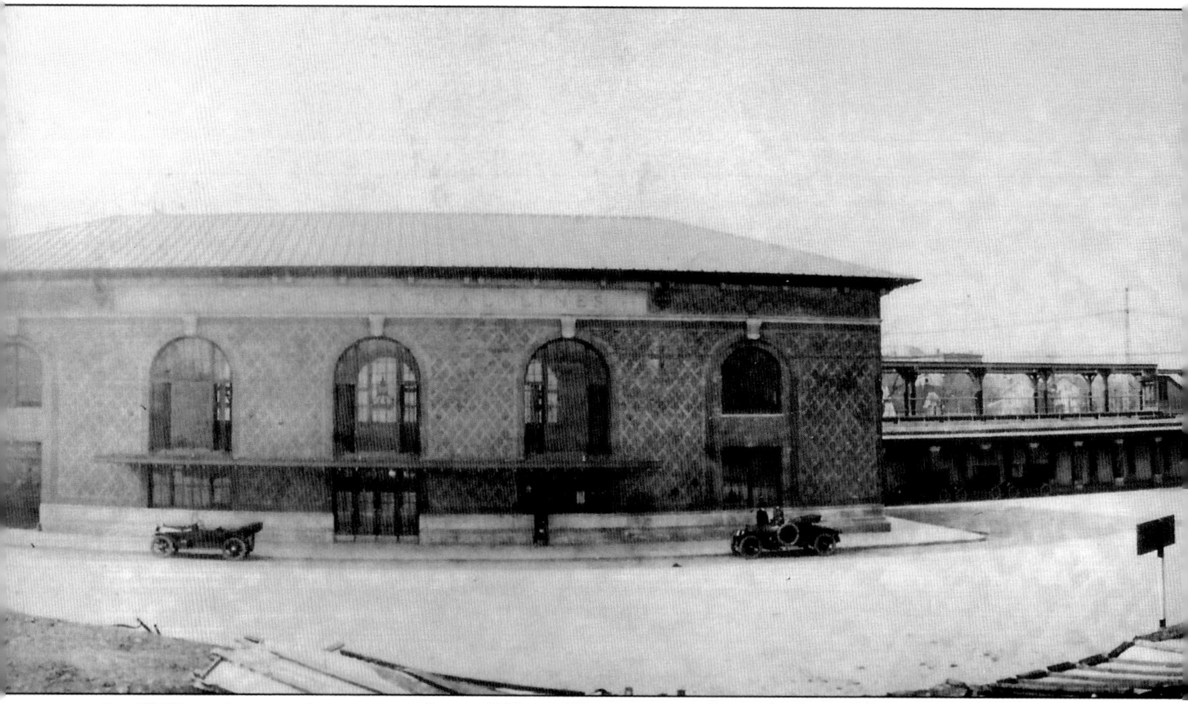

In 1910, trains on the two tracks to White Plains were electrified, and beginning in 1912, work was under way to relocate the railroad tracks 300 feet to the west and to eliminate the grade crossing by elevating the tracks. The new brick station pictured here was designed by Warren

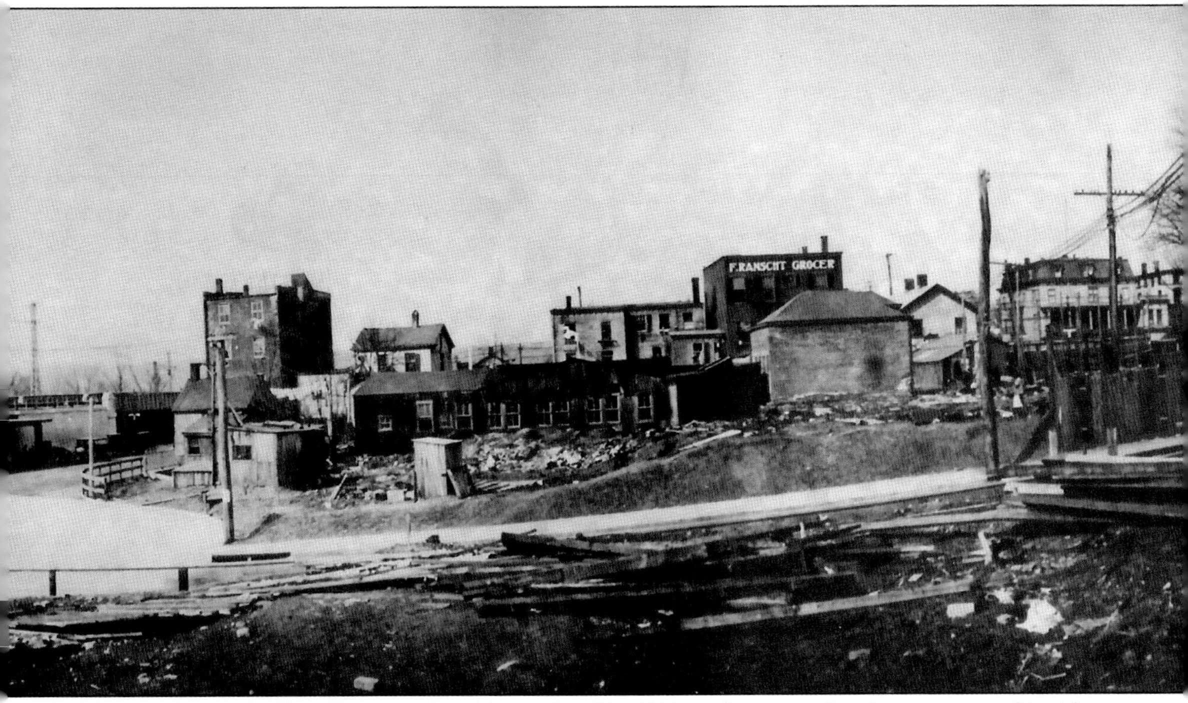

and Wetmore and officially opened on December 20, 1914, with a street-level entrance and inside stairs to reach the platform. (WPCA.)

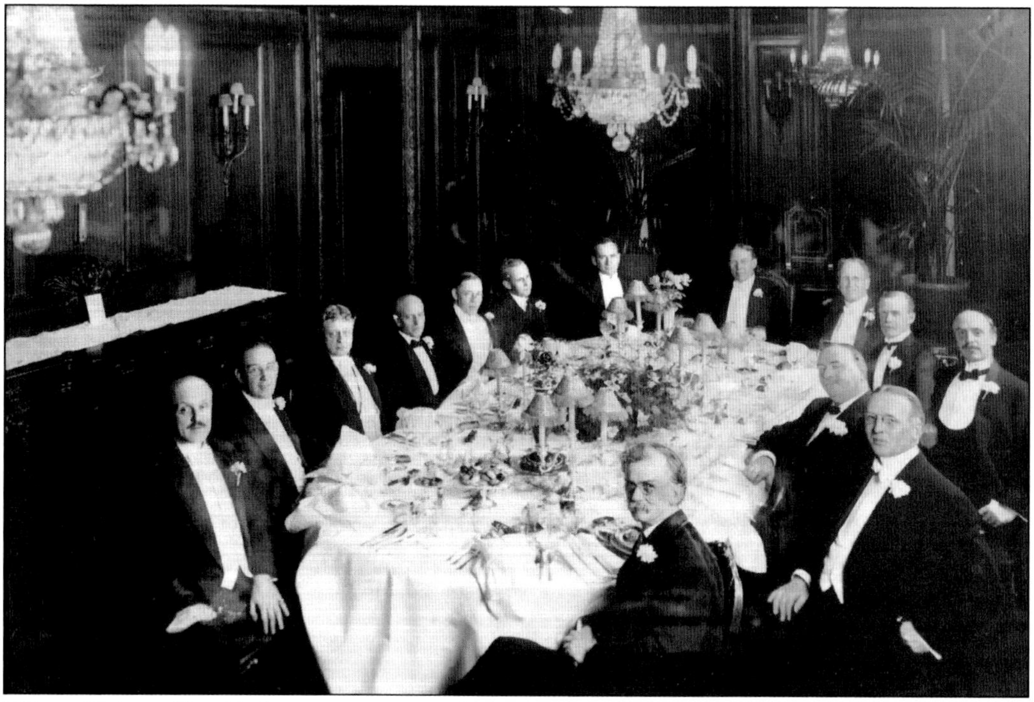

White Plains officially became a city on January 1, 1916. Here, the first mayor, Ffarrington Thompson, is shown sitting at the head of the table with other city officials. Front and center is photographer John Rosch, who was the first city assessor and later city historian. (WPCA.)

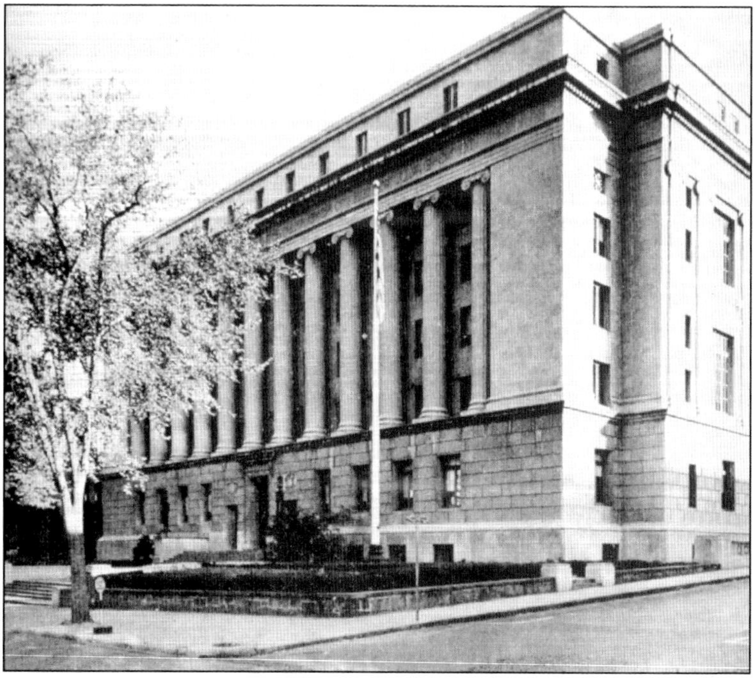

The decade of the 1910s saw many changes along Main Street. On September 3, 1914, Railroad Avenue officially became Main Street at the same time that electricity created a "great white way" along the street. While the mammoth new county courthouse was under construction from 1915 to 1917, White Plains became a city on January 1, 1916. This courthouse was razed in 1977 during the urban renewal era. (WPCA.)

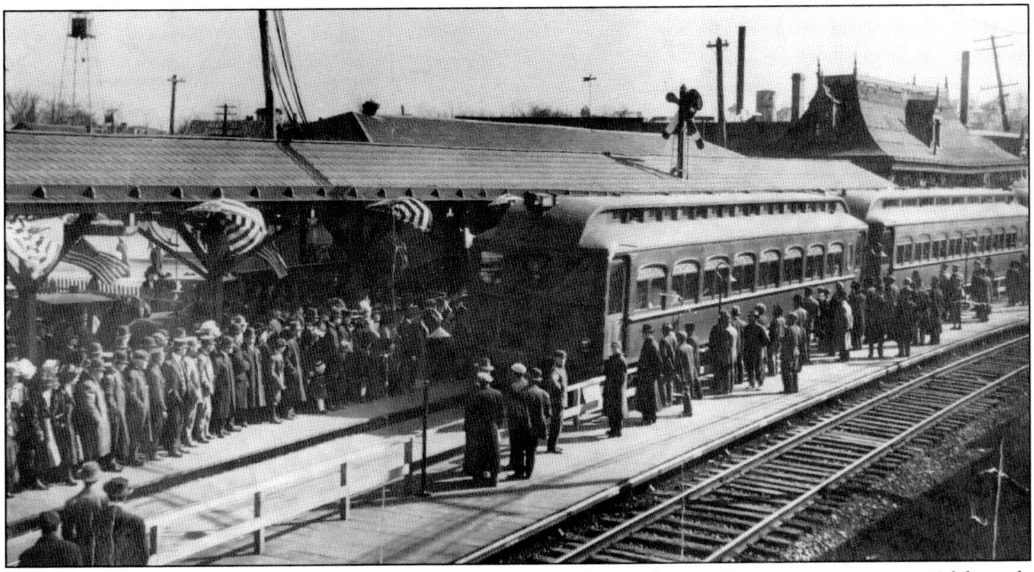

During World War I in White Plains, residents mobilized like their military counterparts. Although Company L, 10th Regiment, from the New York National Guard, was called up to serve in the Army, many other folks in White Plains pitched in to support the American war effort. A large Red Cross chapter was set up, cadets were trained at St. John's, and there were hugely successful liberty loan drives. (WPPL.)

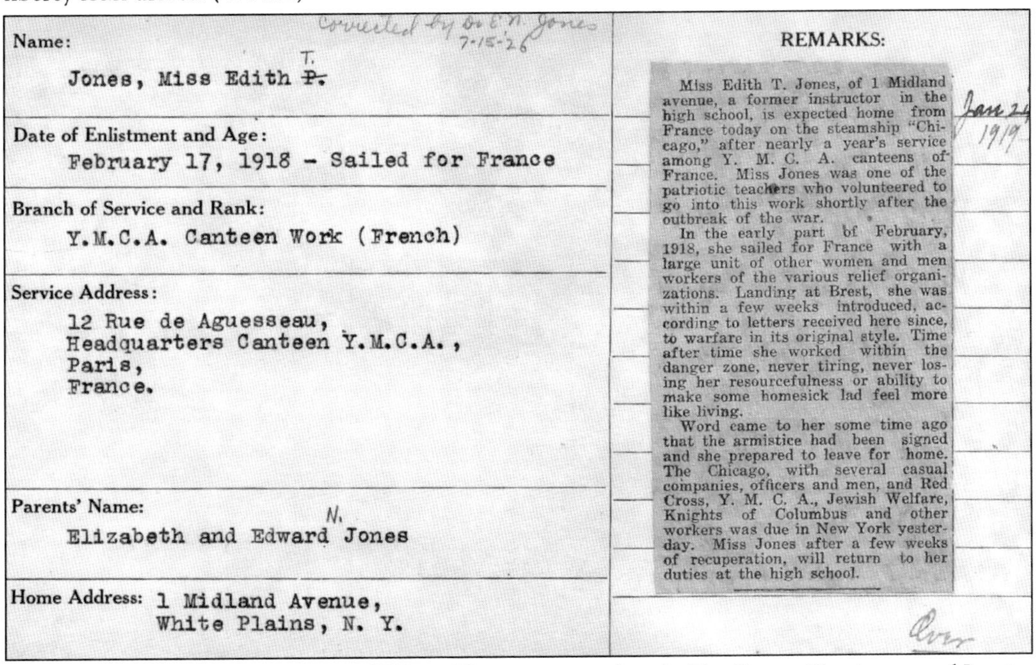

Corrected by Dr. E. N. Jones 7-15-26

Name:
Jones, Miss Edith ~~P.~~ T.

Date of Enlistment and Age:
February 17, 1918 - Sailed for France

Branch of Service and Rank:
Y.M.C.A. Canteen Work (French)

Service Address:
12 Rue de Aguesseau,
Headquarters Canteen Y.M.C.A.,
Paris,
France.

Parents' Name:
Elizabeth and Edward N. Jones

Home Address: 1 Midland Avenue,
White Plains, N. Y.

REMARKS:

Miss Edith T. Jones, of 1 Midland avenue, a former instructor in the high school, is expected home from France today on the steamship "Chicago," after nearly a year's service among Y. M. C. A. canteens of France. Miss Jones was one of the patriotic teachers who volunteered to go into this work shortly after the outbreak of the war.

In the early part of February, 1918, she sailed for France with a large unit of other women and men workers of the various relief organizations. Landing at Brest, she was within a few weeks introduced, according to letters received here since, to warfare in its original style. Time after time she worked within the danger zone, never tiring, never losing her resourcefulness or ability to make some homesick lad feel more like living.

Word came to her some time ago that the armistice had been signed and she prepared to leave for home. The Chicago, with several casual companies, officers and men, and Red Cross, Y. M. C. A., Jewish Welfare, Knights of Columbus and other workers was due in New York yesterday. Miss Jones after a few weeks of recuperation, will return to her duties at the high school.

Jan 24 1919

Over

Following World War I, a group of White Plains women, headed by Grace Harriman and Louisa Lockwood, supervised a house-to-house canvas to identify White Plains residents who served in the Great War. The information collected, called the "War Mothers' Files," was transferred to index cards and arranged in categories, including "women in service." There were cards for 30 women, and one example is shown here. The cards were later deposited in the city clerk's office and are now part of the White Plains City Archives. (WPCA.)

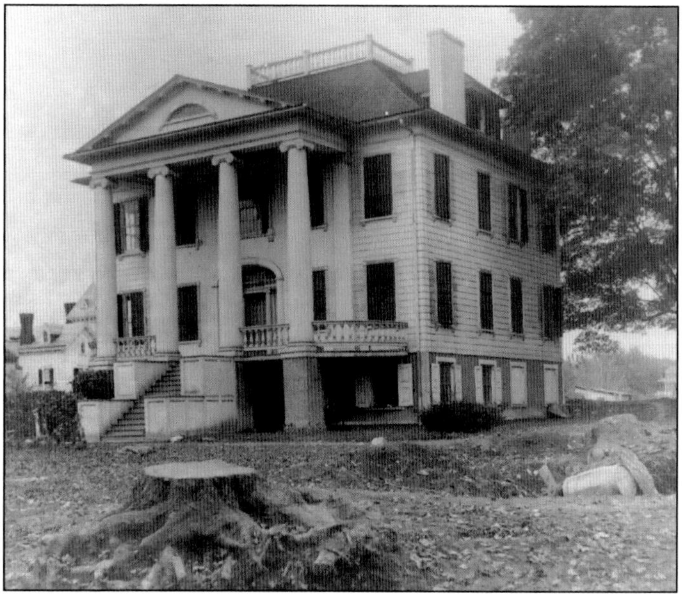

When Minott Mitchell built his home in 1829, Broadway was the center of the village and was called Village Street. Mitchell, a prominent lawyer and town clerk in White Plains from 1812 to 1838, modeled his home after the nearby 1787 courthouse, which stood on the current White Plains Armory site. The large mansion is pictured here in 1915, just before the Greek-pillared home was moved around the corner to Mitchell Place. Since 1949, the Mitchell homestead has been home to the White Plains American Legion Post 135. (WPCA.)

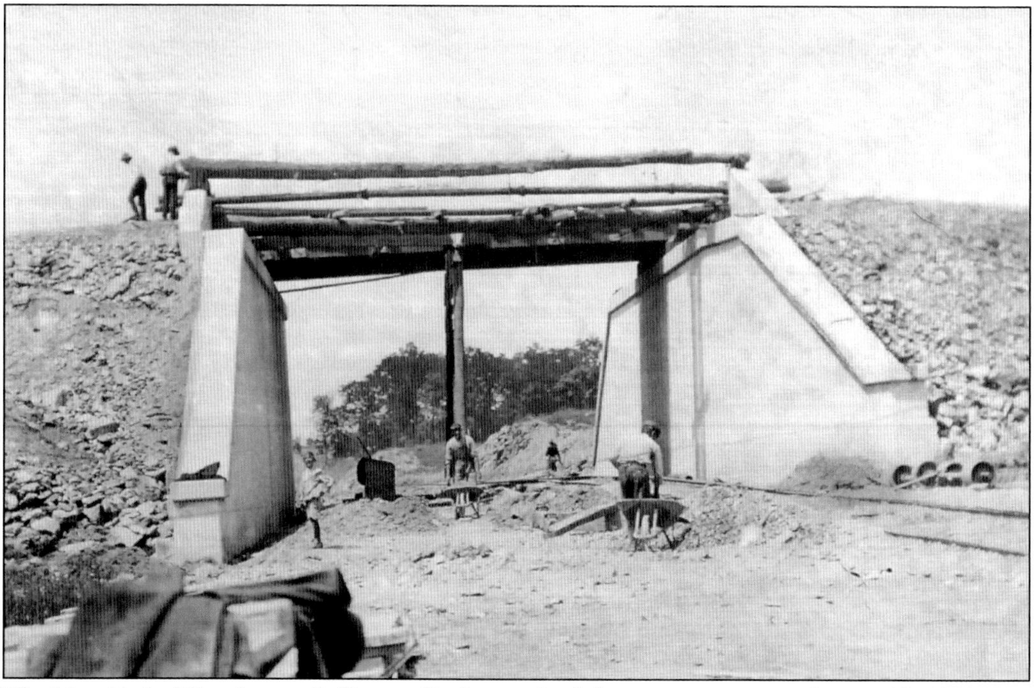

The New York, Westchester & Boston Railway, which began running on August 10, 1912, was the first electrified interurban railway in the country that was designed from the beginning to be electric, rather than converted from a steam system. When construction was completed, over $22 million had been spent to build 18 miles of railway, thus the nickname "million-dollar-a-mile railroad." The railway went bankrupt in 1937. This is construction at the Gedney Way underpass in June 1911. (WPCA.)

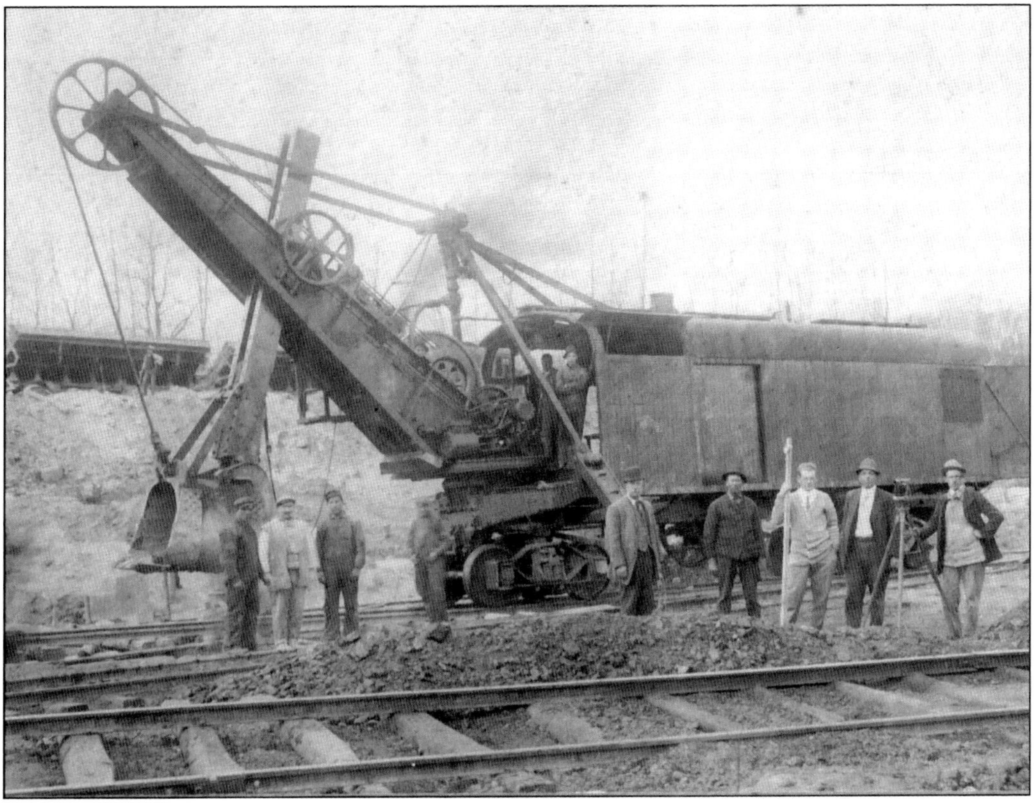

White Plains resident Thomas McParlan was one of the engineers working on the construction of the New York, Westchester & Boston Railway. He is seen here at the extreme right in May 1911 with fellow workers Richards, Taylor, McLaughlin, and Root. (WPCA.)

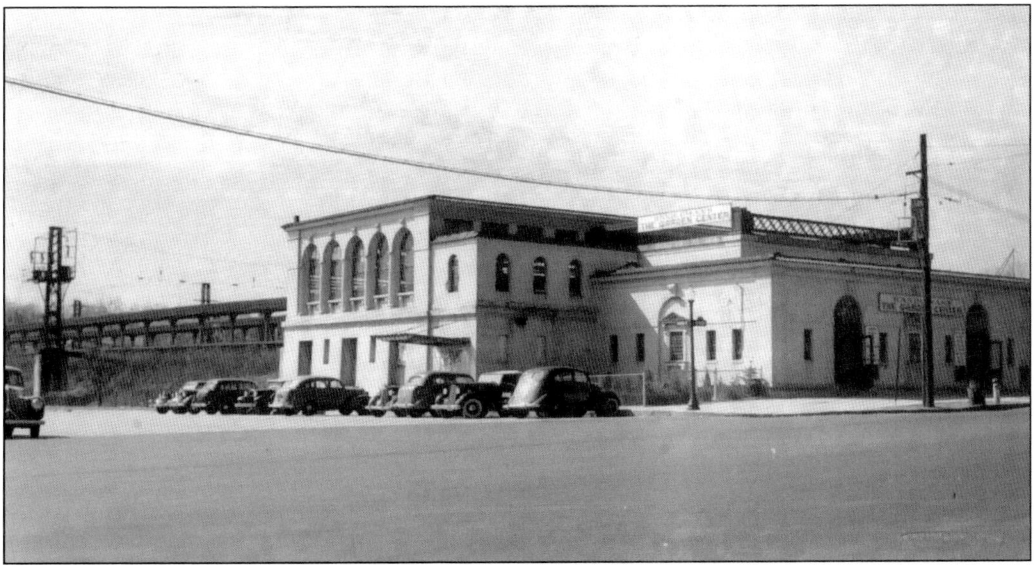

The New York, Westchester & Boston Railway terminal was located on Westchester Avenue, later the site of B. Altman's department store. It is pictured here when the railroad was failing in the 1930s. (WPCA.)

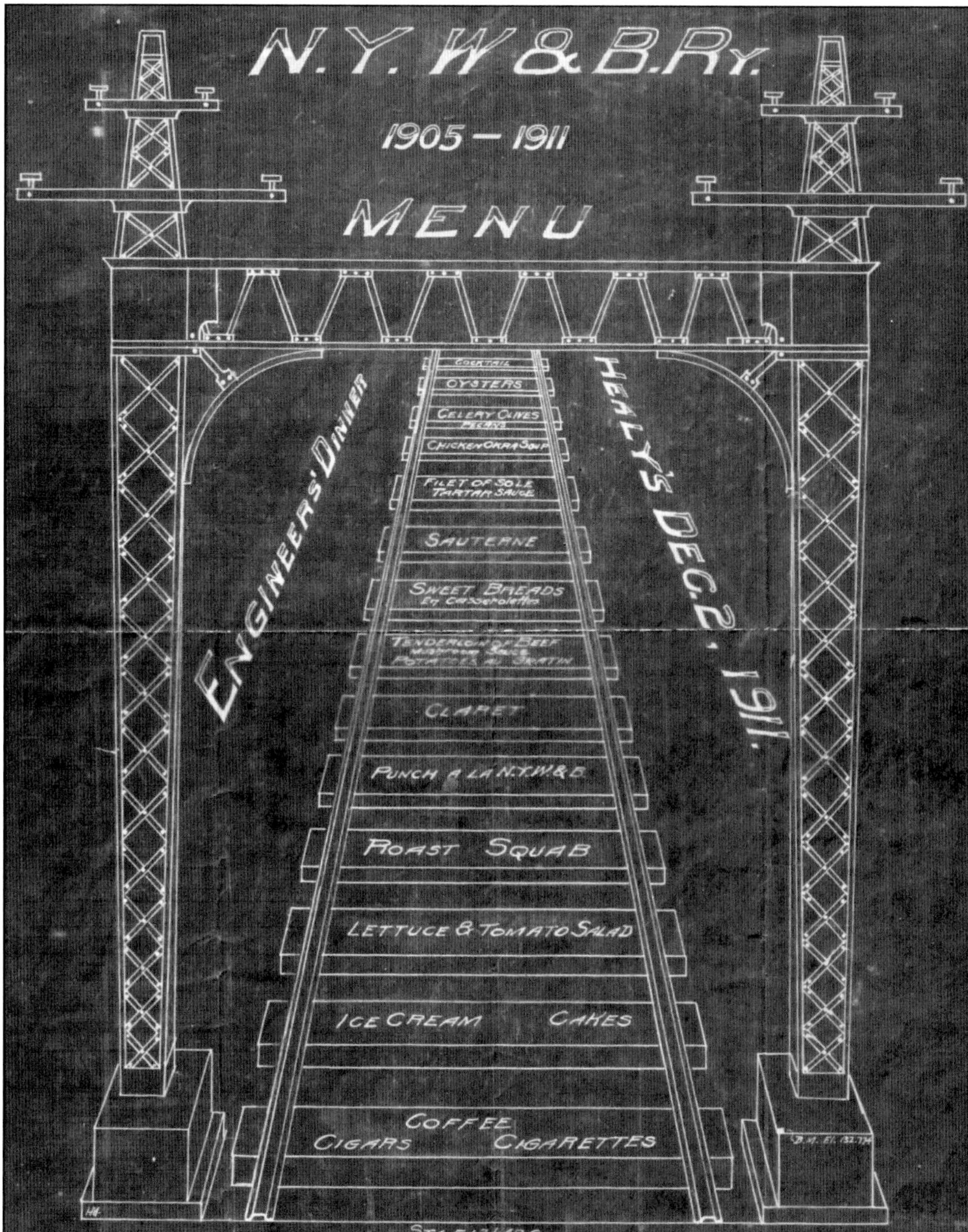

Late in 1911, a group of engineers got together at Healy's Restaurant to celebrate the work they had completed in designing the New York, Westchester & Boston Railway. Thomas McParlan saved the evening's menu, which was printed on blueprint paper. (WPCA.)

Three

The 1920s

The 1920s truly roared in White Plains. The population nearly doubled for the second time in 30 years (as did the county's), a profusion of businesses and professions were housed in ever-taller buildings along Main Street, and a vision of Westchester County as a suburban satellite of New York City took shape through large-scale planning and development efforts. Newspapers, glossy promotional magazines, and professional publications attest to the transformation of White Plains into a "progressive suburban community"—in the words of the *Daily Reporter*—a place where people lived less crowded, though no less productive, lives.

The Bronx River Parkway, completed in 1925, connected White Plains to the southern parts of Westchester and New York City, and was the first concerted effort to make automobile-based travel a central part of county life. Along with a substantial roadway, the Bronx River Parkway reshaped residential and commercial areas along the river, setting a precedent for large-scale government intervention in the built environment of the county. The parkway eliminated ramshackle and often unsanitary conditions along the river and turned the Main Street intersection with the railroad into a space commuters might recognize today. County government grew significantly during this time, driven as much by the desire to bring prosperous business opportunities to the county as it was by the urgent need to control the creation of new buildings and provide for the people who lived in them. Street paving, water, and sewer modernization were top of the list for municipal government, but so was the millions of dollars in tax revenue promised by developers.

One newspaper claimed it was the "second richest city in the state per capita" judging by tax returns, but the era of large estates and country homes was ending, with more apartment houses and small midsize homes for families who wished to live year-round in Westchester. To accommodate all the new residents and buildings in the city, elected officials and civically engaged people created a master plan in 1928. Developed at the height of a prosperous decade of development, the plan quickly became unsuited to the needs of the city when the Depression hit and money for development was lost.

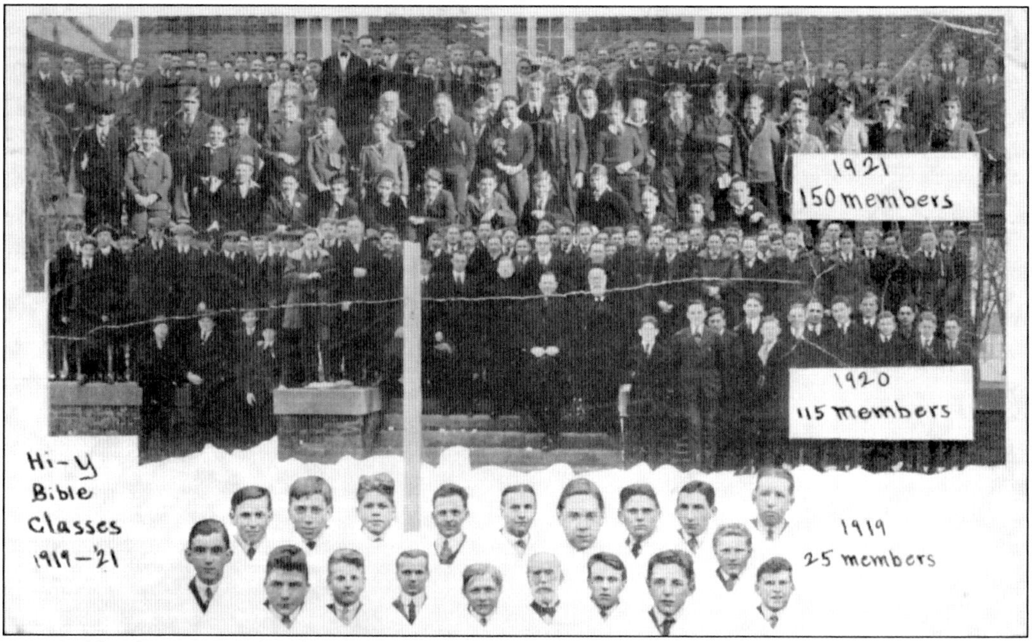

Hi-Y Bible classes were held at the YMCA, which was located on Mamaroneck Avenue near Martine Avenue at the time this picture was taken. The classes were intended to instill Christian principles into young people but also included vocational and recreational pursuits. (WPPL.)

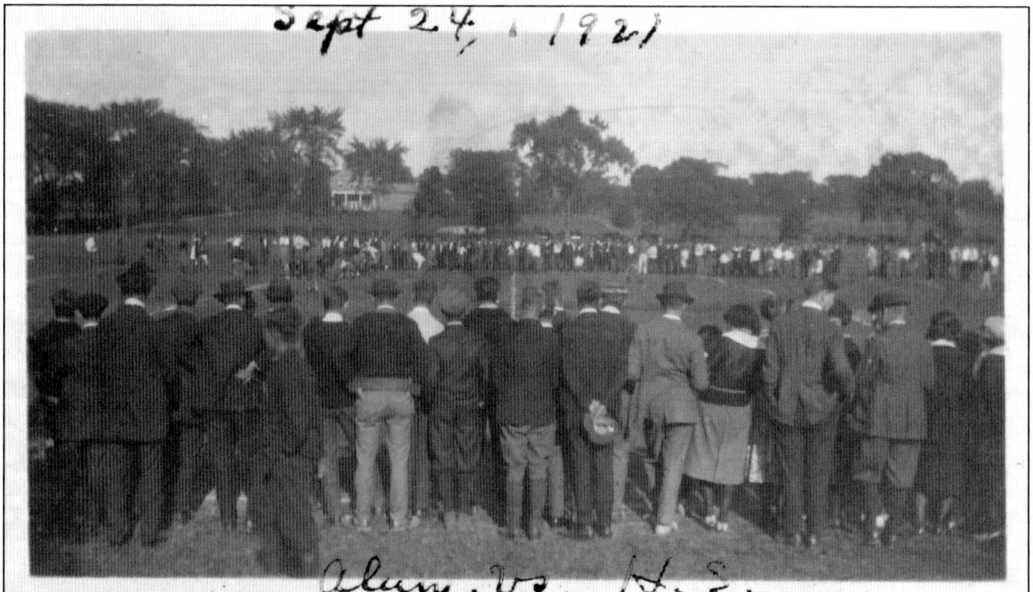

Compared to the teams of the years prior and the very dominant teams of the 1940s and 1950s, the 1921–1922 WPHS football team had a rough go of it. On September 24, 1921, the "alumni [showed] good old WPHS spirit" and defeated the current students' team 20-0. The *Oracle* yearbook noted that overall, the team had gone 113-66 (with only 17 ties) since 1897, a record to be proud of. It is no wonder that enthusiasm and attendance was low at games in 1922, since the three previous years the team had been county champions. "Injuries and eligibility rules took so many out that the team was greatly handicapped," according to the 1922 WPHS *Oracle* yearbook. (WPPL.)

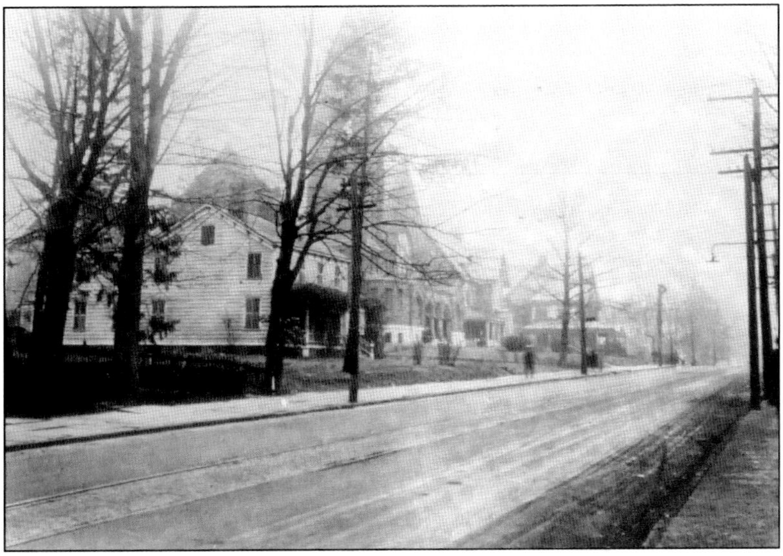

Main Street was changing quickly in the 1920s. Seen here in 1924 is the site of the White Plains Municipal Building, just west of Memorial Methodist Church, with its tall spire and rose window. (WPCA.)

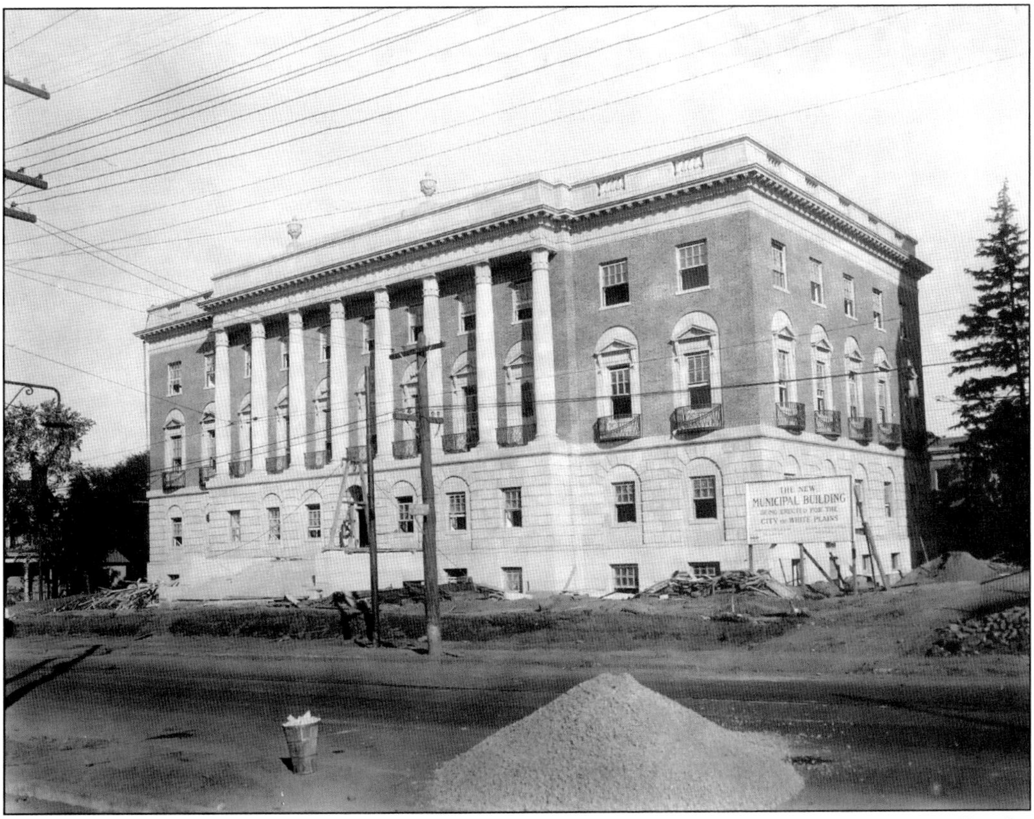

The White Plains Municipal Building was designed in the Colonial Revival style by J.H. Friedlander and echoed the 1917 Westchester County Courthouse just down the street. Part of the impetus for erecting a city building came from the Committee on Memorial for Men in the Service, who, in 1919, recommended to the city council that the memorial take the form of a city hall. Seen here under construction, the building was dedicated on February 22, 1926. (WPCA.)

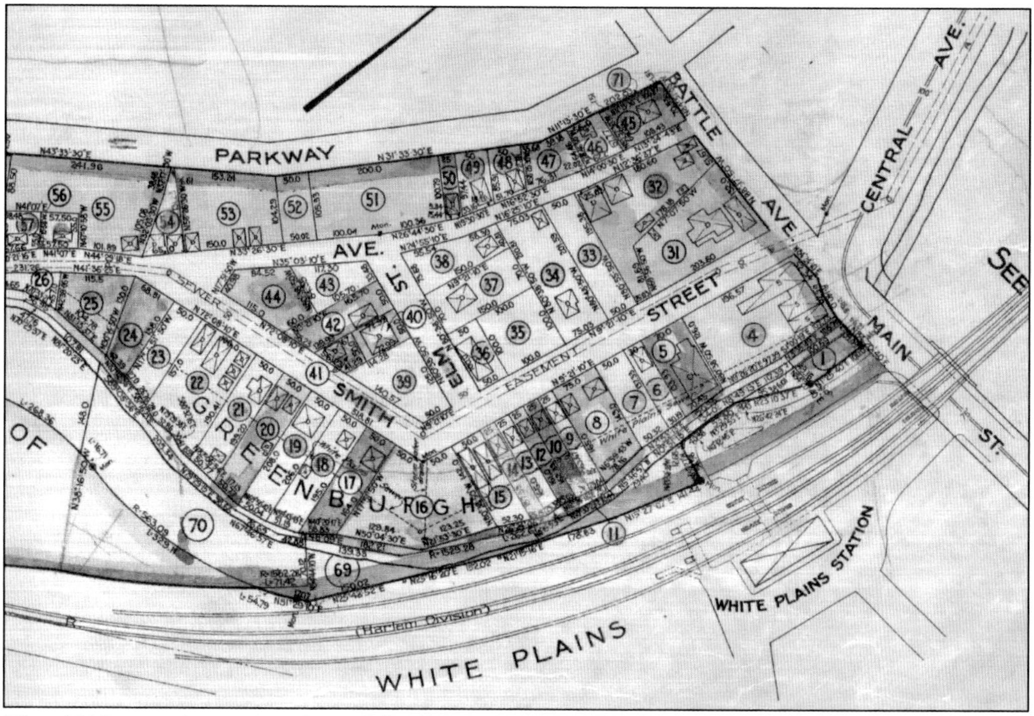

This 1914 map shows the plan of the Bronx River Parkway Commission to purchase over 70 properties owned by all kinds of people and transform them into green space for the parkway. The original site of the Church of Our Lady of Mount Carmel was in this area, along with a mix of single and multifamily homes, at least one saloon, and a hotel. (Courtesy of the Westchester County Archives.)

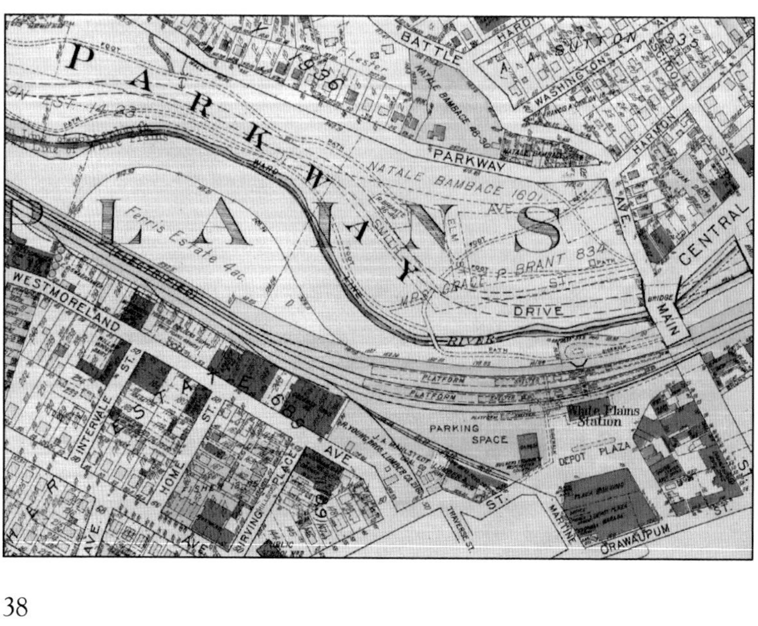

This page from a 1930 atlas shows how the Smith Street area of the Battle Hill neighborhood was transformed by the Bronx River Parkway Commission. The buildings and streets were removed and replaced with green space, meant to create a bucolic atmosphere for people driving along the parkway. (Courtesy of the Westchester County Archives.)

The Bronx River Parkway was the first public parkway designed specifically for automobile use. It began as environmental restoration aimed at transforming the heavily polluted Bronx River into an attractive linear park. Work began in 1906, and the parkway opened in 1925. This 1925 view is from Garth Woods, just south of White Plains. (Courtesy of the Westchester County Archives.)

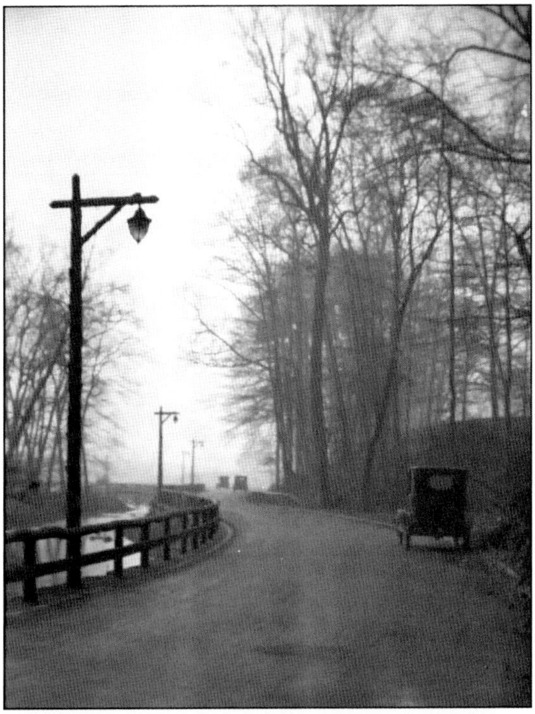

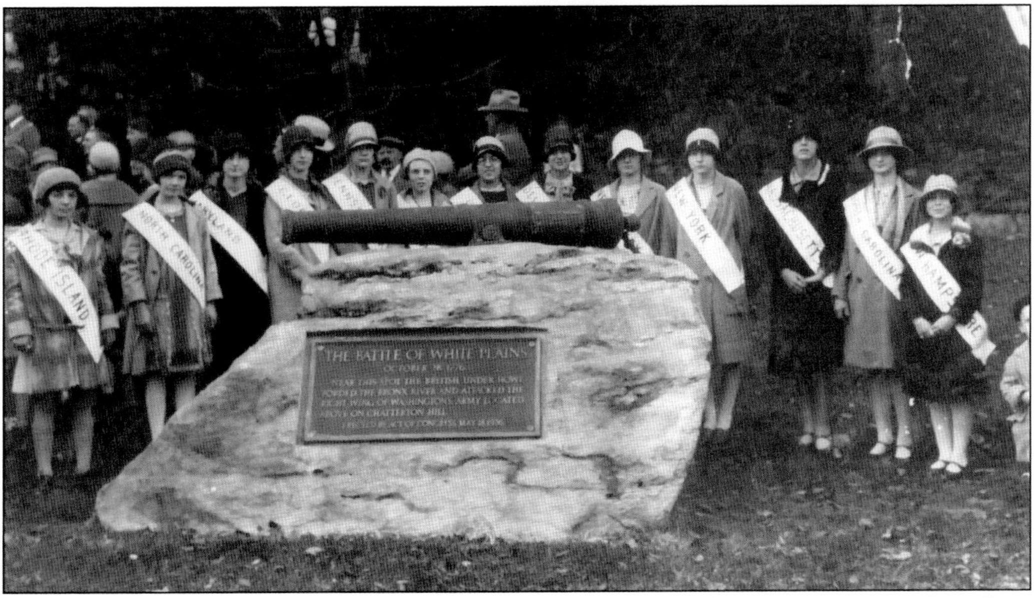

A Revolutionary-era cannon was found in 1890 on Henry T. Dykman's property on Broadway across from Lake Street. Eventually, the cannon was sold to Francis Bannerman in New York City, who dealt in military goods. John Rosch tracked down the cannon to 501 Broadway in Manhattan, where it served as a decoration in a doorway. With $1,000 raised through private contributions, the cannon was purchased and brought back to White Plains. It was placed on the marker pictured here and dedicated on October 28, 1926, on the 150th anniversary of the Battle of White Plains. The cannon was stolen in 1963, recovered, and then stolen again in 1971. A replica now adorns the monument. (WPPL.)

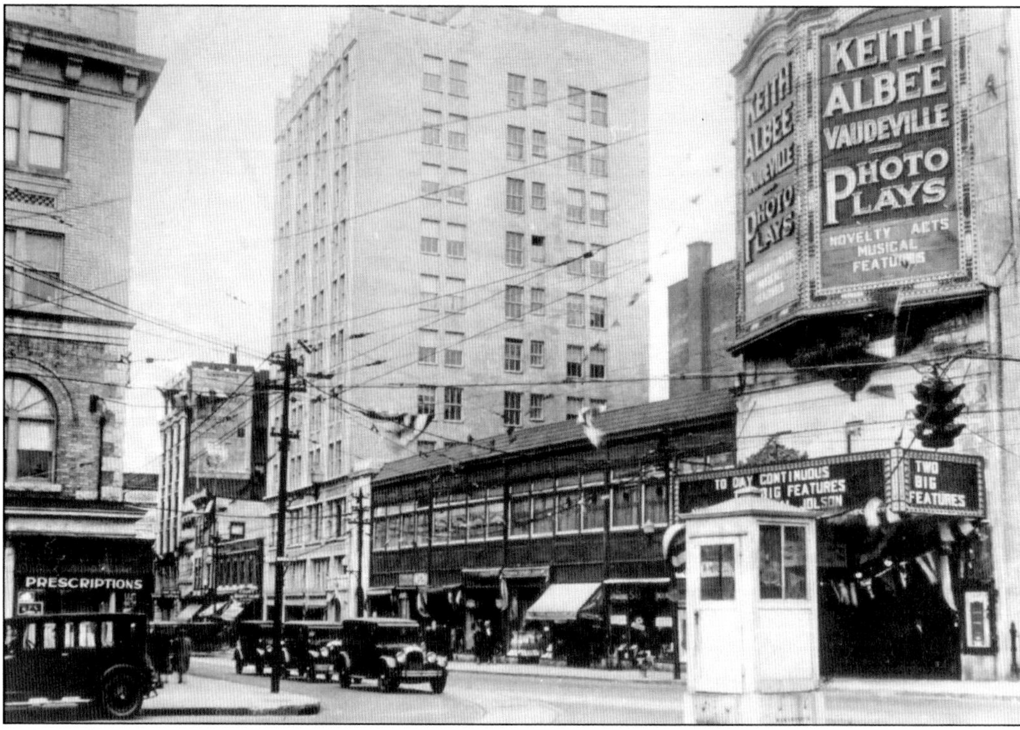

When the Keith's Albee Theatre opened in 1927 at the corner of Main Street and Mamaroneck Avenue, it was the largest theater in Westchester County with 3,012 seats. The marquee shown in this photograph from the 1920s advertises "continuous big features" with Al Jolson, who lived nearby in Scarsdale. (WPCA.)

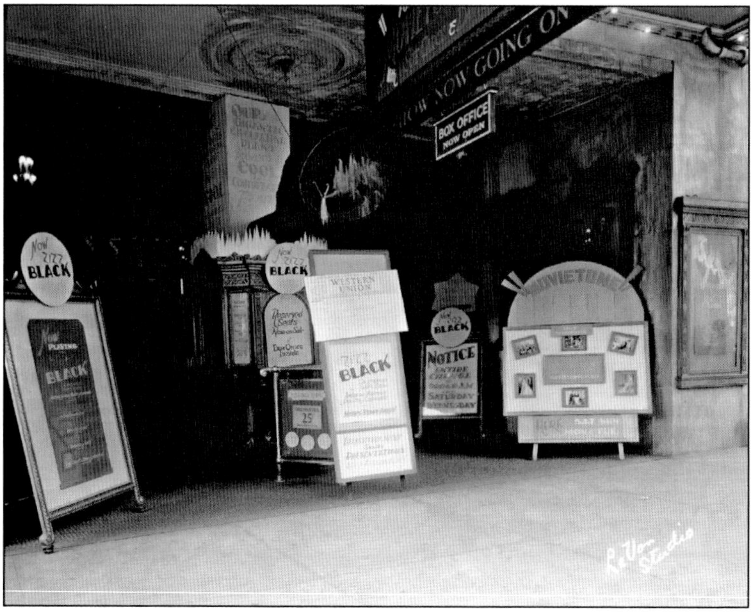

This July 1929 photograph of the entrance to Keith Albee Theatre shows advertisements for "Zizz" Black and movies. Black was the conductor of a popular jazz orchestra that toured the country. The following week, the Marx Brothers' *The Cocoanuts* was shown, and the *Daily Press* noted how a chance to see the film at Keith's in White Plains made "a real Broadway musical available to everybody." (WPPL.)

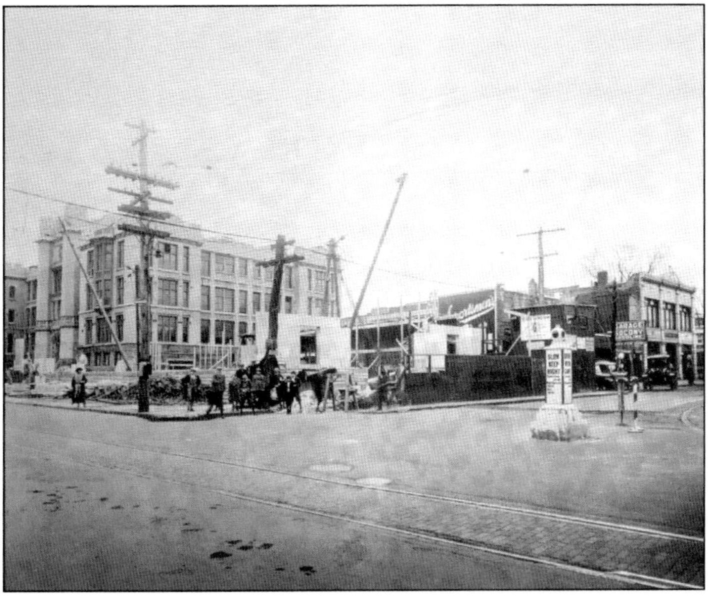

The first savings bank in White Plains, Home Savings Bank, was founded in 1893 and was located on Railroad Avenue. When land was chosen for larger quarters, some thought the corner of Main Street and Mamaroneck Avenue, pictured here, was too far from the central business district, which was closer to the train station. In this photograph, construction had begun on the bank. The large building facing Main Street is White Plains High School, first occupied in 1909. (WPCA.)

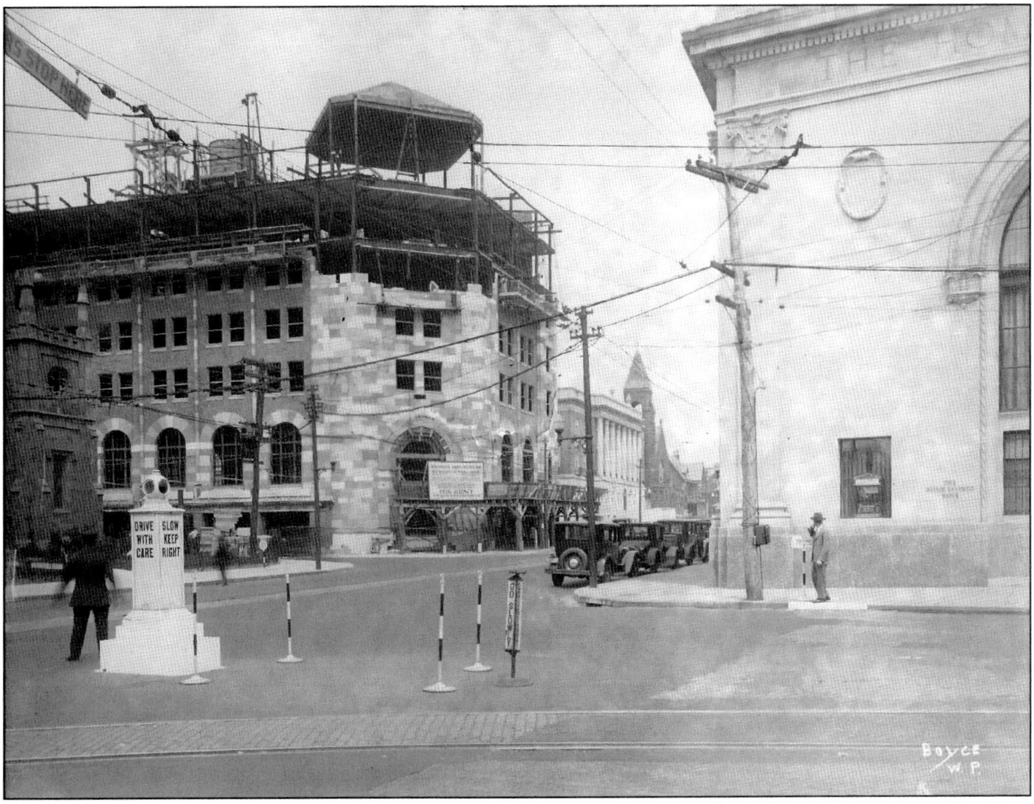

The Lawyers Westchester Mortgage and Title Company was originally in business in a simple office at 160 Main Street, near the courthouse. When its new building was completed in 1926, the company moved into offices outfitted with marble and gold. The architect, Andrew J. Thomas, utilized both Spanish and Romanesque details. Beyond the Lawyers Building, as it was commonly known, is the new White Plains Municipal Building and the Memorial Methodist Church. (WPCA.)

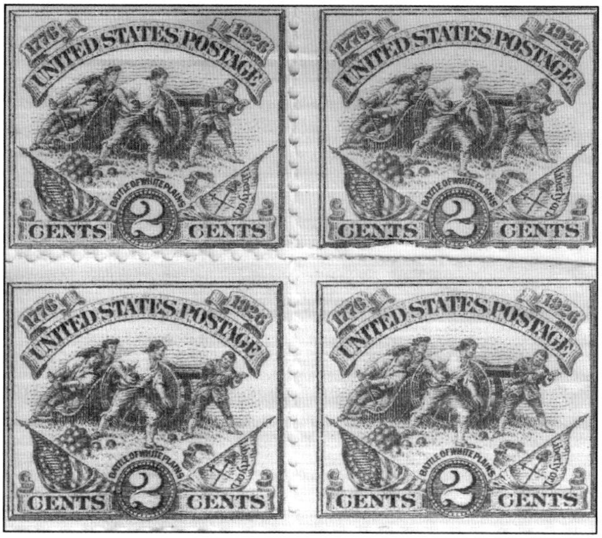

In 1926, White Plains illustrator Edmund F. Ward was asked to design a stamp to commemorate the 150th anniversary of the Battle of White Plains. The first of the 43 million red stamps sold was purchased by Ward's wife, Laura. When Ward was asked to do a mural for the new 1932 White Plains Post Office, he used the same inspiration. (WPCA.)

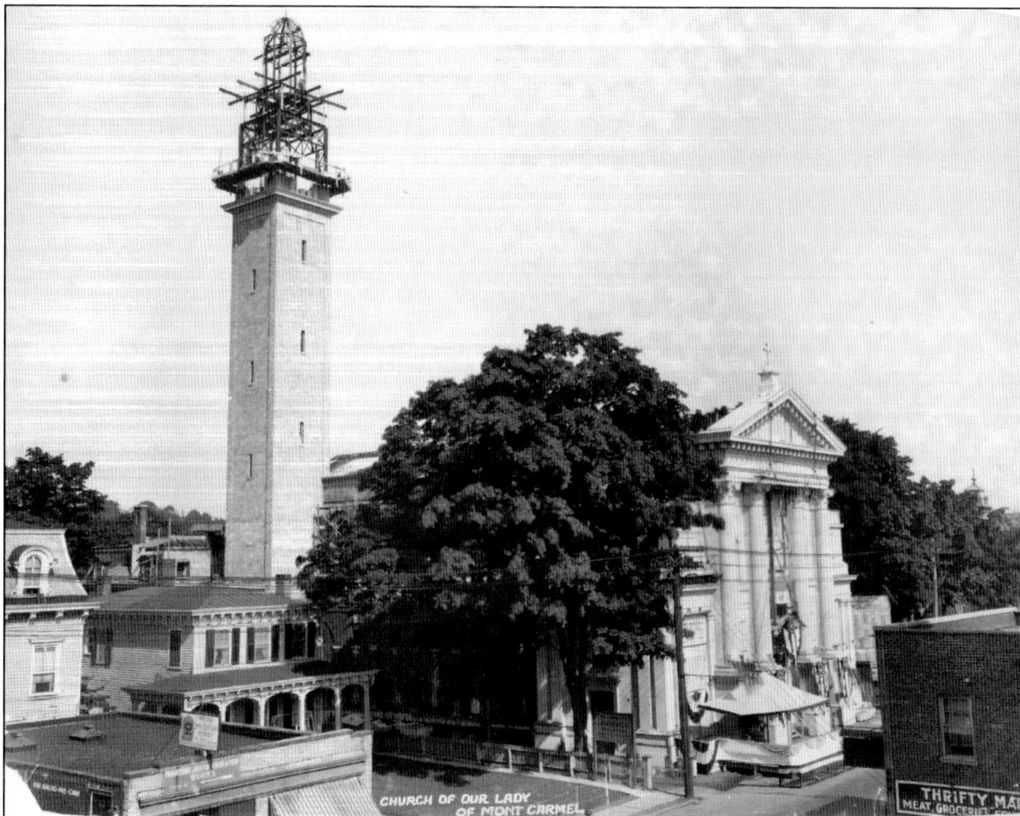

The site of Our Lady of Mount Carmel's first church was near the Bronx River on Smith Street, but it was claimed for the building of the Bronx River Parkway. From 1916 until 1928, the congregation worshipped first on Brookfield Street and then on South Lexington Avenue in a building that had previously been White Plains Hospital. Shown here is the construction of the new church on South Lexington Avenue, just prior to completion in 1928. The 200-foot-high bell tower was designed after the tower of the Cathedral of Lugano in Switzerland. (WPCA.)

Four

THE 1930S

A decade characterized by the stagnation of the Great Depression and the growth of the public sector was met with no corresponding loss of civic pride in White Plains. While the city had its share of Depression-era dynamics—unemployed people, crumbling public infrastructure, stalled real estate market—it did better than many other places in America. Through a mix of New Deal public programs and the relative wealth of the region, by 1936 White Plains was on an economic upswing with growing retail sales and real estate development. The city had a Sears department store and a branch of the B. Altman's store from New York City. The National Recovery Administration (NRA) and Works Progress Administration (WPA) created employment opportunities for millions of unemployed Americans and material benefit to communities throughout the country. White Plains and Westchester were no exception, with significant public works projects and make-work efforts, where jobs in local businesses and agencies were supported by federal funds. The WPA and an extensive, progressive adult education system left no shortage of ways for some residents to survive the unemployment crisis created by the Depression. In 1938, the WPA gave the city $436,800 to support work relief.

The 1930s were a time of stagnation and tension over the future of the city. The booming real estate market of the 1920s completely crashed in the early part of the decade. Even though the city remained the crossroads of the county in many ways, its local identity was contested. The chamber of commerce and some civic leaders called White Plains a "home community," a place for commuters to New York City, but their claim that the city had no industry was false. Still, by the end of the decade, the city had more residents in single-family homes than in apartment buildings. Children went to better, bigger schools and spent summers on the school's playgrounds under the supervision of recreation directors. The 37 police call boxes and 172 fire alarms on city streets never stopped working, giving a constancy and sense of security to the city. A total of 25 bus lines and 200 trains passed through the city every day, and the time to Grand Central Terminal was 38 minutes, much like today.

By the second half of the decade, William L. O'Donovan, city editor of the *Daily Reporter*, could reasonably be believed when he called White Plains the "Ideal Small American City." It was in that year when funds became available for large projects that the era of "slum clearance" began. Although World War II interrupted civic action regarding housing, the facts and narratives established in the late 1930s set the context for the postwar era, when development was set on the course that brought urban renewal to White Plains.

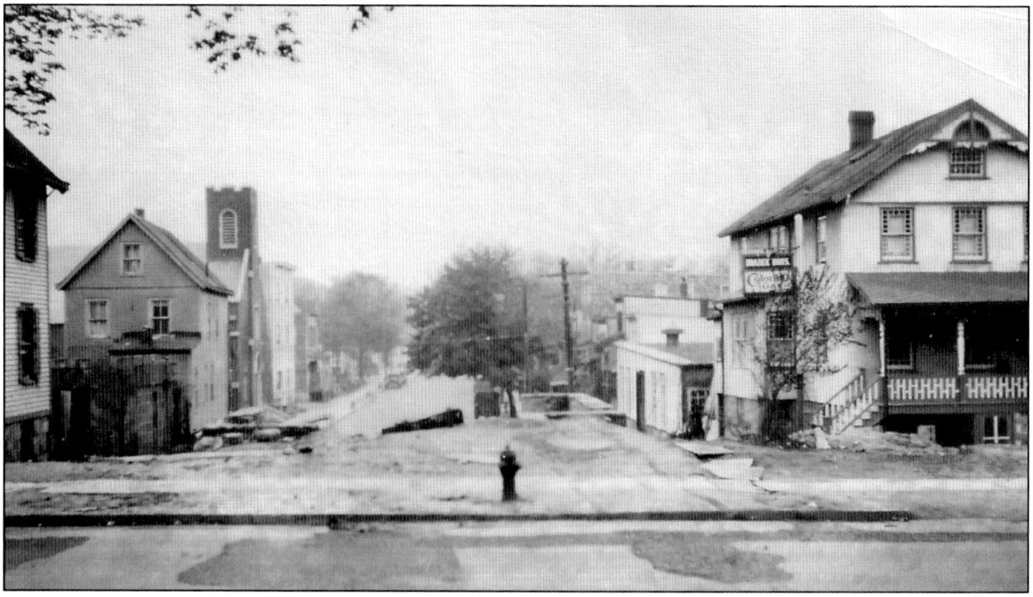

In 1929, the William F. McCabe Contracting Company was awarded the contract to pave Fisher Avenue from Winchester Street to Walworth Avenue, near the Scarsdale line. At the time, Fisher Avenue ended at Winchester Street. This photograph was taken from Grove Street. The crenellated tower of Bethel Baptist Church is visible at left. On the right is a sign for Emil and Louis Hradek's painting business, which had a Grove Street address. (WPCA.)

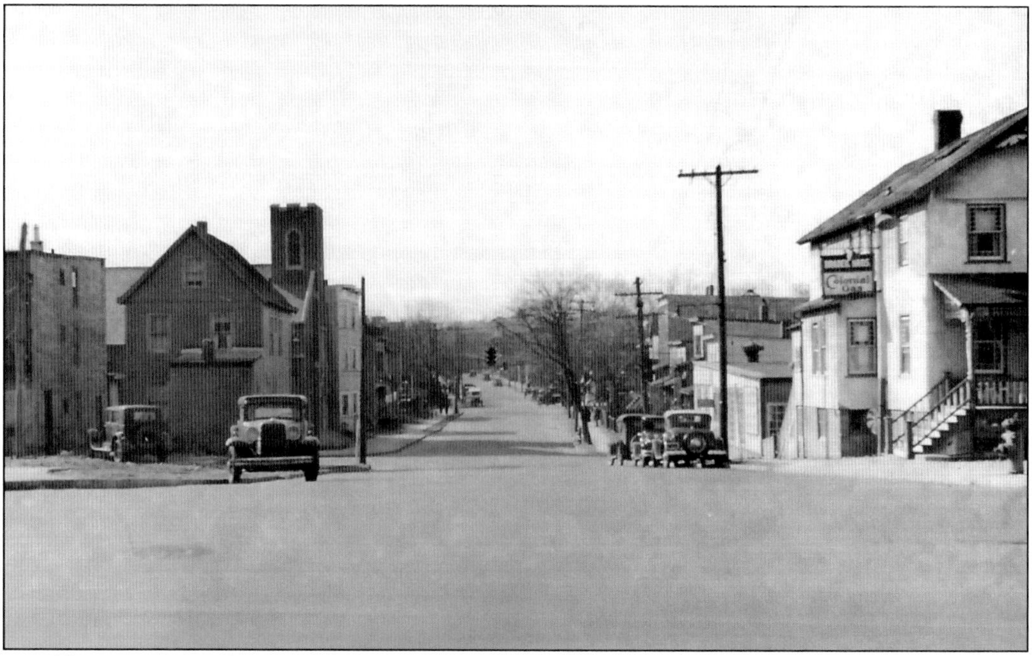

In addition to an asphalt road surface and water and sewer mains, viaducts for telephone wires were installed along Fisher Avenue. By comparing the two photographs, one can also see how the grade of the roadway was leveled and made less extreme. The street was radically altered again during the building of Winbrook, which is why Fisher Avenue now connects directly to Quarropas and Bethel Baptist Church has a Fisher Court address. (WPCA.)

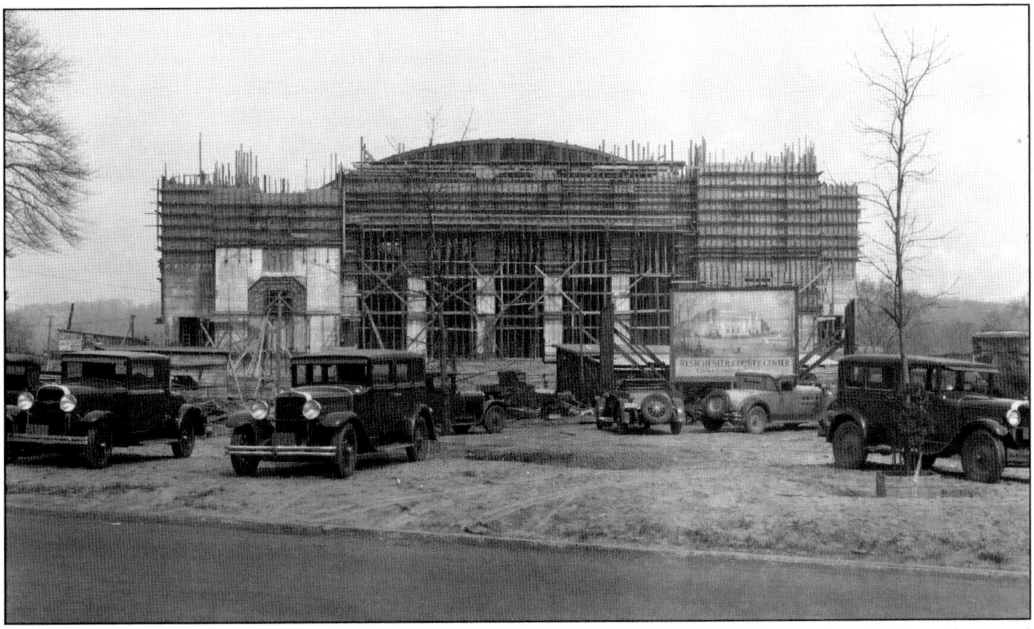

The success of the Westchester County Recreation Commission's music festival in 1926 and a wind storm that threatened its success at the Kensico Dam Plaza led to plans to construct a building for festivals. Well-known architects Walker and Gillette, who had recently completed work on Westchester's Playland, designed the Westchester County Center building in the same Art Deco style as Playland. It opened on May 30, 1930. (Courtesy of the Westchester County Archives.)

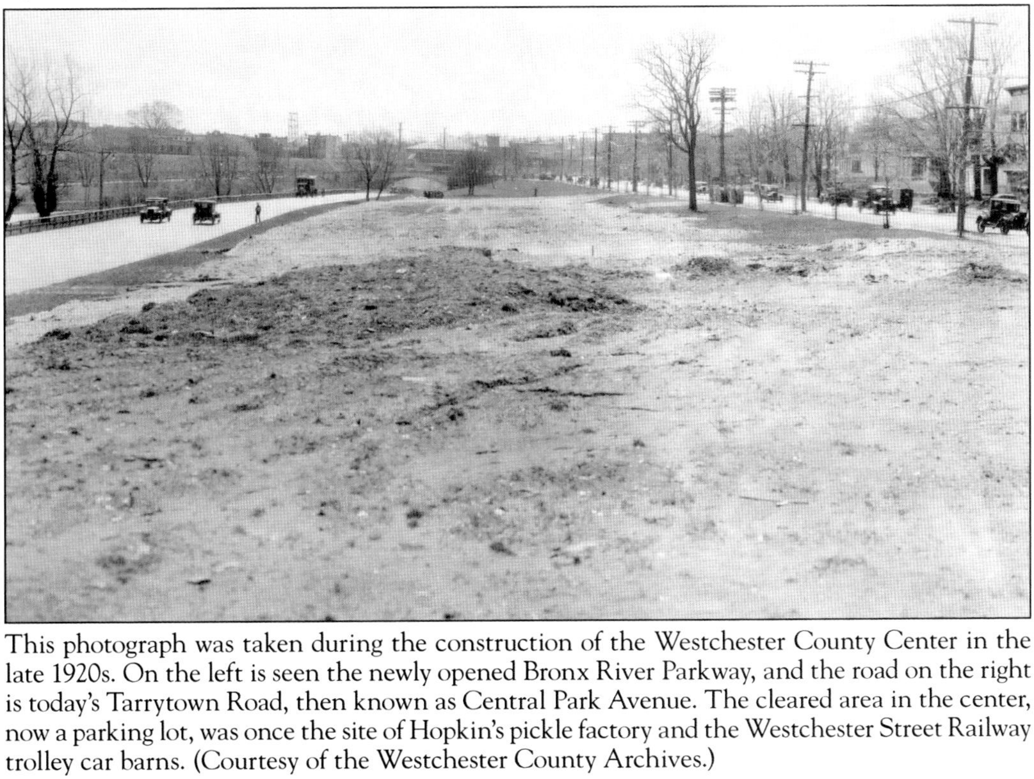

This photograph was taken during the construction of the Westchester County Center in the late 1920s. On the left is seen the newly opened Bronx River Parkway, and the road on the right is today's Tarrytown Road, then known as Central Park Avenue. The cleared area in the center, now a parking lot, was once the site of Hopkin's pickle factory and the Westchester Street Railway trolley car barns. (Courtesy of the Westchester County Archives.)

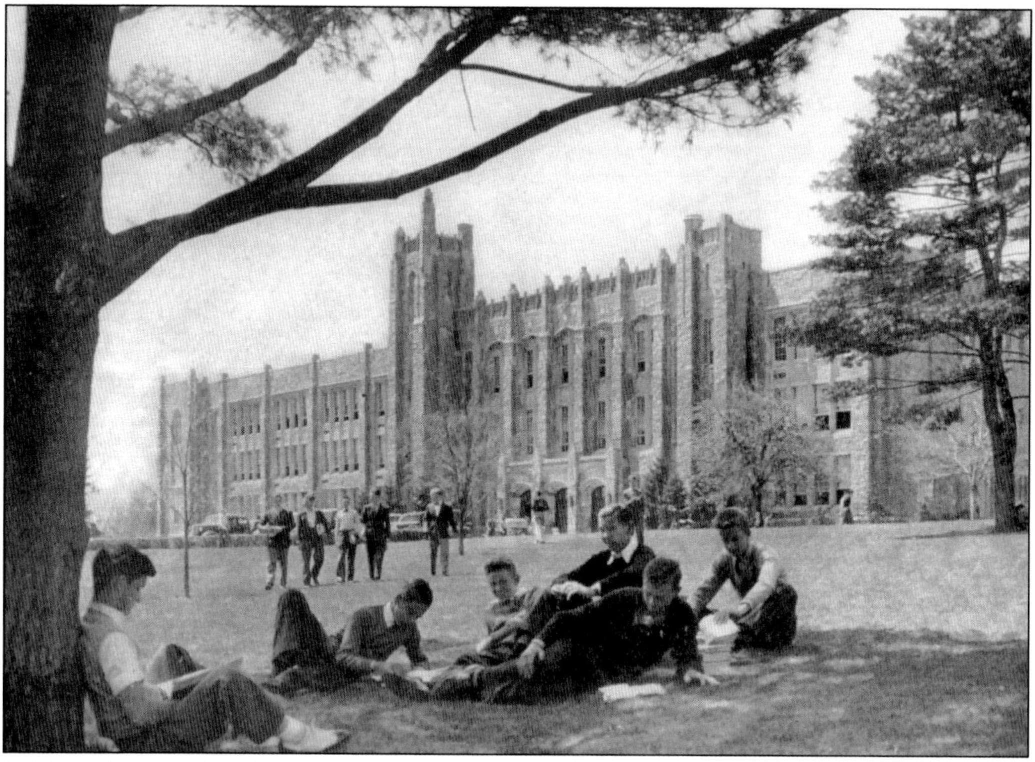

In May 1930, the Westchester County Center opened, B. Altman and Company came to White Plains, and more than 1,000 students started school at the new senior high school that came to be known as Highlands. Ground was broken for the collegiate Gothic-style building in 1928 during a period of tremendous growth in White Plains. Thousands of residents graduated from the building before the next "new" high school was built and opened in 1960 on North Street. At that time, Highlands was converted to use by the middle and junior high grades. (WPCA.)

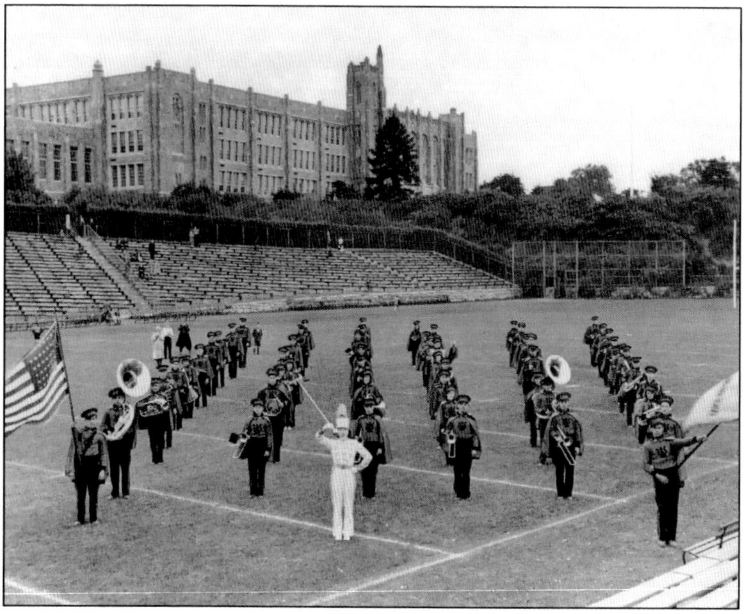

Pictured is the 1938 White Plains High School marching band. Evelyn Dickie, in white, was the first female bandleader and drum major. The 1938 *Oracle* yearbook noted she "did an excellent job of it" and "[proved] an asset." Dickie was also president of Delta Kappa Delta sorority. Parker Stadium was built after Highlands was completed and named for Dr. Jason Parker, who was team physician to the athletes at the school. (WPPL.)

The nine-story Northcourt Building at 175 Main Street was so named as a result of a contest sponsored by the *Daily Reporter.* White Plains attorney Basil Filardi won the $100 prize. He suggested "Northcourt" because the building was across the street and north of the 1917 county courthouse. Designed by Lucian Pisciotta, the Northcourt opened in April 1930 and was the largest office building in Westchester County at that time. Shown here are some details from the elaborate Art Deco exterior. (WPCA.)

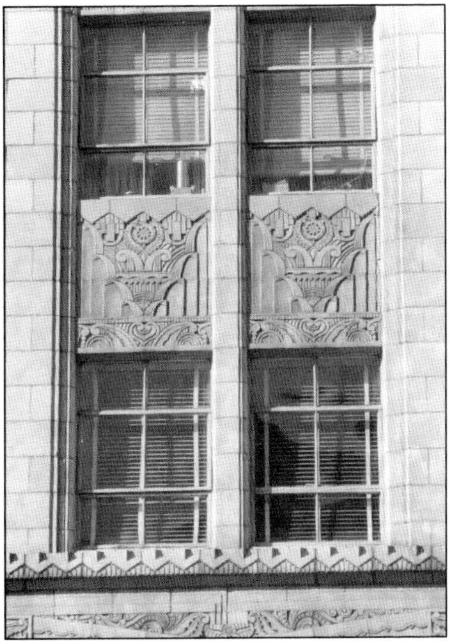

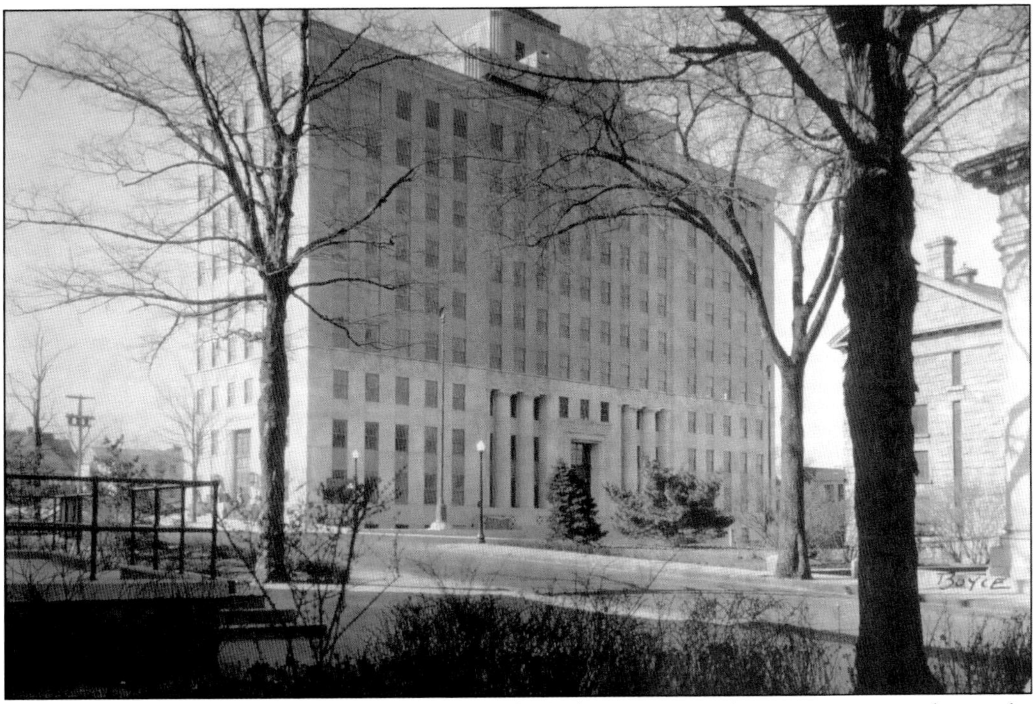

In May 1932, the new County Office Building (COB) on Martine Avenue was opened, months ahead of schedule. The greatest innovation was the Carrier air-conditioning system, which required all the windows in the building to be locked but promised fresh air "to be fine for the health of the workers." The COB was designed by the prominent New York firm of Morris and O'Conner in a simplified Art Deco style. Since 1984, the building has been officially known as the Michaelian Office Building, after former White Plains mayor and county executive Edwin G. Michaelian. (WPCA.)

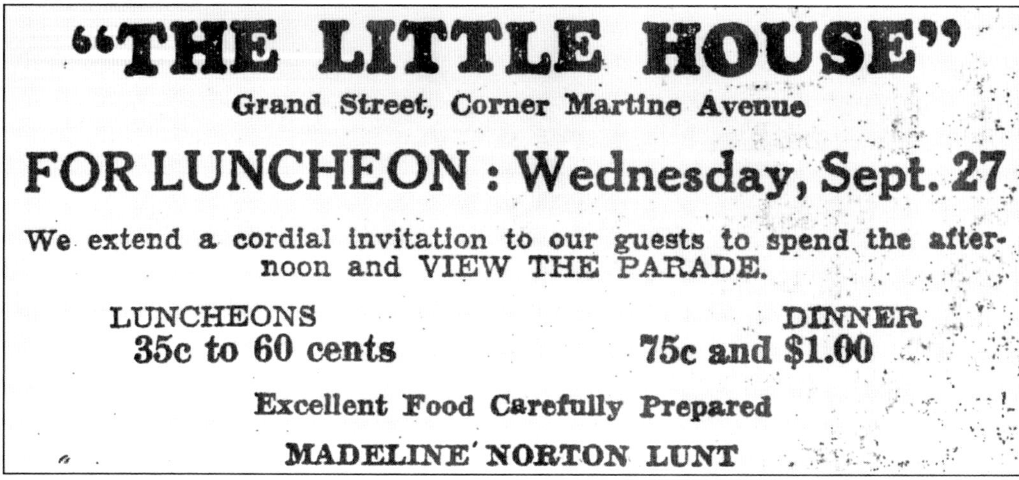

One of the city's grandest parades took place on September 27, 1933, to celebrate the 250th anniversary of the purchase of White Plains from the Weckquaskeck Indians. The Little House Restaurant invited guests to spend the afternoon and view the parade from the restaurant. Mayor Griffen declared a "half-holiday," and schools and businesses closed. Newspapers reported that 50 children from St. Agnes Hospital were guests of the management of the Bar Building and watched the parade from second-floor windows. Rooftops along Main Street were lined with people, and every office window was filled. (WPCA.)

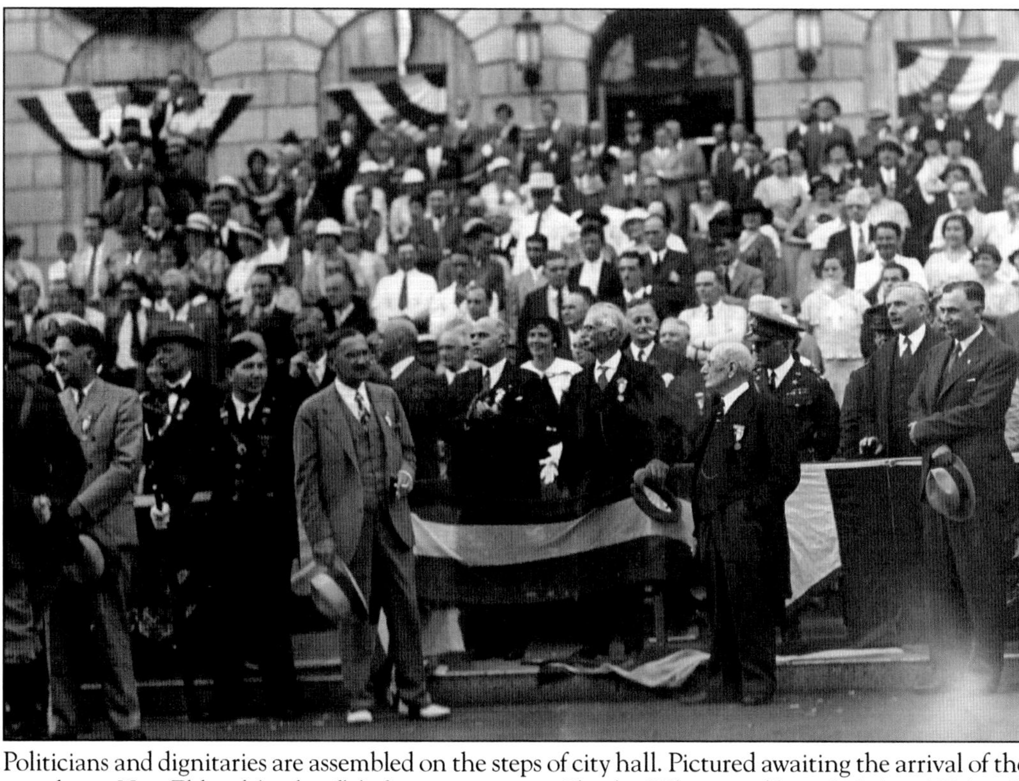

Politicians and dignitaries are assembled on the steps of city hall. Pictured awaiting the arrival of the parade are Hari Eklund (with rifle), former governor Charles Whitman (directly behind Eklund), and, from left to right, former mayor Chauncey Griffen, Gov. Herbert Lehman (applauding), and John Rosch (with cigar). (WPCA.)

Pres. Franklin D. Roosevelt was invited to attend the parade by city historian John Rosch. The president initially declined, but at the last minute, officials received word that his motorcade would stop in White Plains on its way to Hyde Park. The crowds cheered as Roosevelt's car whisked up Main Street. It is seen here approaching the reviewing stand near city hall. (WPCA.)

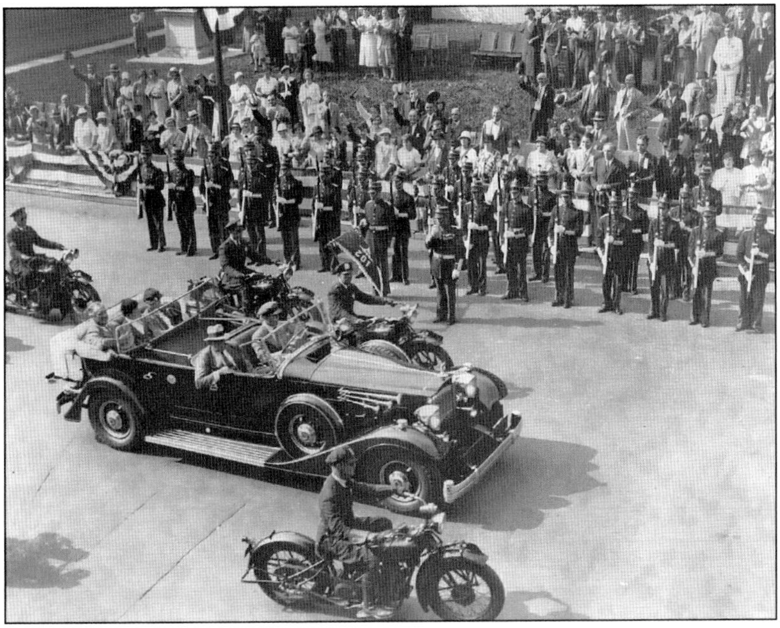

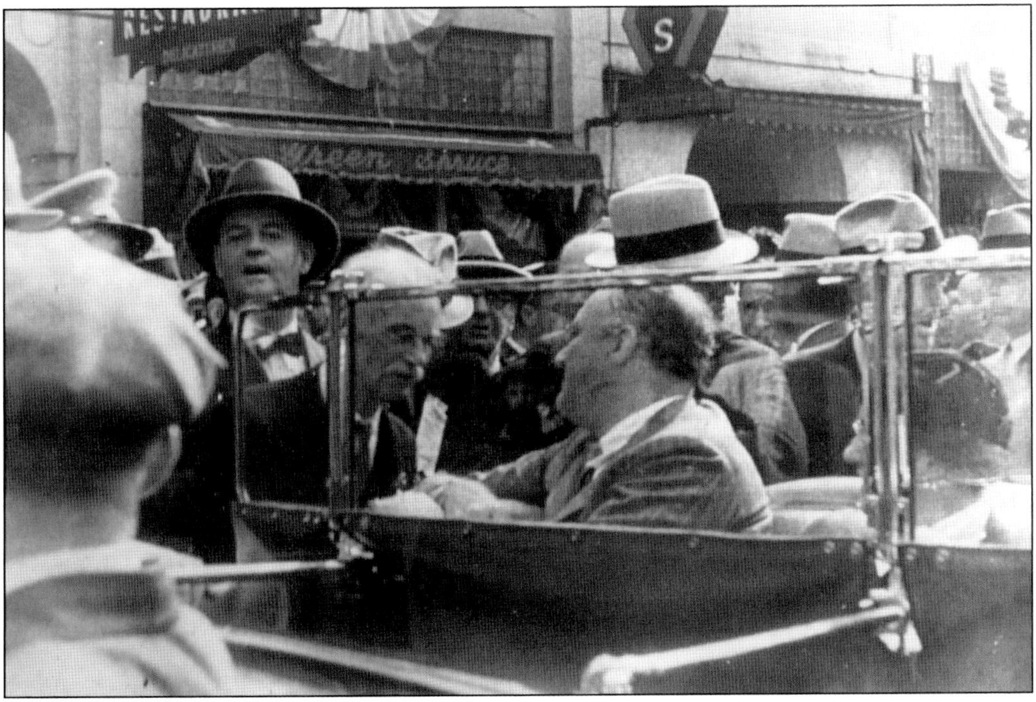

President Roosevelt's car stopped in front of the reviewing stand, and he warmly greeted historian John Rosch. He placed a friendly arm around the elderly man's shoulders and said, "Oh, I am glad to see you. Mr. Rosch, you are doing a fine thing here." The president was asked if he could stay for a while to see the parade, but he deferred to his Secret Service staff and declined with thanks. (WPCA.)

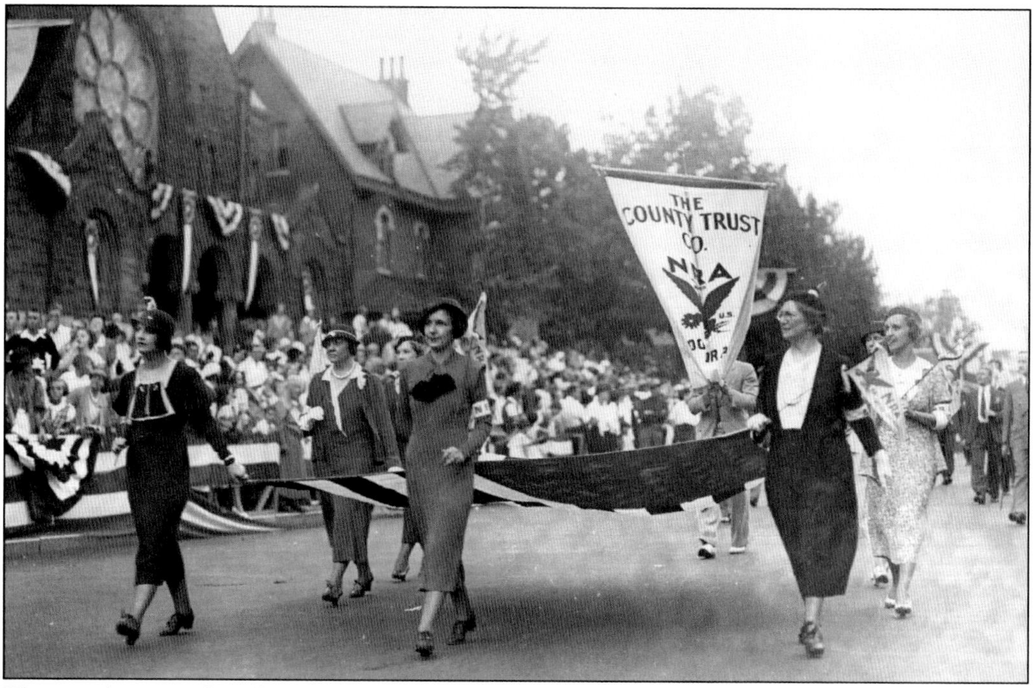

The marchers numbered 5,000, about half of them marching with business groups for the newly formed National Recovery Administration (NRA). In this photograph, workers from the County Trust Company carry the NRA banner past the Memorial Methodist Church on Main Street. (WPPL.)

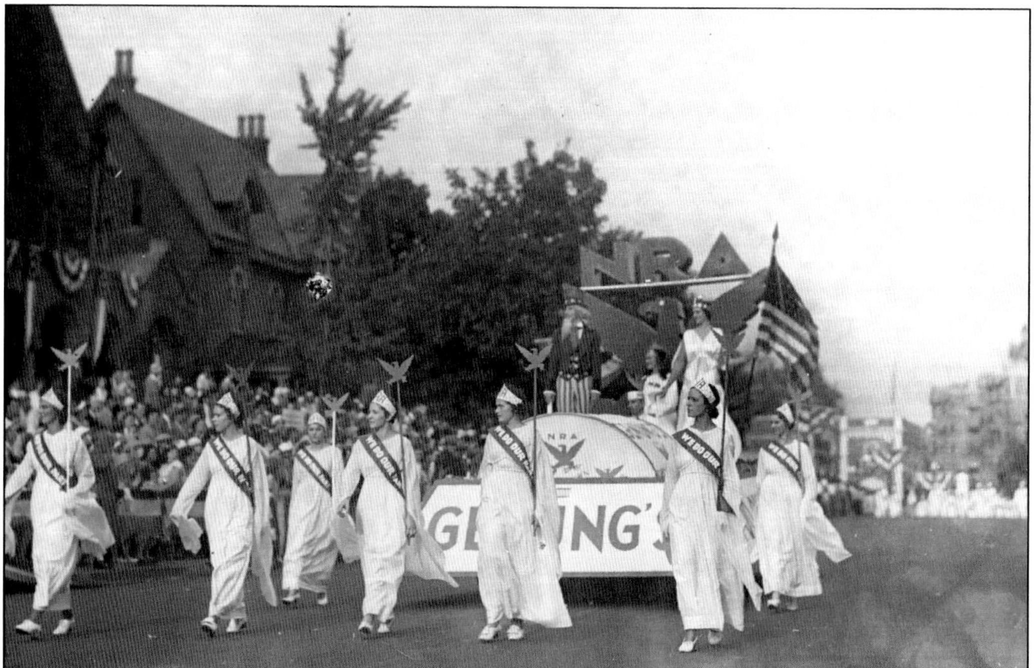

The NRA float, sponsored by Genung's Department Store, was one of the most opulent in the parade. On the float were Ned Coddington dressed as Uncle Sam, Ruth Paulus as Miss Columbia, Jean Atwater as Miss NRA, and Christine Dorn as Miss America. (WPPL.)

President Roosevelt signed a program and gave it to John Rosch. It is now part of the collection of the White Plains City Archives. (WPCA.)

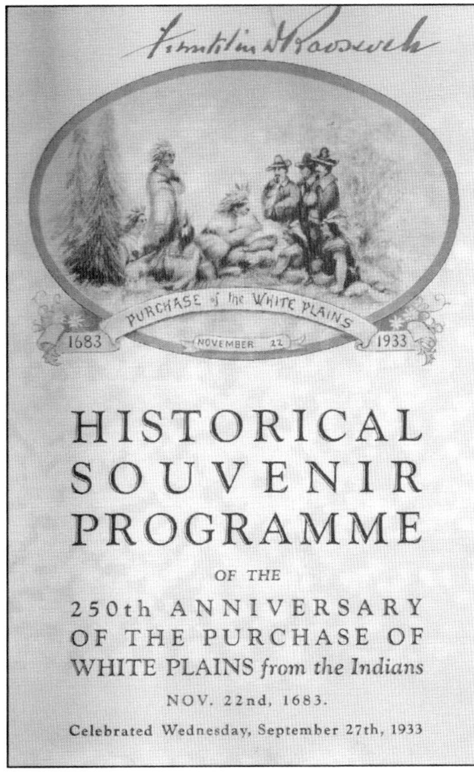

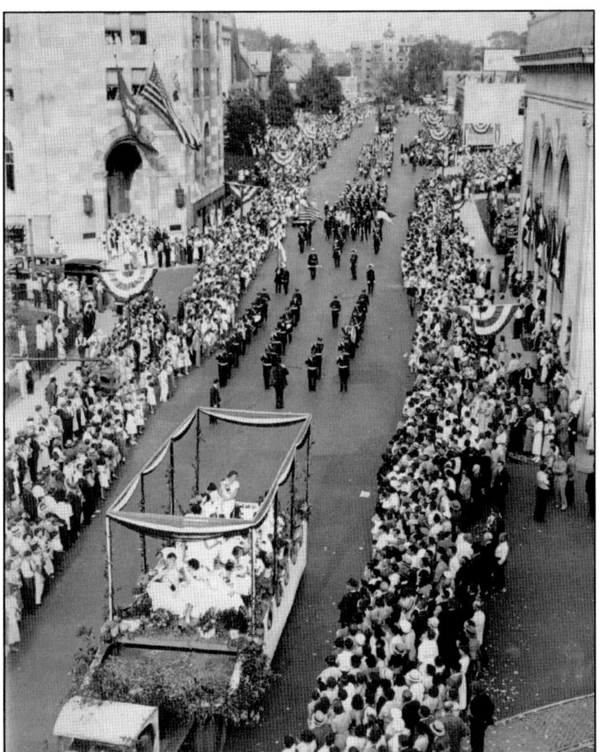

According to the newspaper, the parade drew 60,000 people to the city. There were 25 bands and military units and a dozen floats depicting events of historical significance. At 7:00 p.m., there were fireworks on Ferris Avenue sponsored by the Ferris Avenue Citizen's Club. Later, a costumed ball at the Westchester County Center was attended by over 5,000 people. (WPCA.)

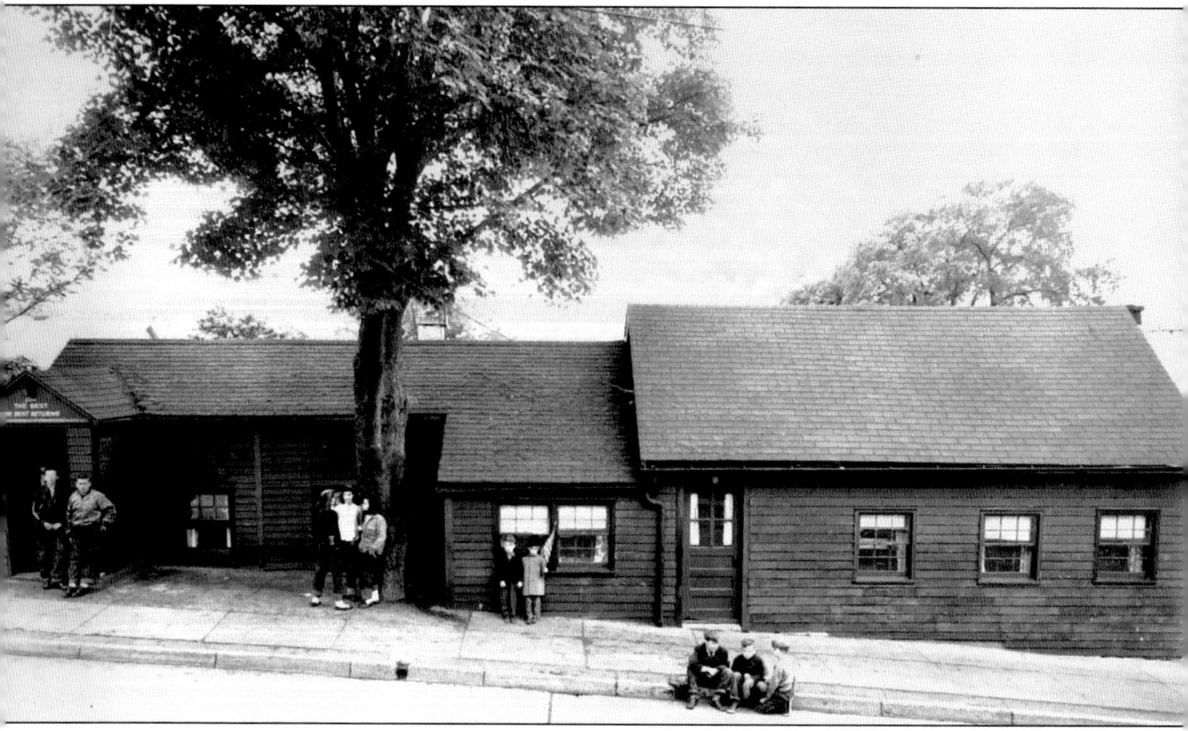

The Rangers Club was formed in 1934 by Amodeo W. Taiano, a probation worker for the Children's Court, who wanted to provide wholesome activities for children to keep them out of trouble. Under Taiano's leadership and support from the YMCA, hundreds of boys (and later girls) became "Rangers" and "Rangerettes." By the end of the 1930s, the Rangers had a substantial clubhouse at 43 Ridge Street thanks to the dedication and commitment of Taiano and the hard work of the Rangers. The principles of the club were simple: learn by doing and help others. Reportedly, not one club member ever appeared in the Children's Court again. Countless Ranger alumni had success and credit Taiano's guidance. He retired in 1968, and in 1970, the clubhouse was sold to the Urban Renewal Agency. The site is now occupied by the Hillside condominiums. (WPCA.)

This photograph shows Teddy Lee Jr. in front of his family's home at 201–203 Brookfield Street. The Lee family's association with White Plains began in the 1910s when Ted Sr. opened a funeral home in the city. Lee's Funeral Home is a touchstone for the African American residents of White Plains, having served as a spiritual and social center for 100 years. (WPPL.)

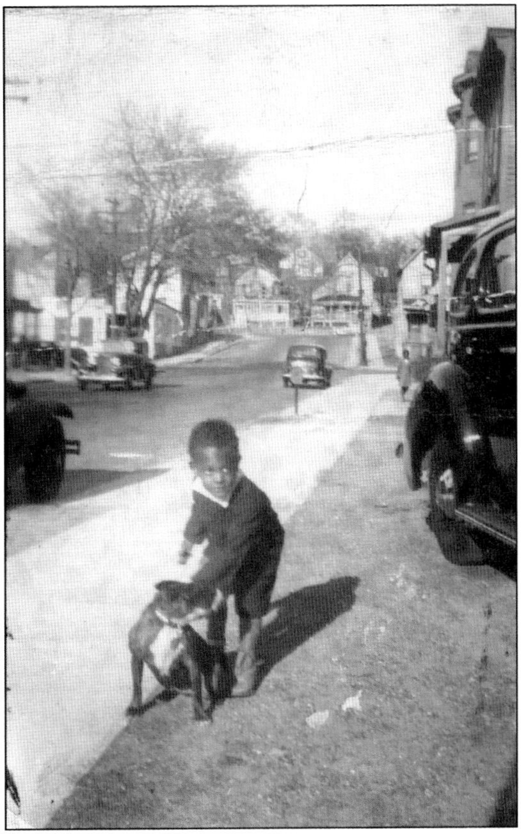

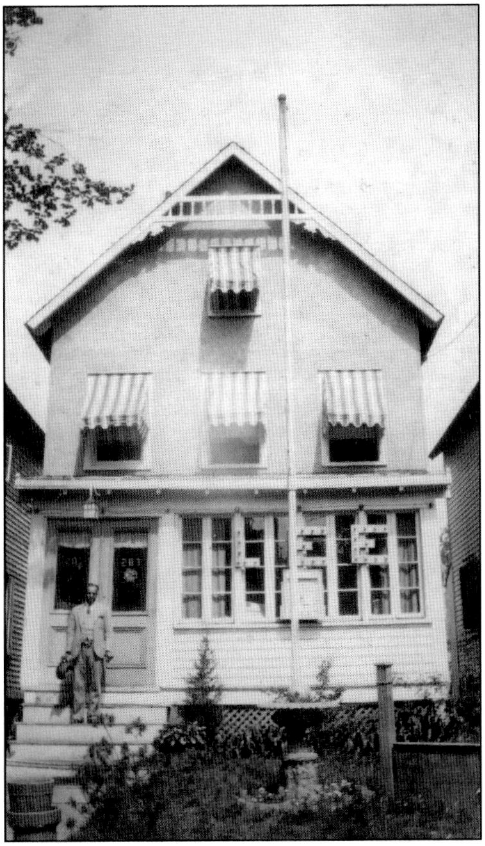

Theodore J. Lee Sr. is seen on the steps in front of his funeral home at 201–203 Brookfield Street. The Lees continue to operate a funeral home, having relocated to various buildings as their business grew and the downtown area underwent urban renewal. Lee's Funeral Home is currently located at 160 Fisher Avenue. (WPPL.)

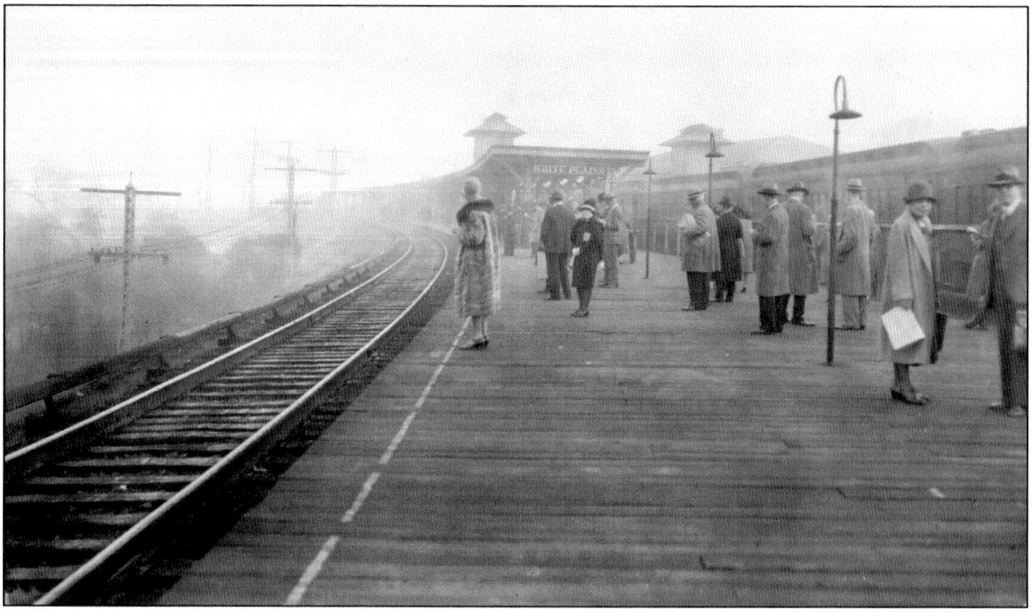

This is a view of the White Plains Railroad Station in the 1930s. The photograph was taken for the Publicity Bureau of the Department of Public Relations for the New York Central System. The roof of the station that sat at the end of Martine Avenue on Depot Plaza is visible above the train on the right. The platform suffered numerous fires and was finally brought up to more modern standards in 1962 when shops and a snack bar were added to the station. (WPPL.)

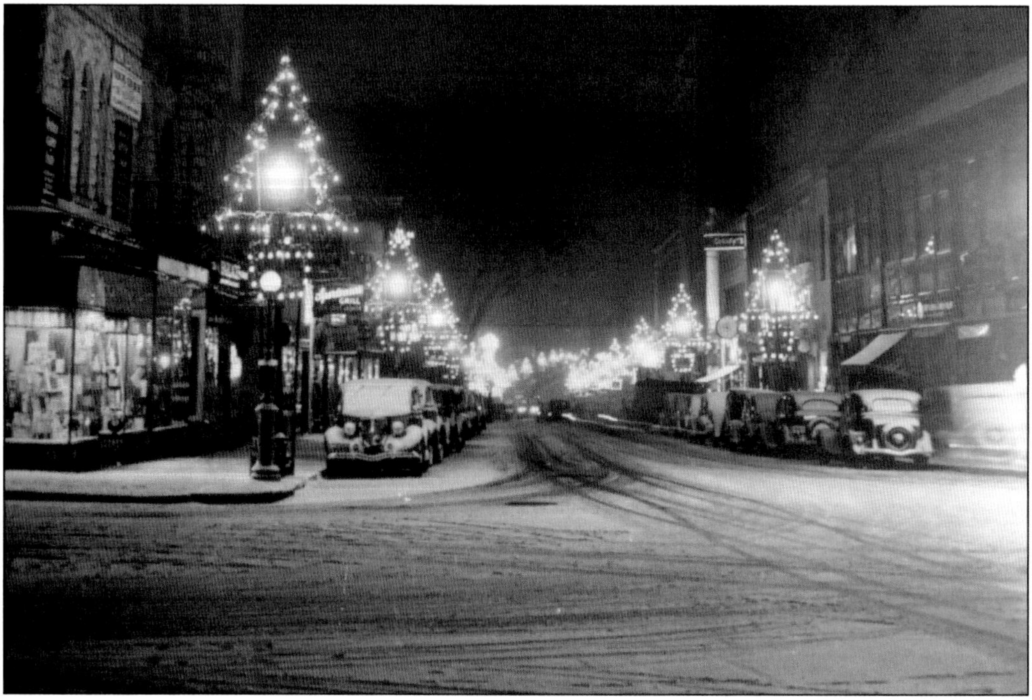

This view is looking west on Main Street on New Year's Eve in 1937. The Auditorium Building at the corner of Mamaroneck Avenue is on the left. It was the first year that Christmas lights decorated the streets in White Plains. (WPCA.)

Five

The 1940s

Mobilization for World War II and an enthusiastic return to local concerns dominated the early and late parts of the 1940s in White Plains, respectively. Seeds planted in the 1940s—demand for housing for growing families, desire for diverse shopping opportunities, automobile-based travel—would not fully manifest until the 1950s.

Many goods were rationed during World War II, including sugar, meat, coffee, building materials, and gasoline. The Office of Price Administration (OPA) issued ration books to individuals a number of times during the war. Folks visited the OPA office in the former high school on Main Street. Blackouts and air-raid drills were another reality of life in White Plains during World War II. On April 6, 1942, the Common Council passed an ordinance authorizing the promulgation of "necessary orders, rules, and regulations for blackouts and air raids." One might think White Plains had little to worry about, but the council felt differently: "WHEREAS, in modern warfare no city, however distant from the enemy is free from attack." Local leaders must have felt strongly about this, as they had Yasuo Matuso, a resident of the city for 40 years, detained with other county residents of Japanese descent after Pearl Harbor. In 1944, the Navy arranged to use the Westchester County Center as a manufacturing center. The building was emptied to prepare, but the Navy operation never materialized.

After the war ended, people returned to White Plains and did not necessarily want to move back in with their parents or families. The demand for housing reinvigorated the "slum clearance" projects of the late 1930s and led to the construction of Winbrook, a large public housing project set on land in the downtown area. Priority for apartments was given to veterans, but some were also set aside for those who were displaced by the razing of the old neighborhood.

In 1943, in the midst of the war, 10 shoe stores, 3 furriers, and 22 apparel stores were advertised in a transportation schedule published by the White Plains Chamber of Commerce. More stores and larger stores were added through the decade, with a commensurate demand for improved infrastructure and building conditions. Even though the chamber sponsored the largest Christmas light operation covering 22 blocks in 1947 and successfully lobbied to have signs that hung over the sidewalk removed by ordinance, there were fundamental issues with the downtown area that could only be addressed by major redevelopment. A portent of things to come, in 1949 Macy's replaced older, smaller shops with a large store on Main Street.

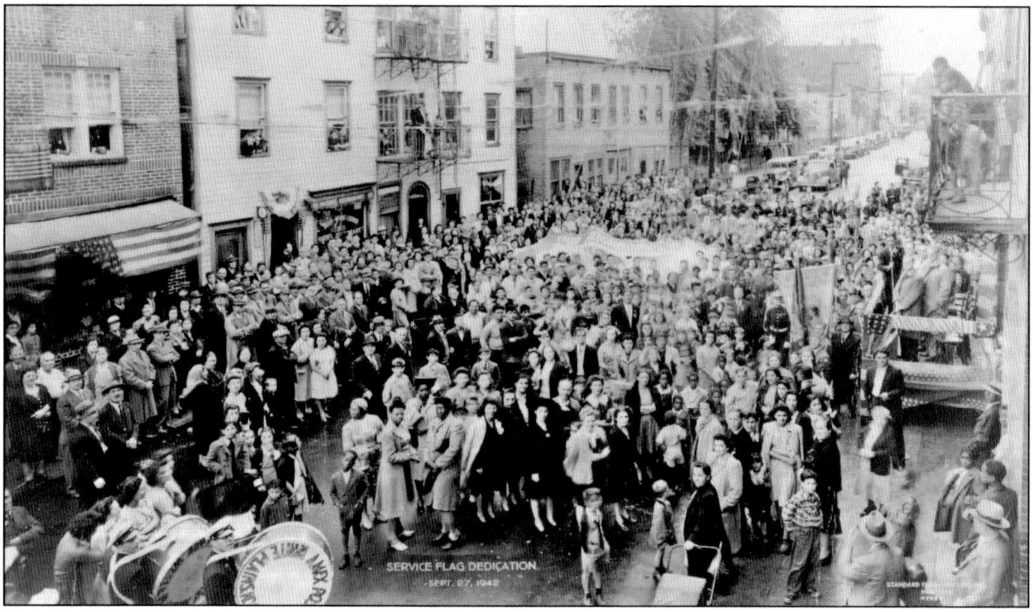

On September 27, 1942, the residents of the Ferris Avenue neighborhood held a service flag dedication for their 100 boys serving in the armed forces. It rained, but nearly 1,000 people still turned out to see the banner with 100 stars paraded along the street. In this photograph, the 12-by-20-foot flag is being carried by the marchers and is paused in front of the reviewing stand. Pastor Louis Zuliani of Our Lady of the Assumption Church blessed the flag. (WPCA.)

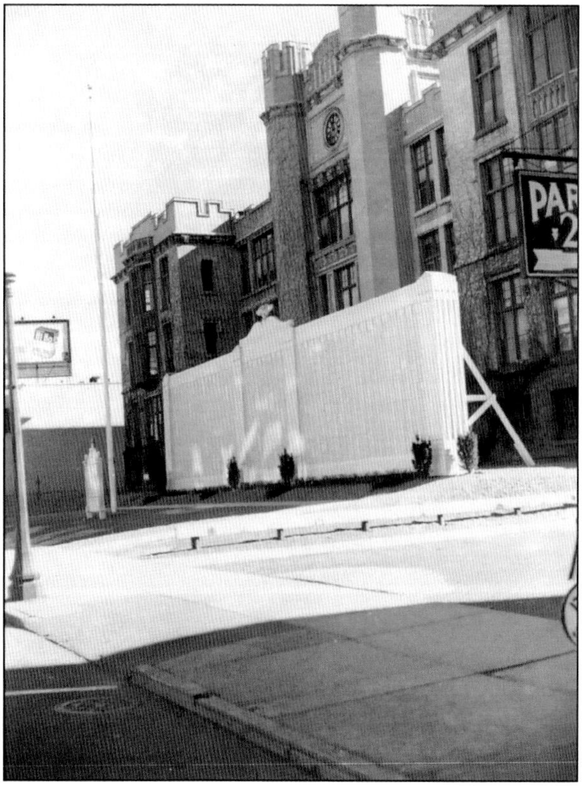

This Honor Roll to the over 3,000 men and women from the city in the armed forces was dedicated on February 12, 1943. It sat in front of the old high school on Main Street, also the location of the draft board and Office of Price Administration (OPA), which was in charge of rationing food and goods in the city. Most people were familiar with the OPA and would have visited to claim ration tickets or report issues with obtaining items. This photograph was included in a set sent to a serviceman during World War II. (WPPL.)

Boyle's Bookshop was located at 134 West Post Road and was owned by Norman L. and Edith B. Boyle. It was one of five bookshops in White Plains at the time, with three on Mamaroneck Avenue, one on Main Street, and Boyle's on West Post Road. This photograph was included in a set sent to a serviceman during World War II. (WPPL.)

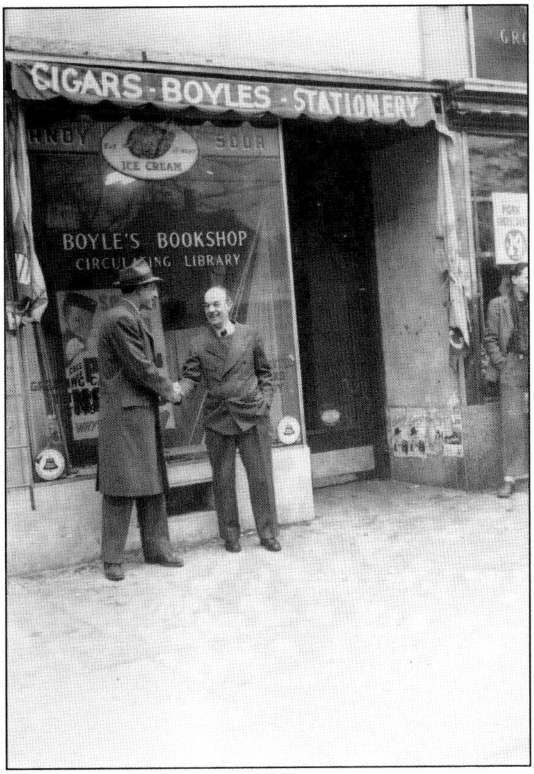

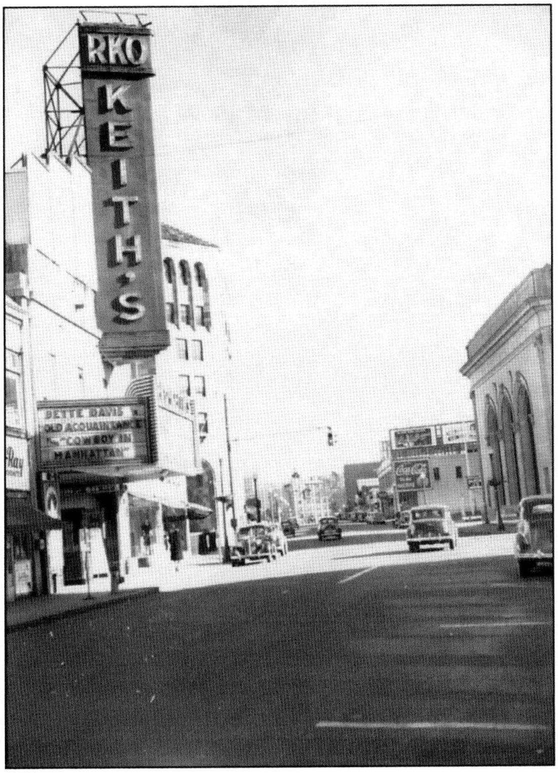

In August 1945, the streets in downtown were flooded with people on the night Truman announced the surrender of the Japanese. Just 10 minutes after the announcement, a boisterous scene developed, with all ages out, young girls barefoot on the sidewalks, and a few adults injured in brawls. This photograph was included in a set sent to a serviceman during World War II. (WPPL.)

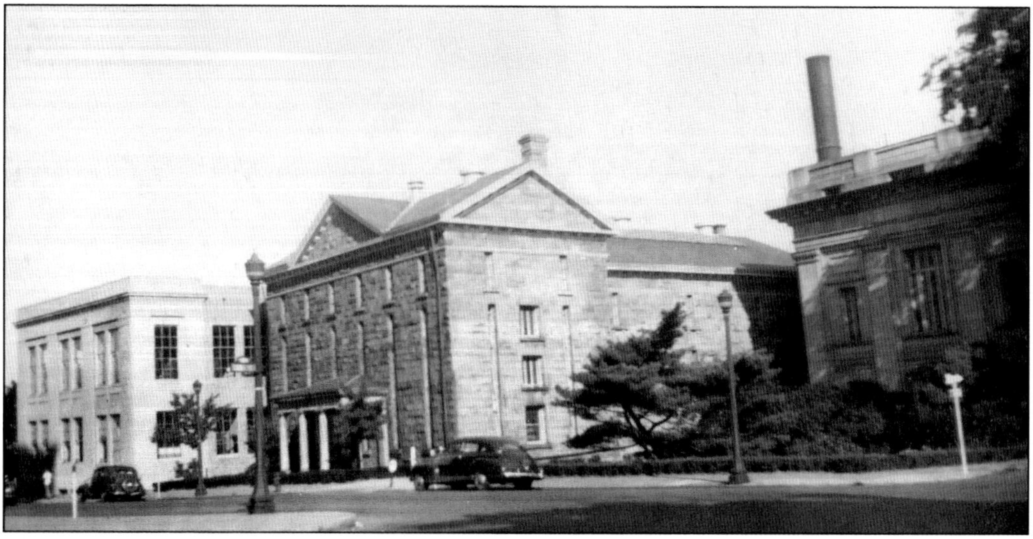

This view of the first Westchester County Jail is from 1943. Situated on Martine Avenue, directly across from the County Office Building, it was opened in 1857 with a new wing added in the 1880s to house females and a hospital ward. In this photograph, the jail is flanked by the Hall of Records annex at left and the 1907 Supreme Court Building on the right. (Courtesy of the Westchester County Historical Society.)

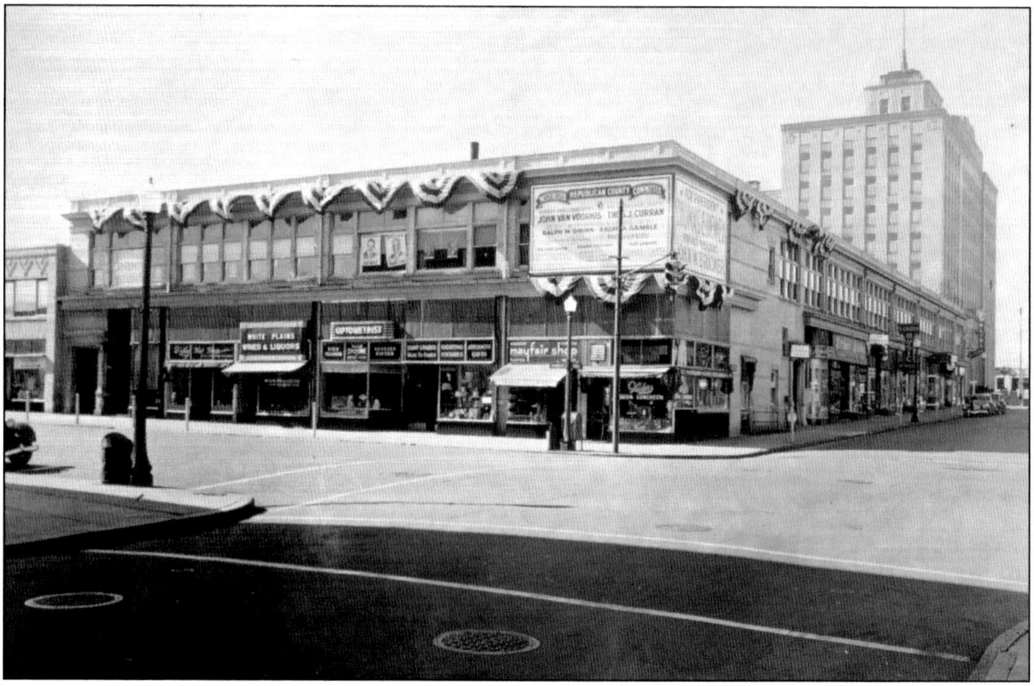

This building at the corner of Mamaroneck and Martine Avenues was constructed in 1910 by John Miles and still stands today. It was named the Tod Building for Miles's son, while a matching structure in the next block was named Marion for his daughter. The Marion Building contained the famous Tod Market, an early supermarket. Seen here in 1944, the County Office Building looms overhead in the distance, having replaced the Marion Building. John Miles had extensive real estate holdings in White Plains, and Miles Avenue was named for him. (WPCA.)

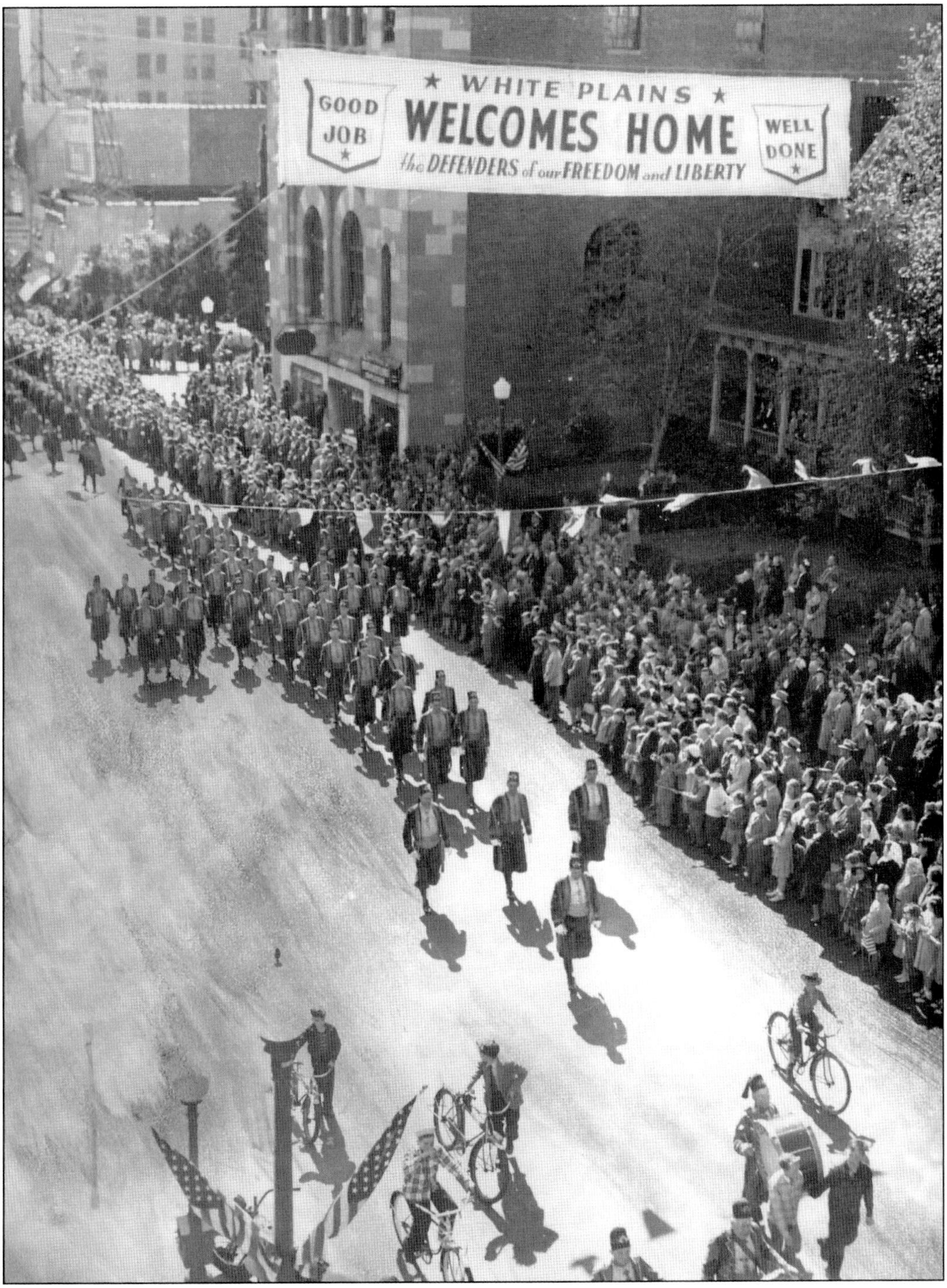

On April 28, 1946, a homecoming parade for veterans of World War II was held in White Plains, with "an estimated 100,000" people in the city, according to the *Reporter Dispatch*. John Rosch, over 90 years old, was the honorary chairman of the parade and designed a victory float that included a replica of the Liberty Bell. Here, Shriners parade past the building at the corner of Church and Main Streets on their way to city hall. (WPPL.)

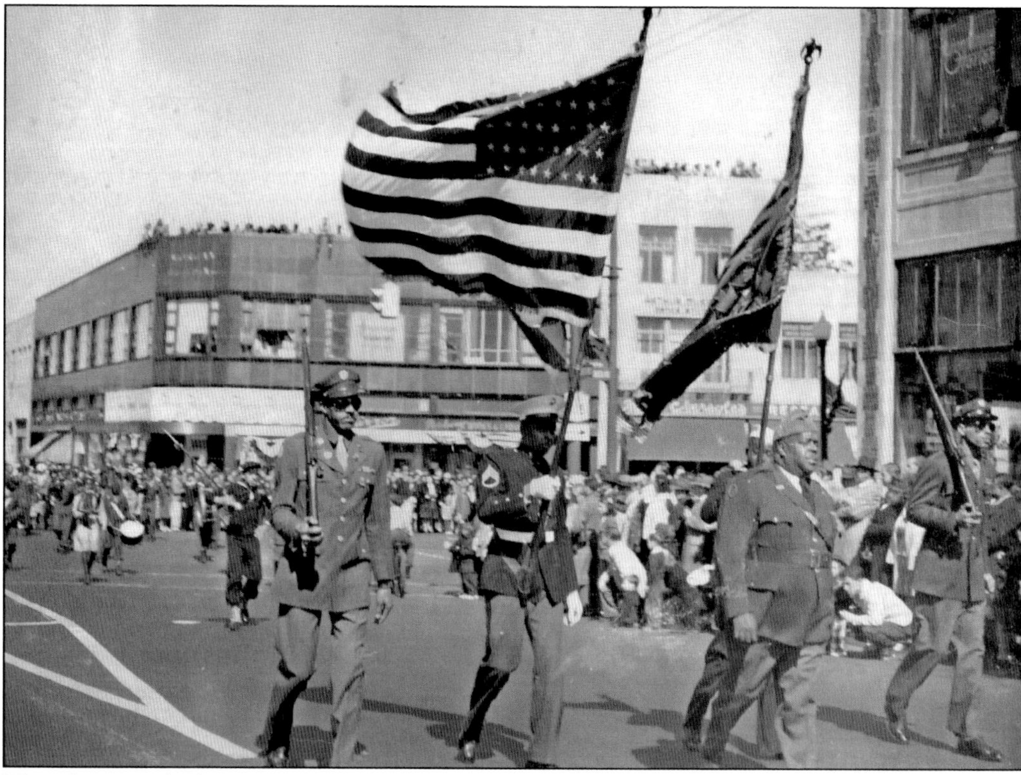

This photograph shows representatives from the Captain Frederick W. Cobb Veterans of Foreign Wars Post No. 3262 led by Comdr. William T. Rogers passing along the parade route. (WPPL.)

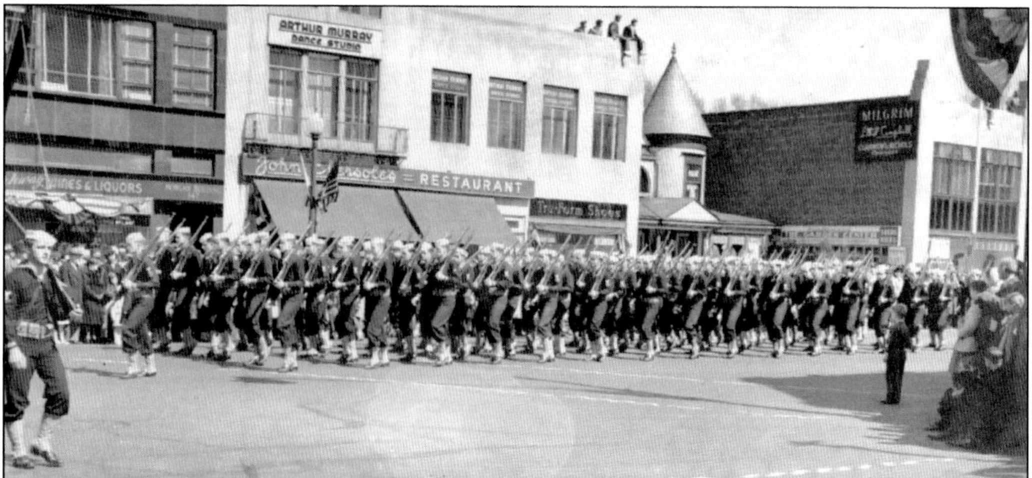

Here, sailors march along Post Road. At the end of the parade, a large party was held at the White Plains Armory. (WPPL.)

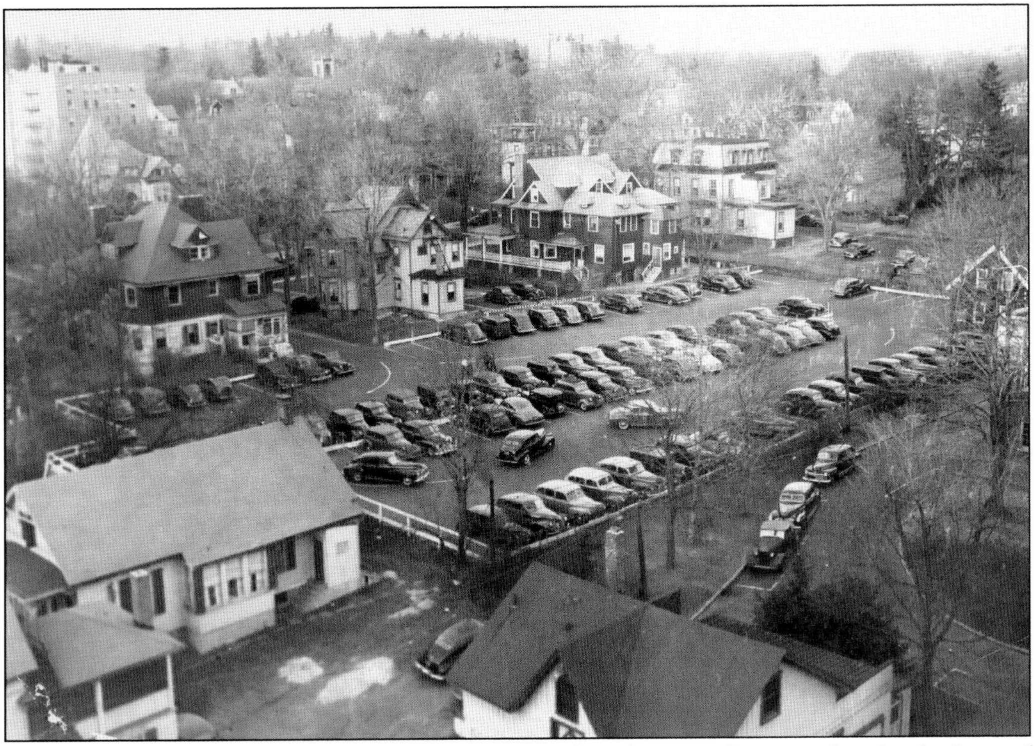

The White Plains Parking Authority was the first such authority to be created under the Laws of the State of New York and became a model for other jurisdictions. White Plains installed curbside meters in 1938 with one hour costing 5¢. Located between Hamilton Avenue and Main Street, this lot was reportedly the first in the United States to have parking meters. It opened in 1946 and had parking for 94 cars. (WPCA.)

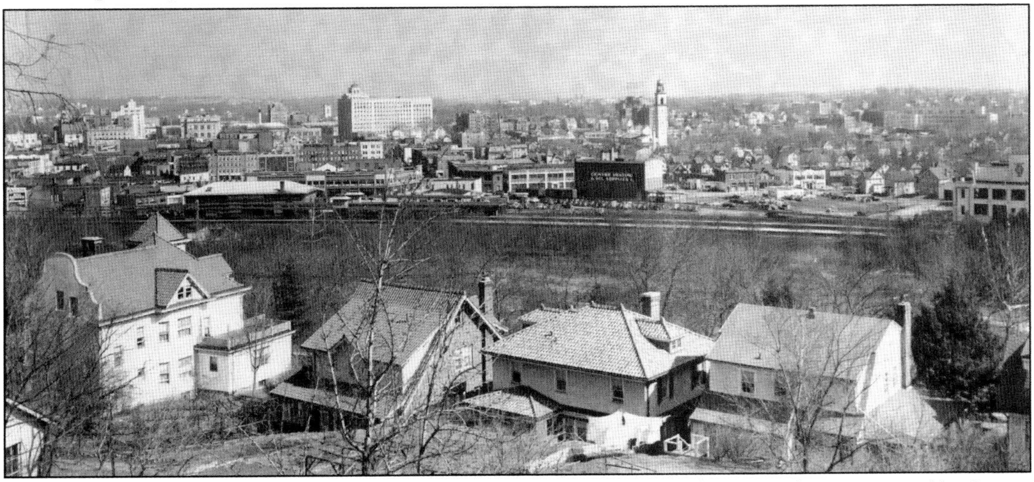

This is a view of White Plains from Chatterton/Battle Hill. The photograph was printed by James Nevins, a photographer at 300 Main Street. Houses along Chatterton Parkway are visible in the foreground, with the Bar Building, Peoples' Savings and Trust, the County Office Building, the Roger Smith Hotel, and Our Lady of Mount Carmel's bell tower (the highest) sticking up along the skyline. Depot Plaza, the large commercial and industrial area at the base of Martine Avenue, is visible to the right of the railroad station, which was demolished in 1984. (WPPL.)

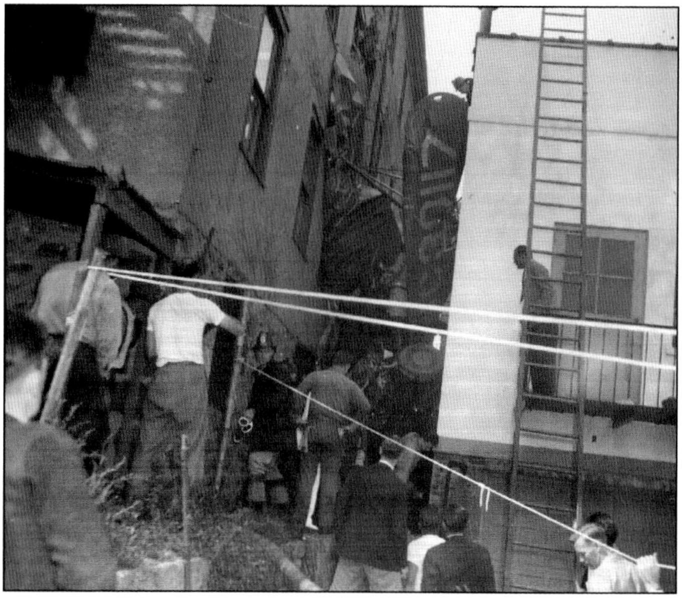

October 5, 1946, was a memorable day along West Post Road. It was just past noon when witnesses reported seeing a small plane circling overhead at a low altitude. It was flying over White Plains Hospital. Reportedly the engine was off when the red, single-engine plane struck the side of 85 West Post Road between the second and third floors. It came to rest between an apartment building and the smaller structure next door. (Courtesy of the Westchester County Historical Society.)

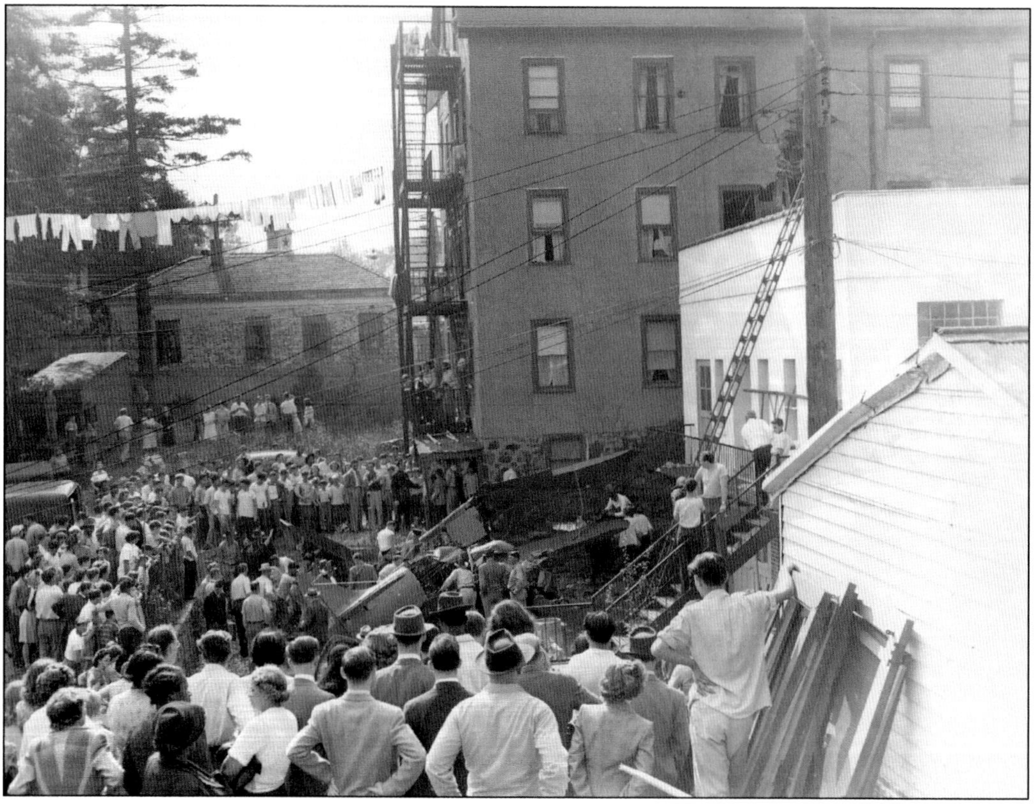

The pilot and lone occupant of the plane, Raymond J. Heraux, 33, of Astoria, Queens, New York, died in the crash. The New York State Police investigated for the Civil Aeronautics Administration. They reported that Heraux had rented the plane at the airport in Teterboro, New Jersey, and that he had a three-hour supply of fuel when he left the airport. He had been in the air less than one hour when the crash occurred. (Courtesy of the Westchester County Historical Society.)

The police investigation concluded that there was nothing wrong with the plane and that the accident was the result of "poor judgement" by the pilot. (Courtesy of the Westchester County Historical Society.)

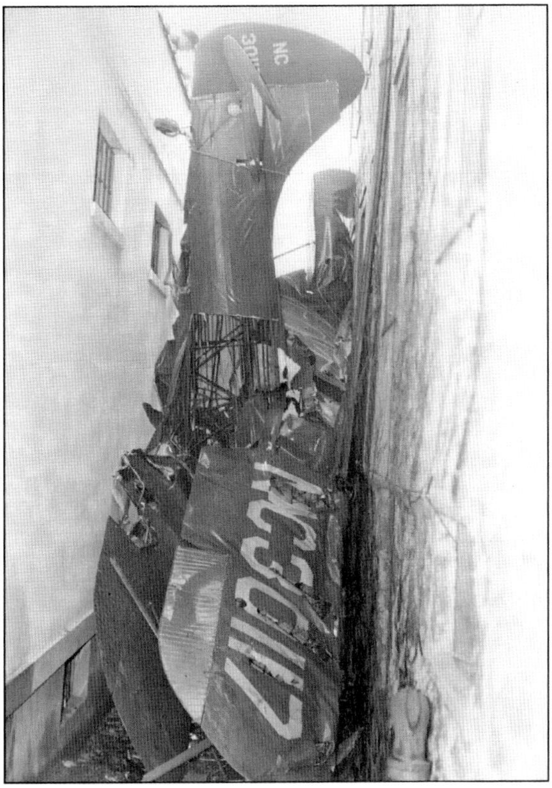

Several newspaper accounts of the crash pointed to the fact that the pilot's estranged wife, Harriet, was living with a friend at the West Post Road apartment building. She was home at the time of the crash. (Courtesy of the Westchester County Historical Society.)

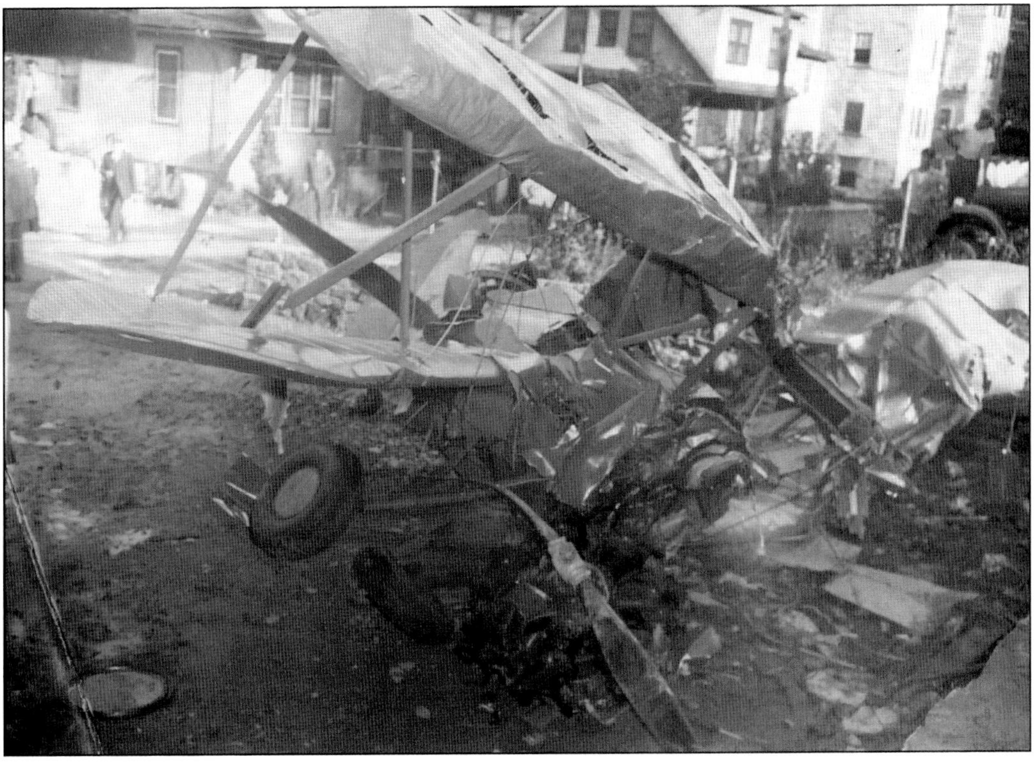

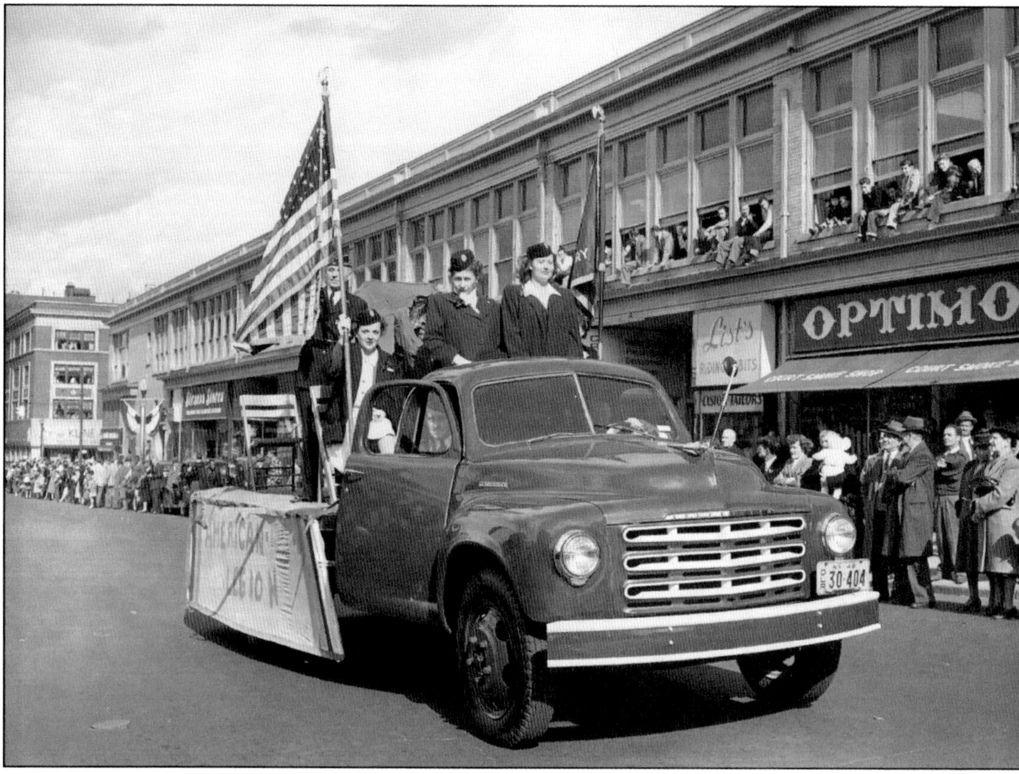

In May 1948, the Parade of Progress was put on to show the "American way of life" as the "greatest hope of mankind" and to demonstrate that "White Plains has the best of everything." Open houses at all types of public and private establishments and lectures by fashion and food experts took place throughout the city during the 10 days. The American Legion Auxiliary is shown passing the Tod Building on Martine Avenue during the parade. (WPPL.)

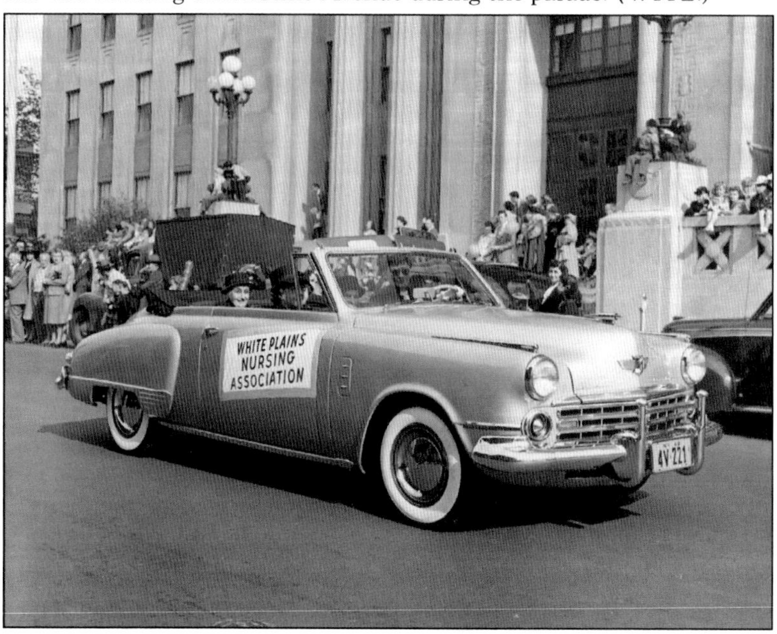

Representatives of the White Plains Nursing Association pass in front of the County Office Building during the Parade of Progress. The General Motors Science Show was part of the 10 days of activities, on display at Eastview Middle School. (WPPL.)

William H. Evans and William O'Connor were marshals for the Parade of Progress. They are pictured here heading down the hill on Martine Avenue. The parade was sponsored by the Civic and Business Federation of White Plains and the Brand Name Foundation. It was intended to demonstrate the "value and quality of brand name merchandise and its influence and establishing and maintaining the American way of life." (WPPL.)

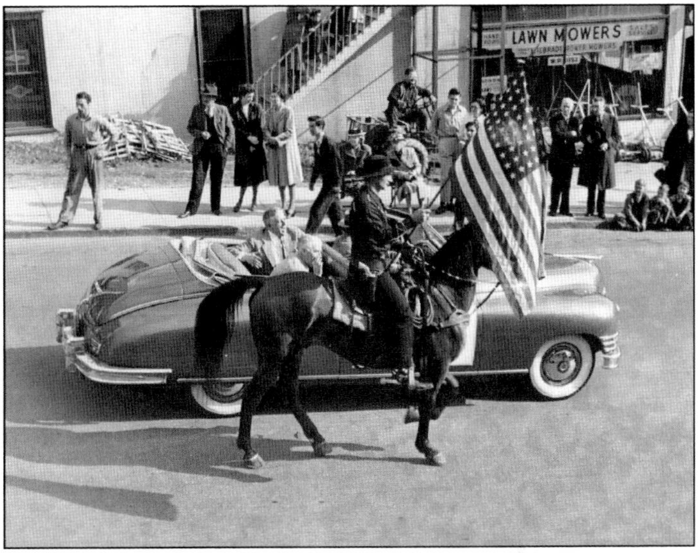

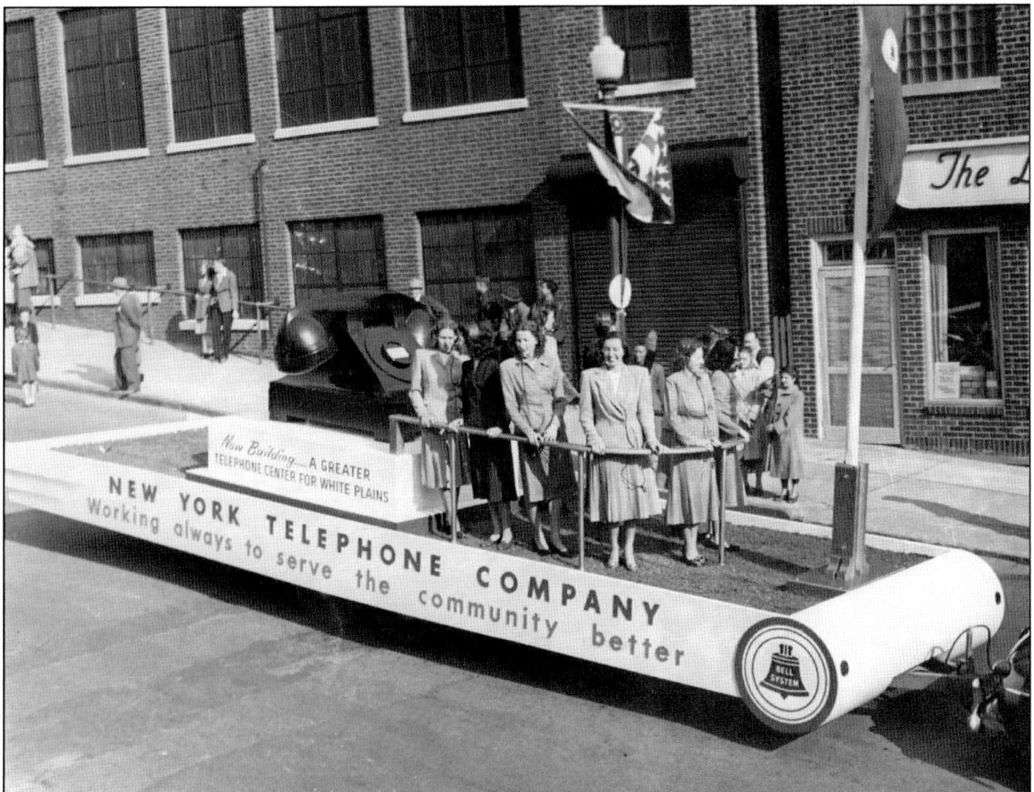

Representatives from New York Telephone Company are shown heading down Martine Avenue. The company also sponsored a demonstration of microwaves at the New York State Institute of Applied Arts and Sciences during the 10 days of activities. The institute was one of five opened by New York State in 1946. The institute operated out of Battle Hill School until 1953, when agreement was reached between the city, county, and state to transform it into Westchester Community College. (WPPL.)

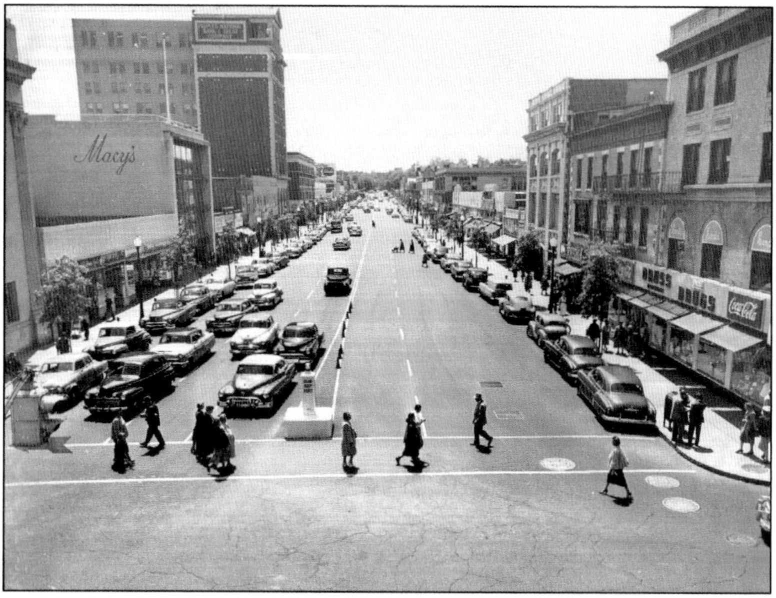

Another view of Mamaroneck Avenue from the intersection with Main Street shows how busy the primary shopping district of the city was in the late 1940s. A mix of apartments, beauty salons, interior decorators, and gift shops occupied the right side of the street up to Genung's—one of White Plains's older local department stores. (WPCA.)

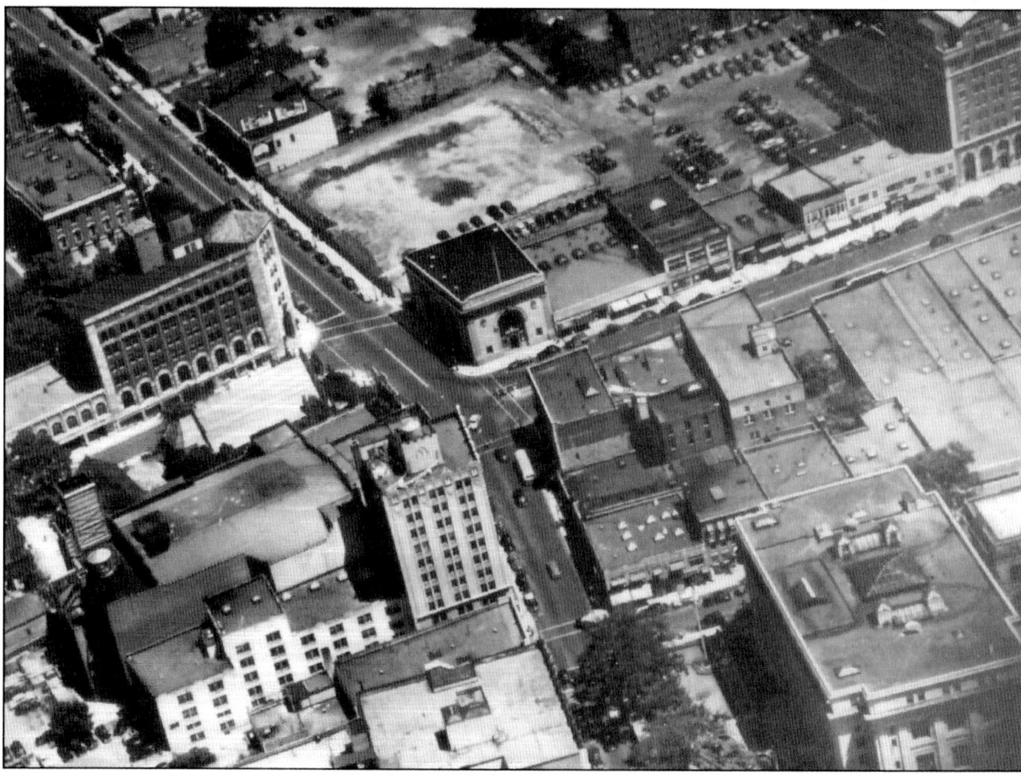

This photograph shows the intersection of Main Street and Mamaroneck Avenue. The large cleared area where the high school stood behind the Home Savings Bank became the site of Macy's Department Store. Between the Home Savings Bank and the People's National Bank on the other end of the block, a variety of shops, including ones for shoe repair, corsets, cigars, dry goods, tailoring, and radios, occupied various buildings, only some of which were replaced with Macy's first location in White Plains. (WPCA.)

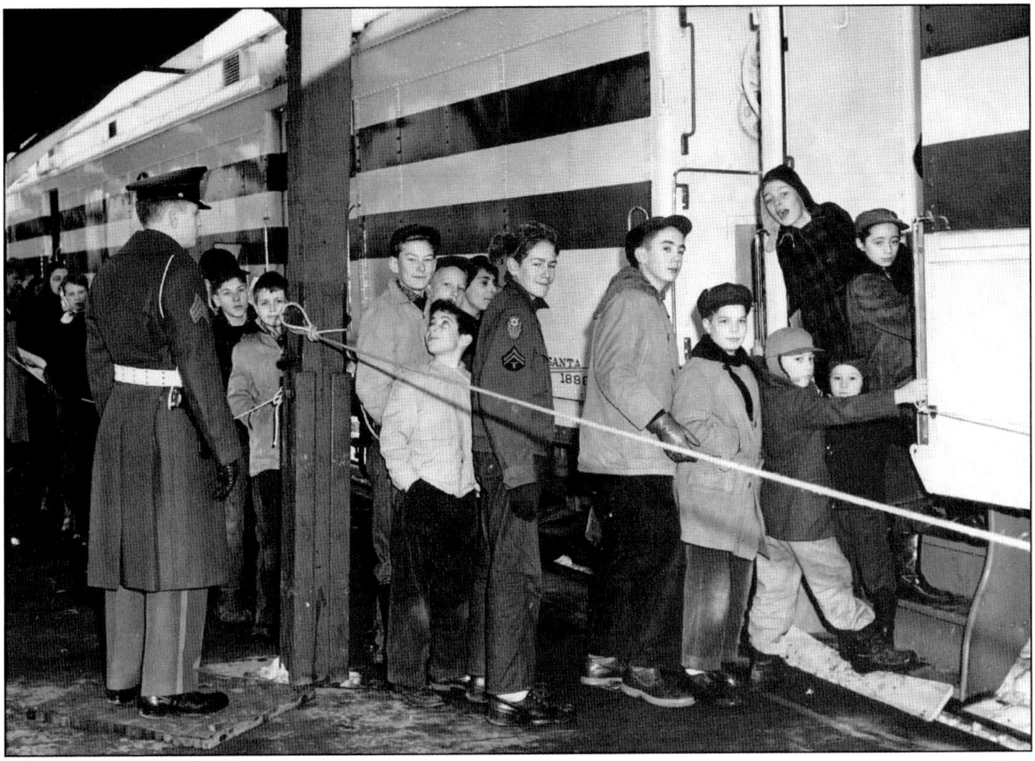

On December 22, 1948, the Freedom Train rolled into White Plains with its "cargo of priceless Americana" in three exhibit cars. The train completed a 3,000-mile nationwide tour and visited other locations in Westchester County. Some controversy was stirred by the $3,500 the city had to pay to have the train visit, though the tour was nominally sponsored by the American Heritage Foundation. (WPPL.)

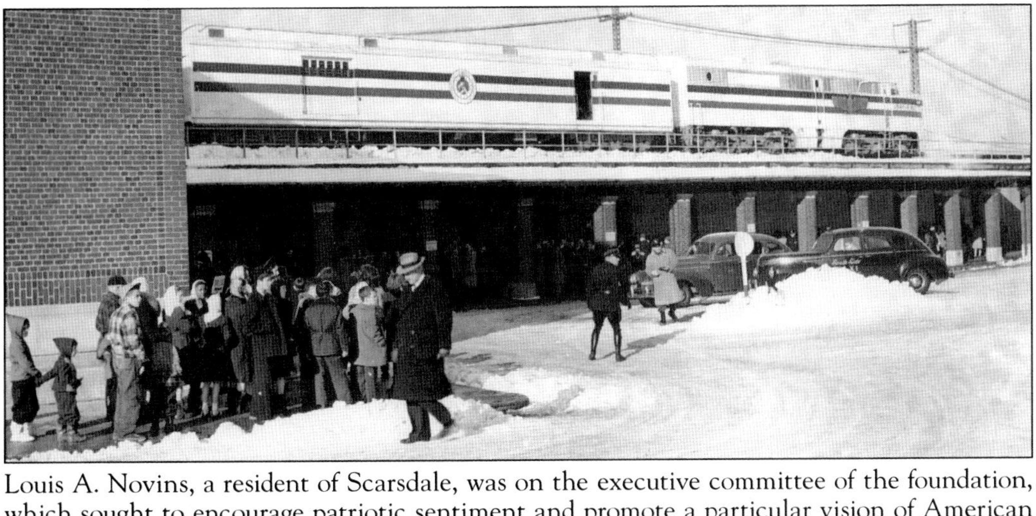

Louis A. Novins, a resident of Scarsdale, was on the executive committee of the foundation, which sought to encourage patriotic sentiment and promote a particular vision of American identity. An editorial in the *Reporter Dispatch* warned, "Just because our democratic government has sheltered us since the day we were born is no assurance it can't be snatched away by the subversive forces seeking to undermine it," setting the stage for the Red Scare and Cold War eras in Westchester. (WPPL.)

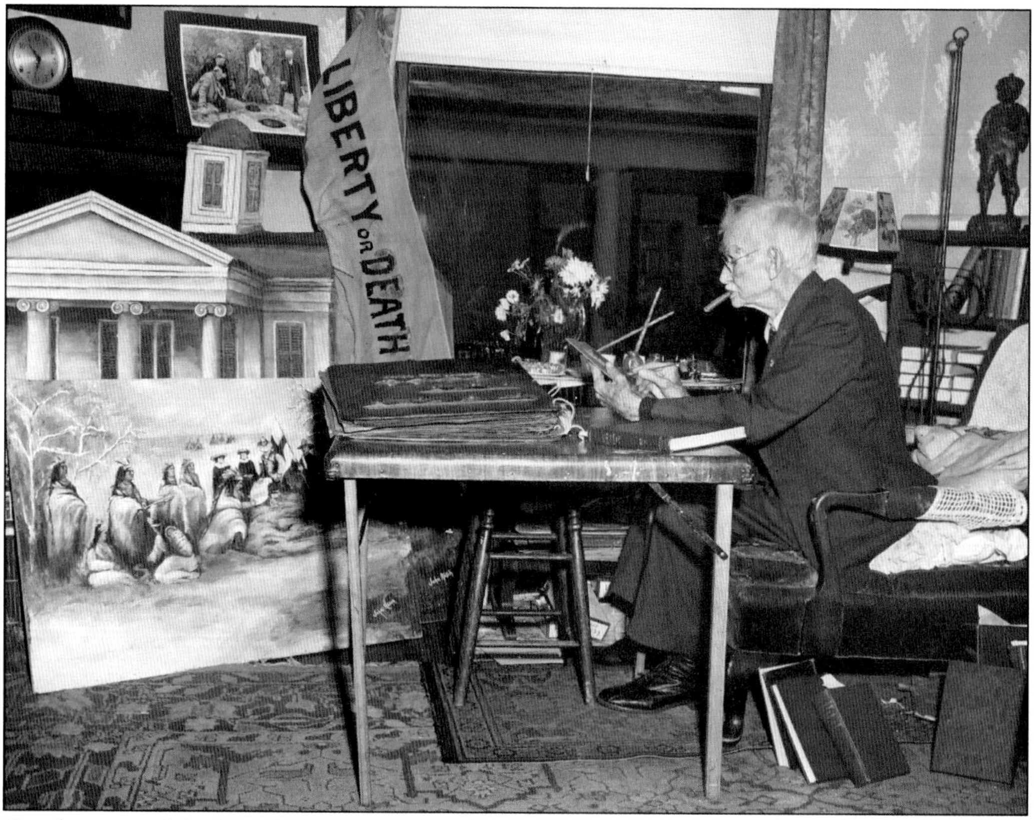

City historian John Rosch (1854–1949) is shown here at work on his scrapbooks in what may have been his study. At left is his imagining of the scene when English settlers from Rye met with Weckquaskeck Indians to sign a deed for the land White Plains now occupies. Rosch's historical work, while often creative and sometimes filled with contemporary bias, is invaluable and did much to establish a tradition of local history in White Plains. (WPPL.)

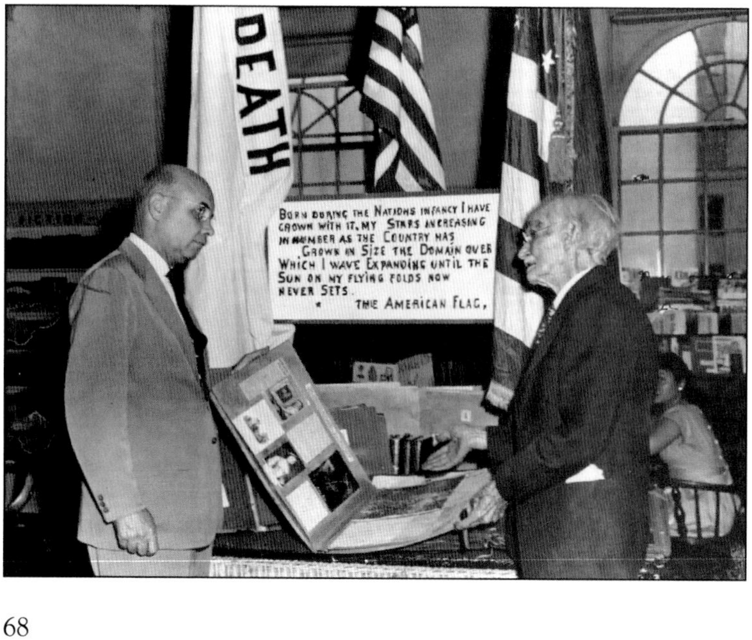

This is city historian John Rosch showing his scrapbooks to Mayor Silas S. Clark at the Grand Street location of the White Plains Library in 1948. Rosch operated a photography business from 1874 until 1929. His scrapbooks contain many wonderful pictures and are works of folk art, filled with his stories and drawings. (WPPL.)

Six

The 1950s

The last great population boom in the city occurred between the end of World War II and 1960. The baby boom and postwar economic prosperity came to White Plains as elsewhere. White Plains's dual identity as a suburb to New York with its own internal urban-suburban dynamic solidified in the 1950s. Urban renewal was seized upon by civic leaders as a chance to bring millions of mostly federal dollars to the city for redevelopment of areas that had suffered since the Depression from underinvestment and poverty. Housing segregation was clearer than ever, with most of the downtown area occupied by black business and home owners as well as renters.

Nestle (1952) and General Foods (1954) both created large headquarters in White Plains, beating the competition to land that would grow in value over the next 30 years. When I-287 was built (1957–1960), the land around the interstate was rezoned and made ready for the corporate office parks that relied on workers driving their automobiles to get to work. Strikes and pickets by workers were not an uncommon occurrence during the 1950s. At various times, bakers, barbers, AT&T employees, and newspaper printers took to the streets to demand changes in their working conditions.

Citizens like Rosa Kittrell, who came to White Plains from North Carolina in the 1930s, undertook transformative action to address social problems. In the mid-1940s, Kittrell partnered with Dr. Thomas Brennan from Grasslands Hospital to form the highly successful White Plains Mental Hygiene Group, which had specific goals. Kittrell traveled to spread her progressive message that people should "look upon mental illness as they do upon physical illness," presaging our contemporary understanding of mental illness. In addition to putting her energy into national reform efforts, Kittrell dedicated the majority of her time in the late 1940s, until her death in 1967, to social activism in White Plains. Kittrell's "war on poverty" started long before Lyndon Johnson declared the eradication of poverty a national priority. In 1945, Kittrell established the Carver Community Center to serve young people in downtown White Plains, and in 1952, she founded the Kittrell Nursery School for the children of working mothers, modeling a strong commitment to civic life that many people followed from the 1950s on, until nearly every person in White Plains was associated with some kind of civic or social organization.

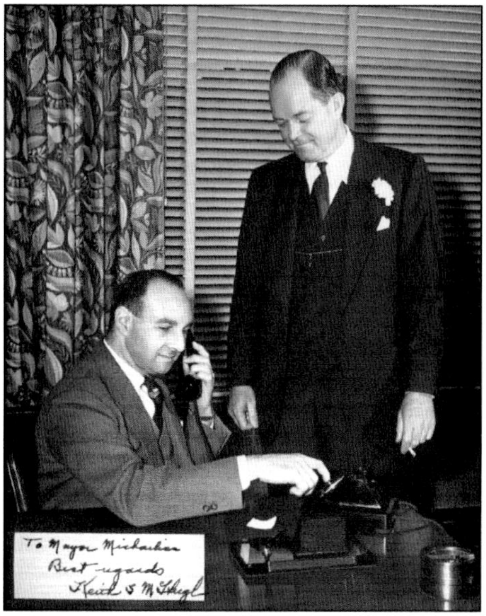

Pres. Keith S. McHugh of the New York Telephone Company is shown here teaching Mayor Edwin Michaelian the new dial system for White Plains. On April 22, 1950, the new White Plains 6 Dial System became operational, allowing subscribers to dial directly without speaking to an operator. Mayor Michaelian successfully placed a call to San Francisco in 15 seconds. (WPCA.)

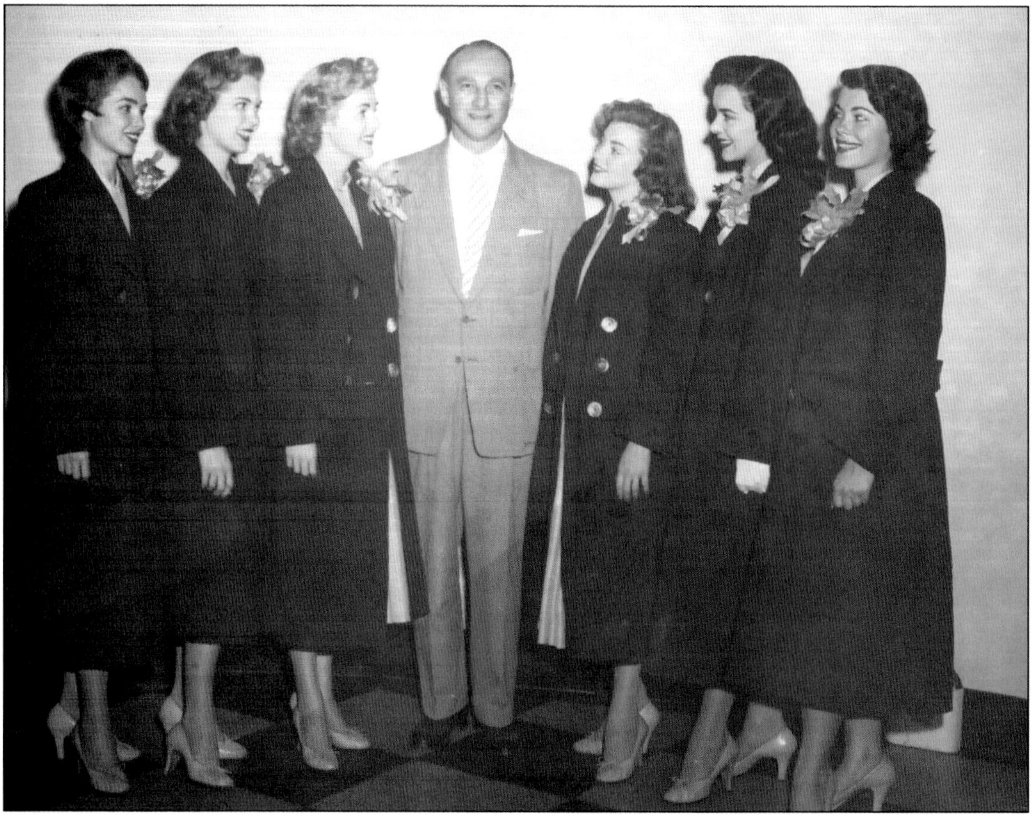

From the early 1940s until 1965, a highly anticipated annual event in New York and New England was the Miss Rheingold contest. Chosen by popular vote after a six-week campaign, the reigning Miss Rheingold was featured in the Brooklyn-based beer's advertising, including billboards, posters, and television commercials. The candidates for Miss Rheingold 1955, including the winner, Nancy Woodruff, are shown here posing with White Plains mayor Edwin Michaelian. (WPCA.)

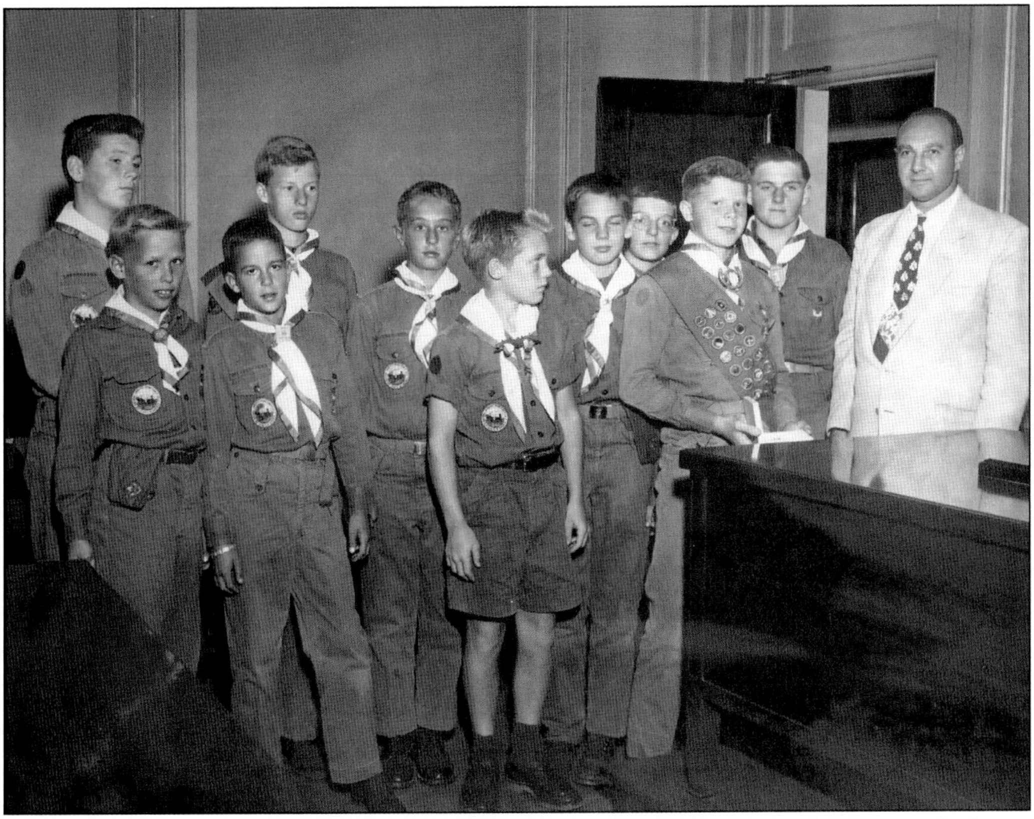

In 1953, White Plains Boy Scout Troop 1 made a trip to the national Scout Jamboree, which was held in California. They returned with a gift of gold nuggets for New York, which they presented to Mayor Edwin G. Michaelian, who was the president of the New York State Conference of Mayors. The mayor called the Scouts, headed by Eagle Scout Daniel Veber, "a credit to our city." (WPCA.)

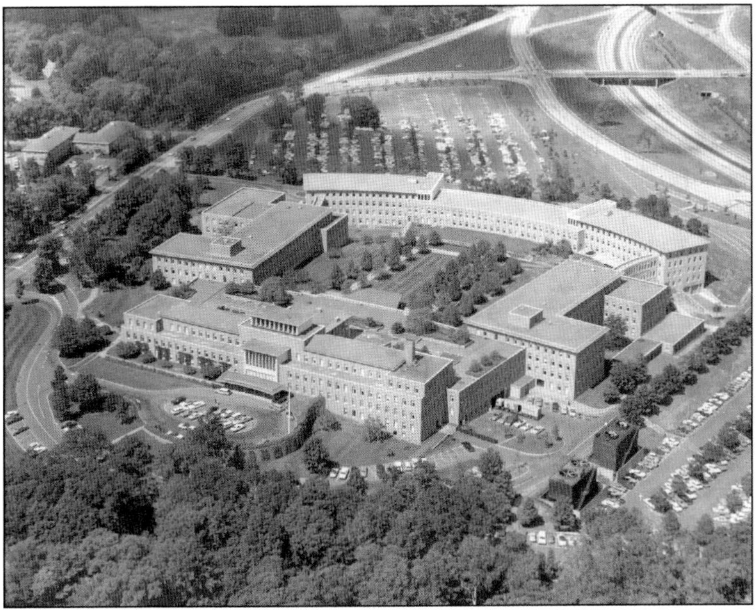

General Foods relocated its corporate headquarters to a new facility on North Street in 1954. It was one of the first large corporations to move out of midtown Manhattan and establish a suburban campus. The Benjamin Lyon house, a Colonial-era home of a Revolutionary War veteran, was relocated during the construction. (WPCA.)

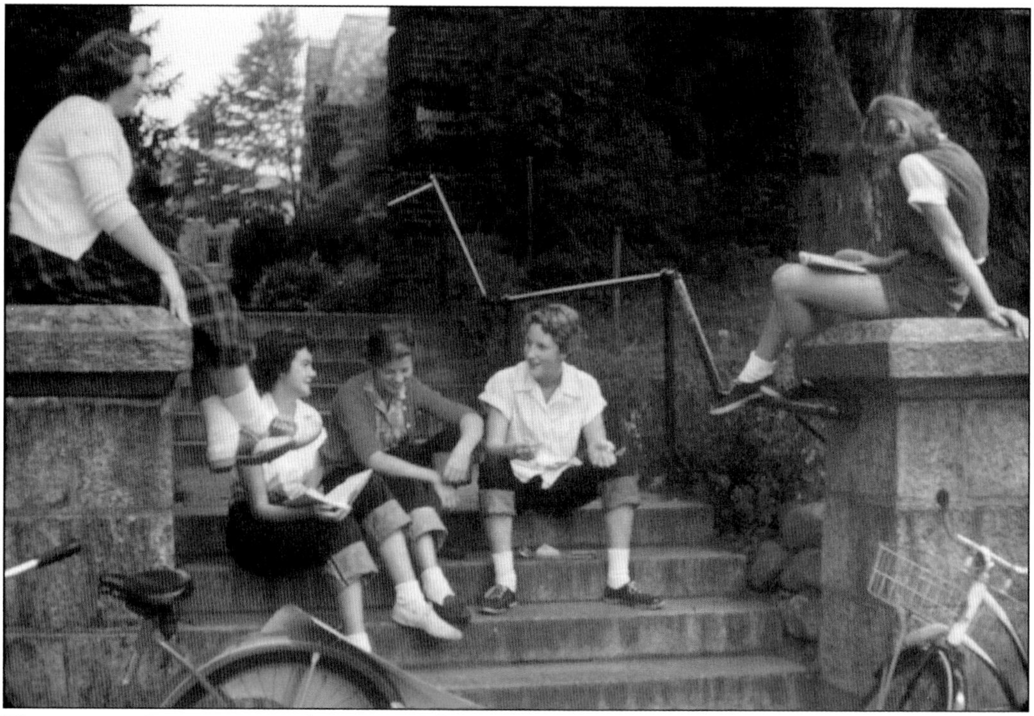

This image of teenagers on the steps of the Broadlawn apartment complex on North Broadway came from a slideshow created by the White Plains Public Library in the early 1950s. The caption read, "Adolescence is a troubled time . . . teenagers and parents alike find guidance and self-understanding in books." White Plains manifested all the typical aspects of the baby boom generation's developing youth culture—places to purchase the records and clothes marketed to a younger clientele, gathering spaces like soda fountains and sports facilities, and spaces for demonstrations about the Vietnam War or civil rights later on. (WPPL.)

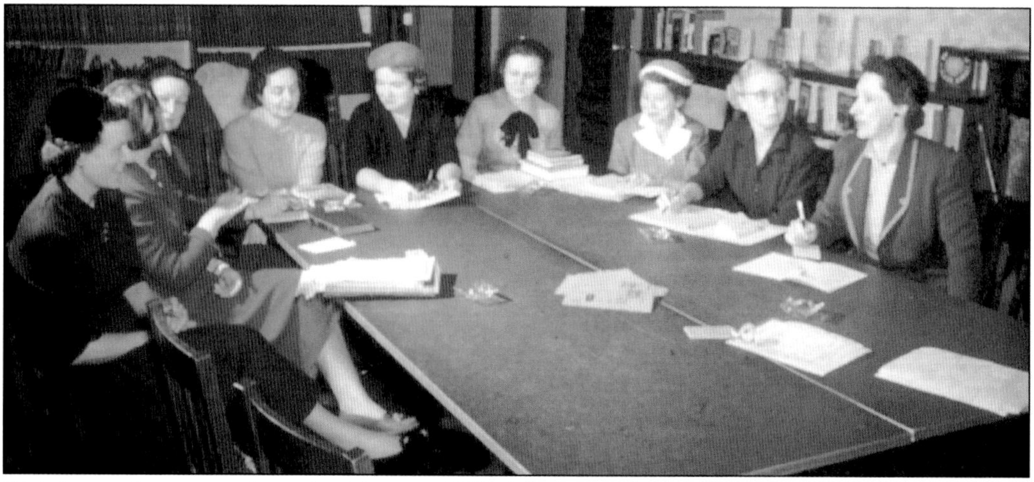

This is another image from the library's 1953 slideshow. The League of Women Voters (LWV) is shown meeting in the library, keeping "up to date on current issues through the use of such library resources as the newspaper index, pamphlets and magazines," according to the caption. Founders and early members of the LWV came from Westchester, and some of the organization's roots can be traced to suffrage activities in White Plains and the county. (WPPL.)

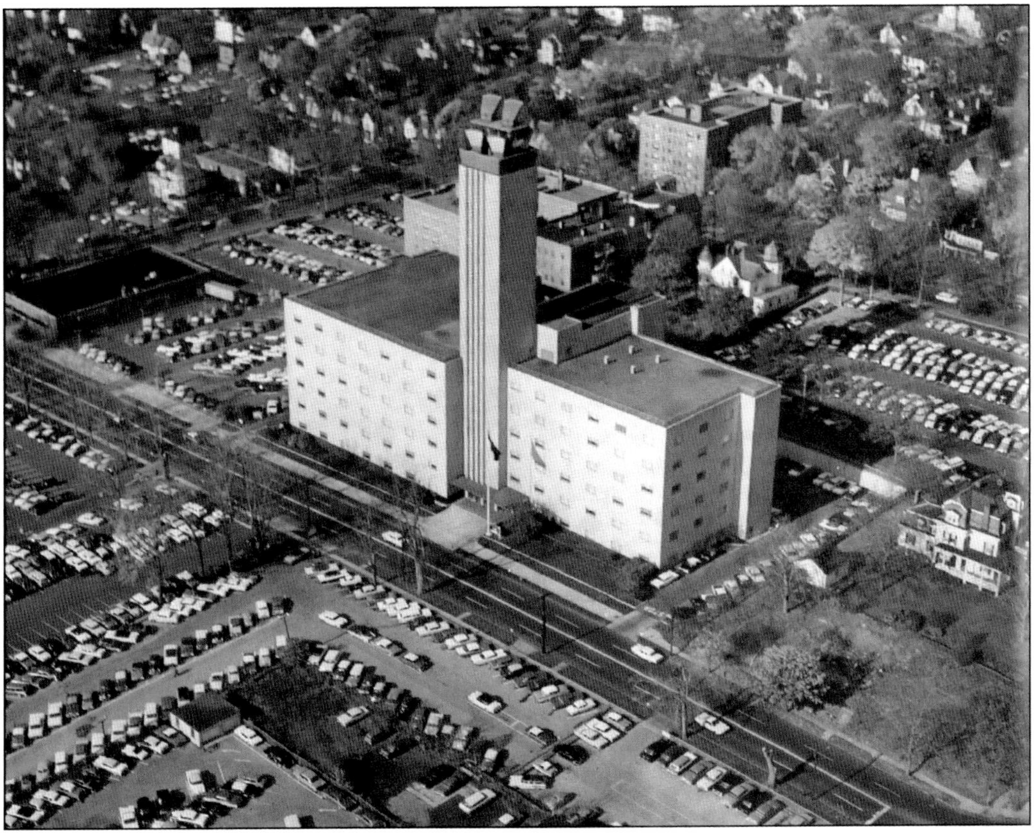

Since 1907, White Plains has been a central point for handling long-distance calls. In 1954, AT&T's Long Lines division constructed a new building on Hamilton Avenue to serve as a long-distance switching center. It was topped by a 204-foot radio relay (microwave) tower, serving as a radio relay link. (WPCA.)

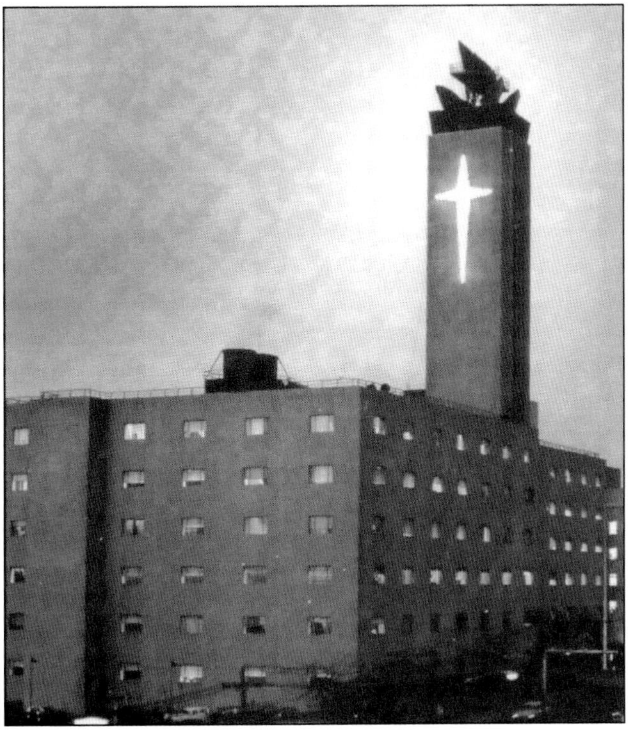

The new Long Lines Building at 400 Hamilton Avenue also became the office headquarters for the eastern area of Long Lines, making it a major employer in White Plains, with over 1,000 employees. Many will remember its annual Christmas star. (WPCA.)

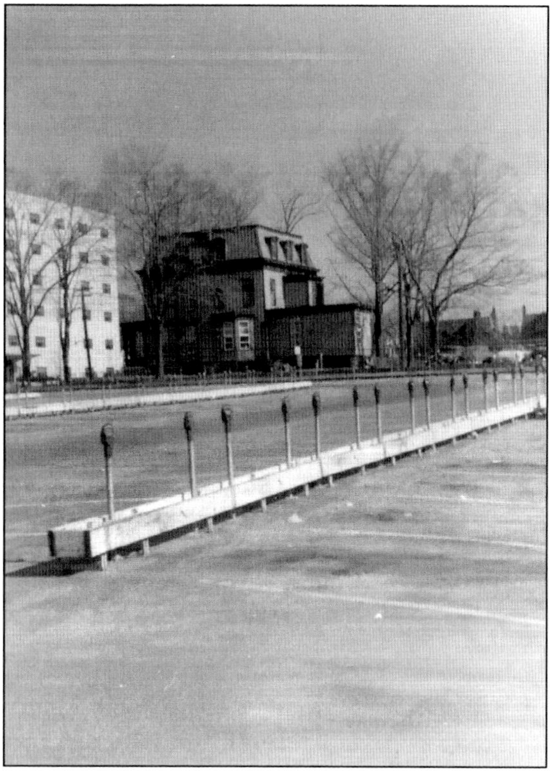

The "last house on Hamilton" survived the creation and expansion of this parking lot between Hamilton Avenue and Main Street during the 1950s. (WPPL.)

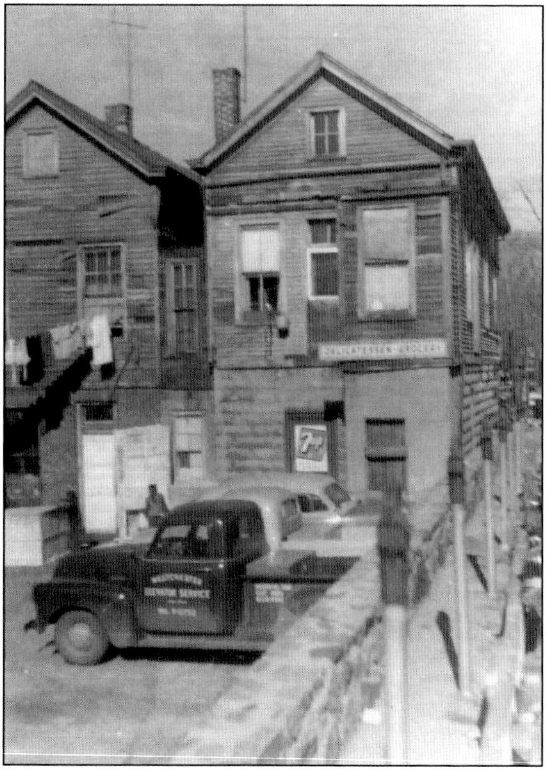

The buildings shown here were located at 239 Hamilton Avenue and abutted one of the first large parking lots the city constructed in the 1950s. By 1955, the city had 17 lots spread across the city and was acquiring land for more parking. The truck belonged to the Westchester Elevator Service, which was owned by a man named Edwin J. Hansen. (WPPL.)

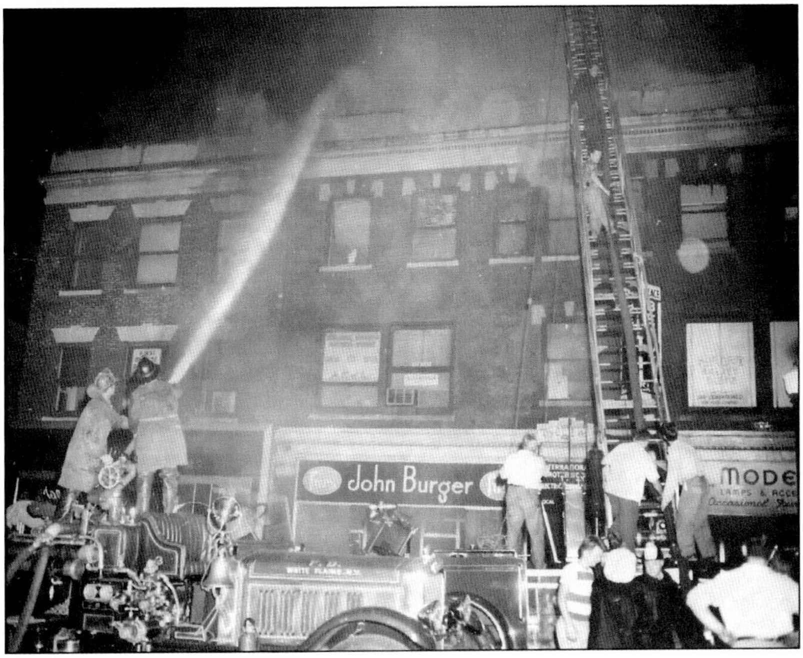

Many fires plagued the aging stores on Main Street during the 1950s and 1960s. Firemen are seen here on the night of July 31, 1954, fighting a fire at 112–114 Main Street, which brought out every piece of firefighting apparatus in the city. It claimed the lives of two White Plains firemen, Salvatore Galasso, age 27, and Bernard Callahan, age 39. (WPCA.)

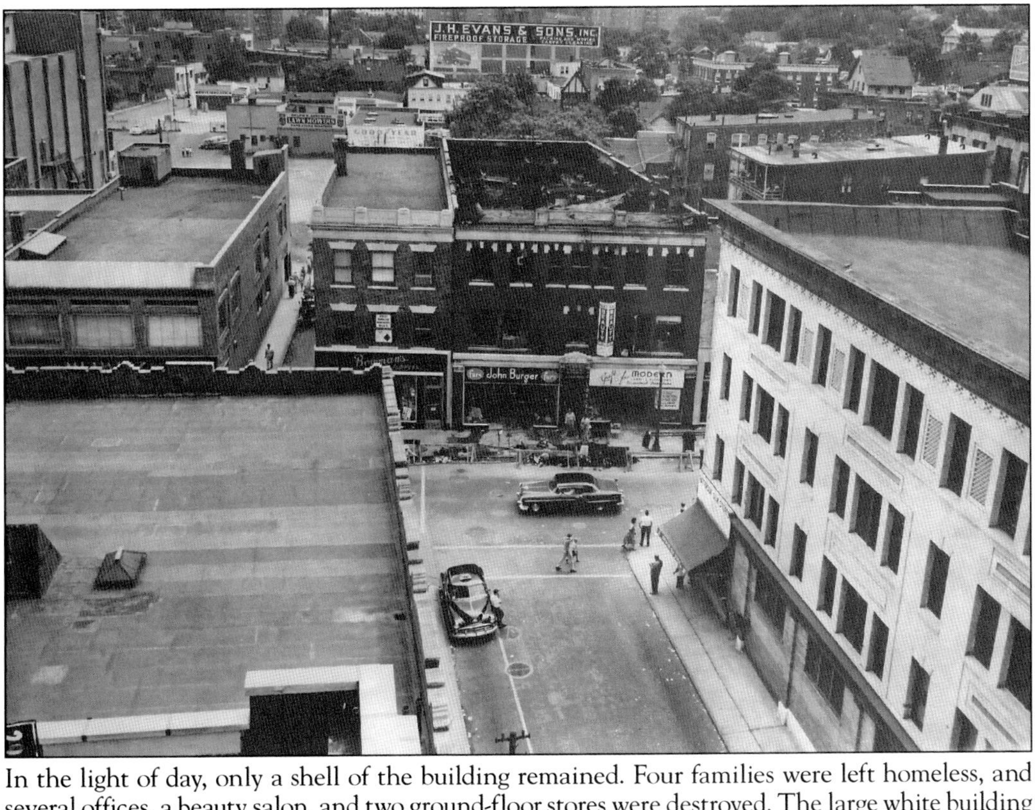

In the light of day, only a shell of the building remained. Four families were left homeless, and several offices, a beauty salon, and two ground-floor stores were destroyed. The large white building in the lower right, Patterson Silk Store, was destroyed in a fire in 1966. (WPCA.)

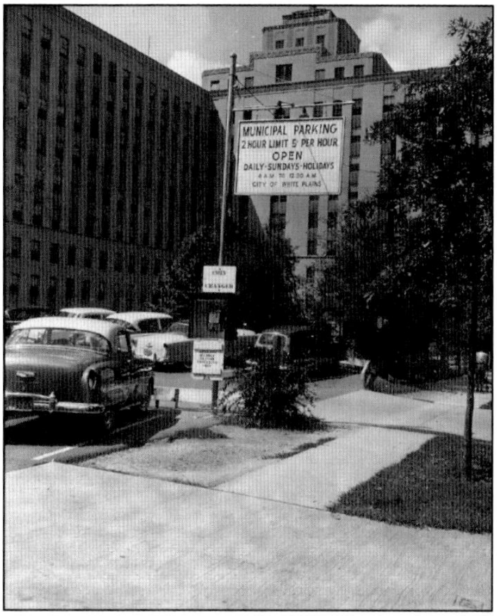

In 1938, parking meters were installed at the curb on downtown streets, and in 1946, a lot was opened for 94 cars. The need for additional parking in downtown grew as White Plains increasingly became a destination for shoppers. This lot, at the corner of Court and Quarropas Streets, served the public visiting the County Office Building (seen in back) and the public library. (WPCA.)

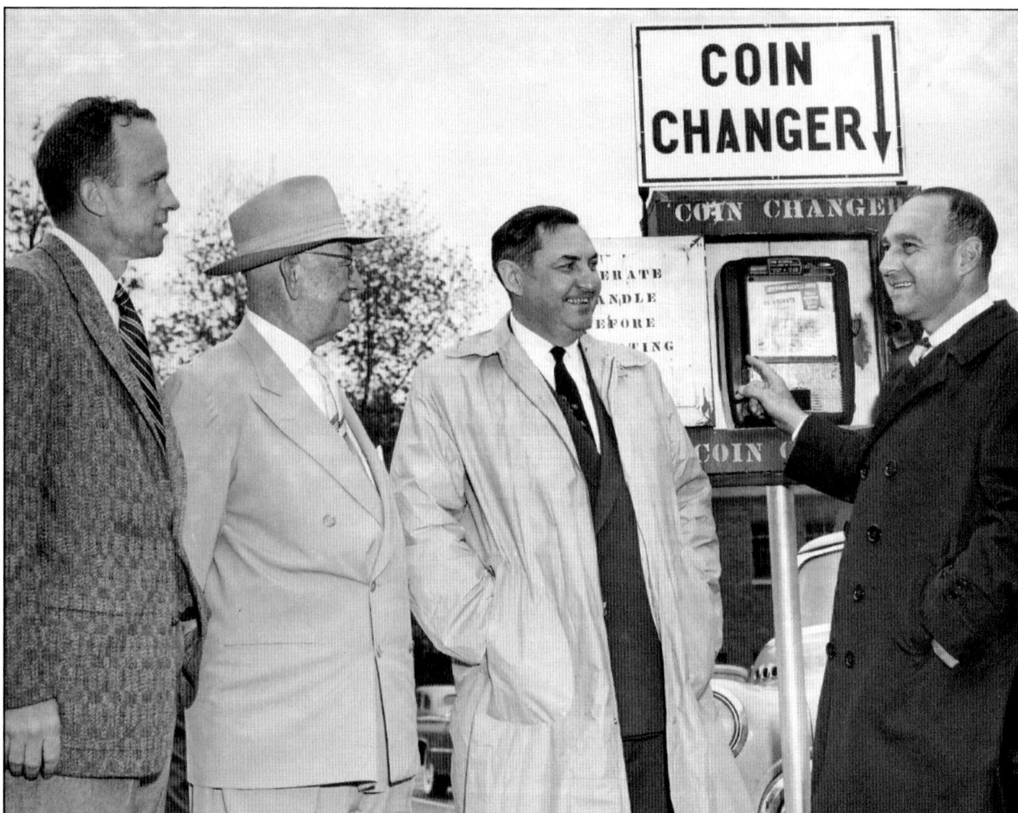

To accommodate the public, coin changers were installed in every lot. In June 1955, Mayor Edwin G. Michaelian (far right) showed off the first coin changer to members of the American Municipal Association's Parking Committee, who noted that White Plains was recognized nationally as a pioneer in municipal off-street parking. The committee recommended "double-decking" some lots. (WPCA.)

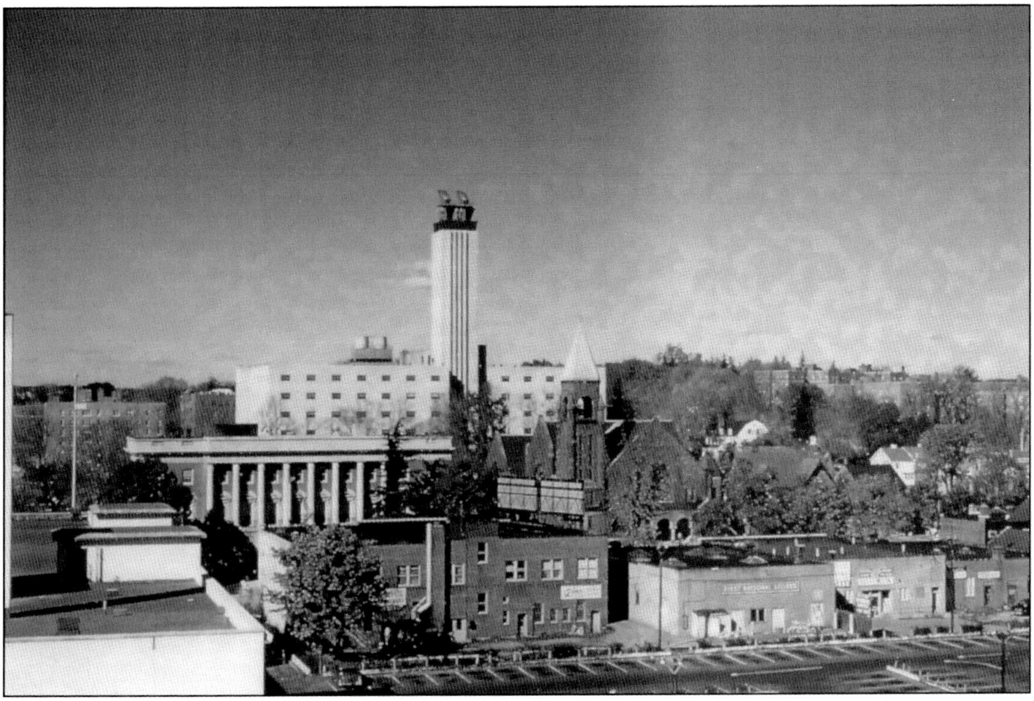

This photograph, taken from atop 210 Martine Avenue in 1957, could not be reproduced today. The street-level parking became the Main-Martine parking structure and later the City Center parking garage. The white building in the lower left was Macy's and is now the site occupied by two sets of twin towers, City Center and Trump Towers. The spired church seen in the center was razed in 1959. (WPCA.)

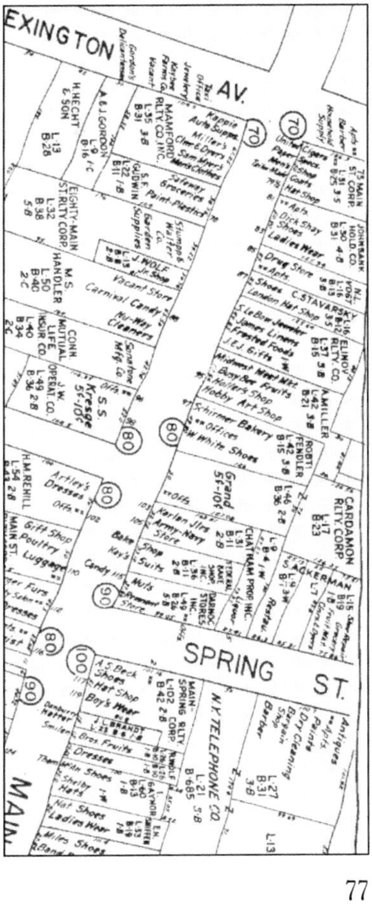

Nirenstein's National Realty Map Co. published a large-format map and photographic document in 1956. The map focused on the downtown area and the dense, varied businesses. In the era before department stores completely dominated retail, each trade and craft had its own store—one for hats, one for shoes, one for jewelry, and the like. (WPCA.)

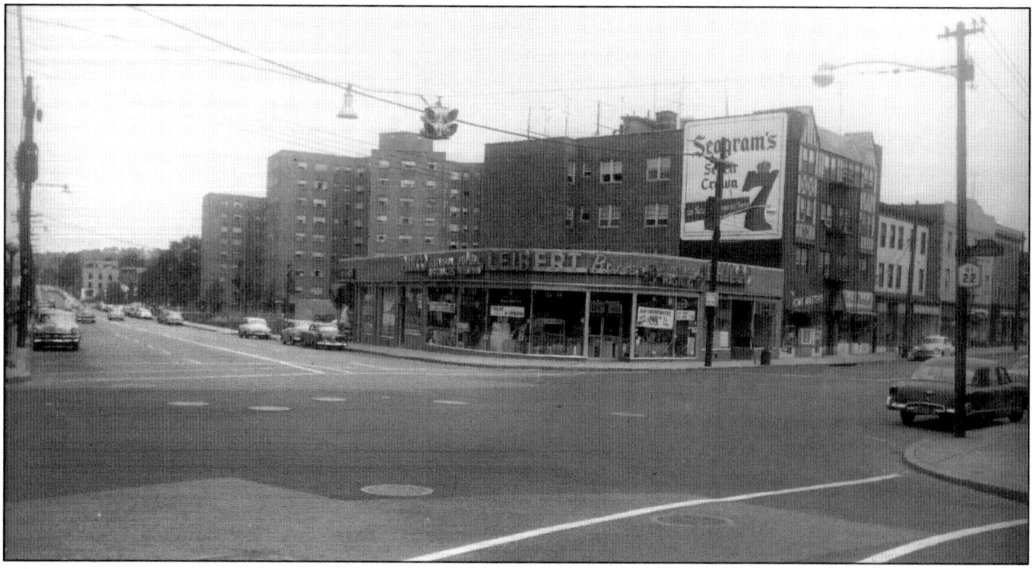

This view of the corner of South Lexington Avenue and West Post Road, captured on June 17, 1956, looks surprisingly similar today. The building on the corner still stands, and the run of shops and apartments along Post Road across from White Plains Hospital is one of the few intact, pre–urban renewal blocks where one can feel what the city was like before the 1960s. Winbrook still stands in the back, though it is being replaced with new buildings. (WPPL.)

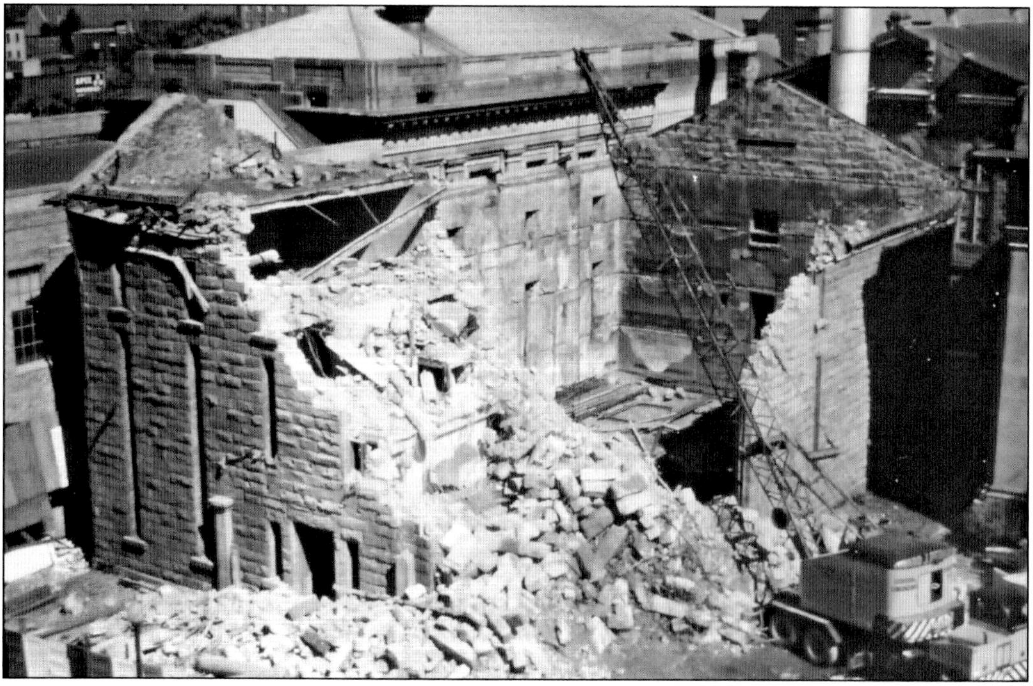

A "Bridge of Sighs" crossed the courtyard between the Westchester County Jail and the 1856 courtroom, lessening the possibility of a prisoner escaping on his way to trial. It was in that courtyard that four executions by hanging took place, the last in 1884. A new county jail was opened in Valhalla in 1932, and the White Plains jail was used for storage of government records until it was razed in July 1957. (WPCA.)

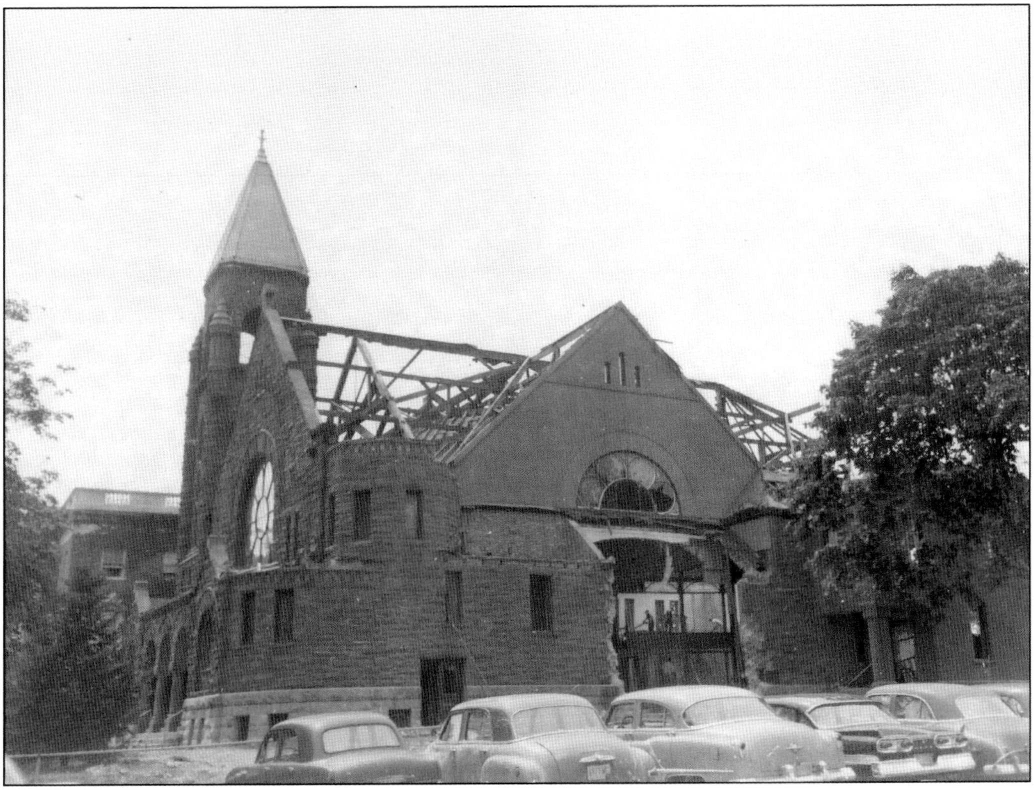

The Methodist Memorial Episcopal Church was built on Main Street in 1903. Behind at left is the top of the 1926 White Plains Municipal Building. The church was demolished in the summer of 1959 to make way for the new Sears and Roebuck store. (WPCA.)

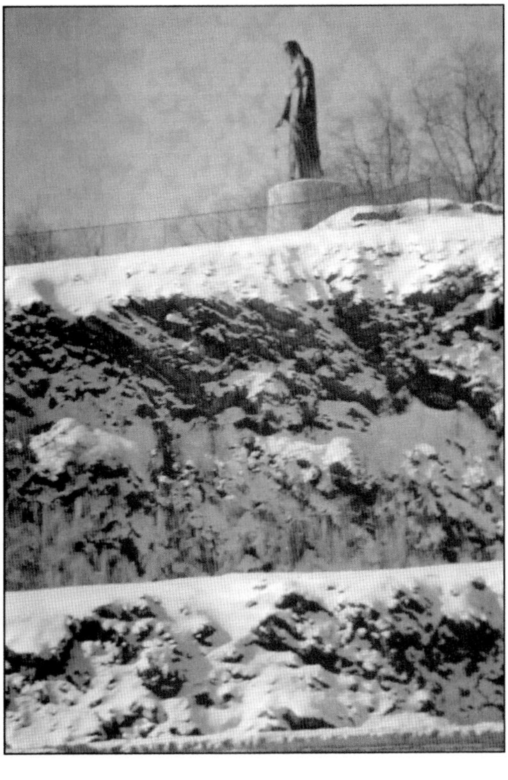

For 17 years, beginning in 1959, westbound motorists on Route I-287 viewed a statue of Our Lady of Fatima, which stood 100 feet above the expressway. The 30-foot, 6.5-ton bronze statue was the gift of the William A. Dunphy Council of the White Plains Knights of Columbus to the Sisters of the Divine Compassion and stood on the campus of Good Counsel College. Known to many as "Madonna of the Highway," the statue was sculpted by New Rochelle artist Lumen Martin Winter. After the Good Counsel College campus was taken over by Pace University in 1976, the statue was moved to the grounds of the Salesian Fathers in West Havestraw, New York. (WPCA.)

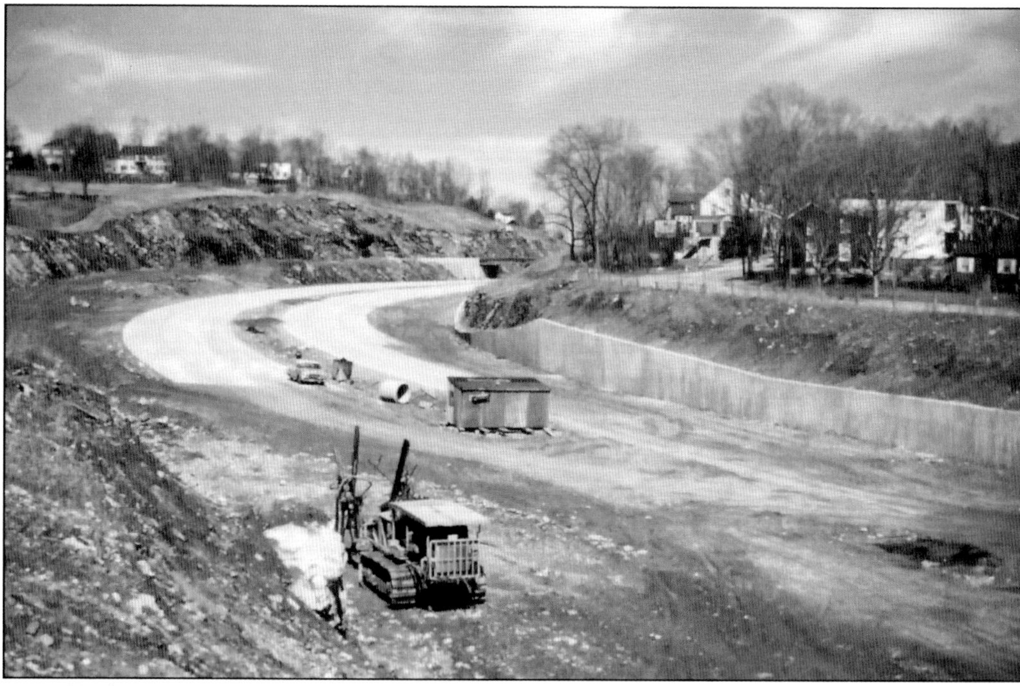

In 1955, the Tappan Zee Bridge opened and plans were under way for a new east–west route through Westchester. Route I-287 is shown here under construction in April 1959. This view is facing west from Lake Street toward, on the curve, the rear of Good Counsel College, where the Madonna of the Highway later stood. (WPCA.)

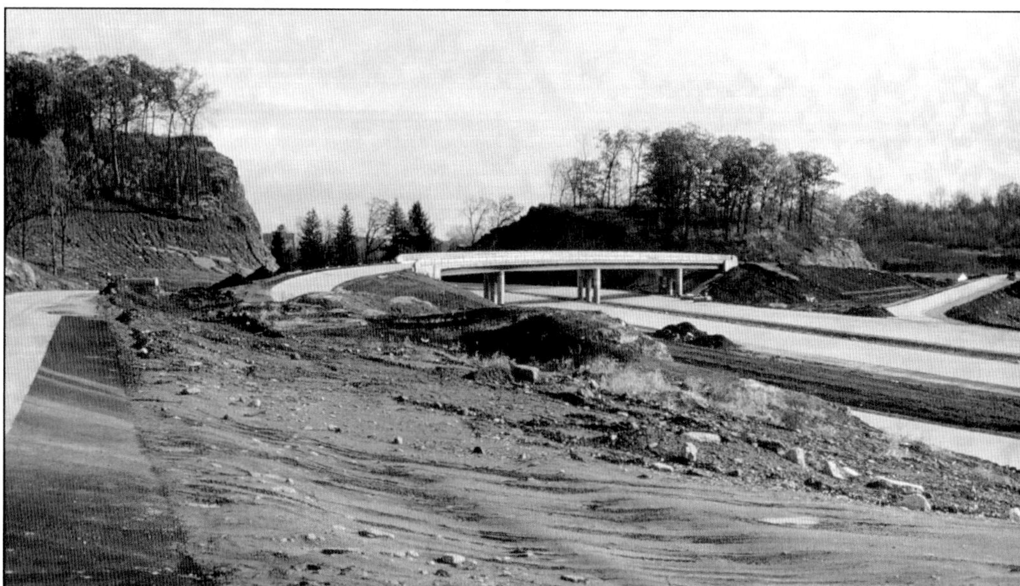

Shown here at right is the eastbound exit ramp at exit 5 on Route I-287. At center is the entrance ramp coming from Route 119. Known as the Cross Westchester Expressway, Route I-287 became an important connection to White Plains, which enabled its growth as a center for shopping, education, and health facilities. (WPCA.)

In 1957, printers of the International Typographical Union went on strike to protest the firing of a fellow union member. The *Reporter Dispatch* and many other papers in Westchester were published by Westchester Publishers, Inc., and were eventually sold to Gannett. (WPPL.)

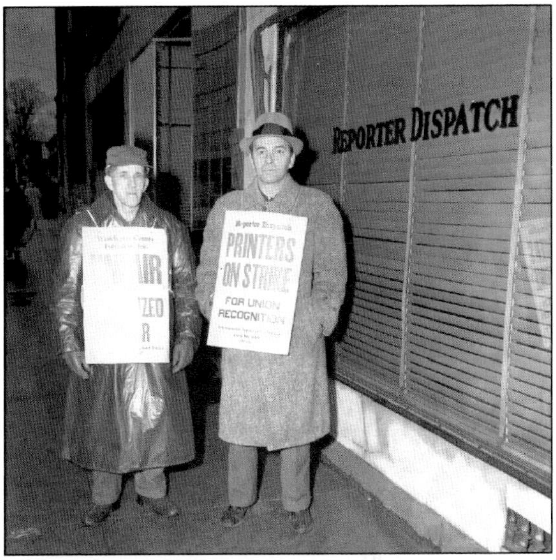

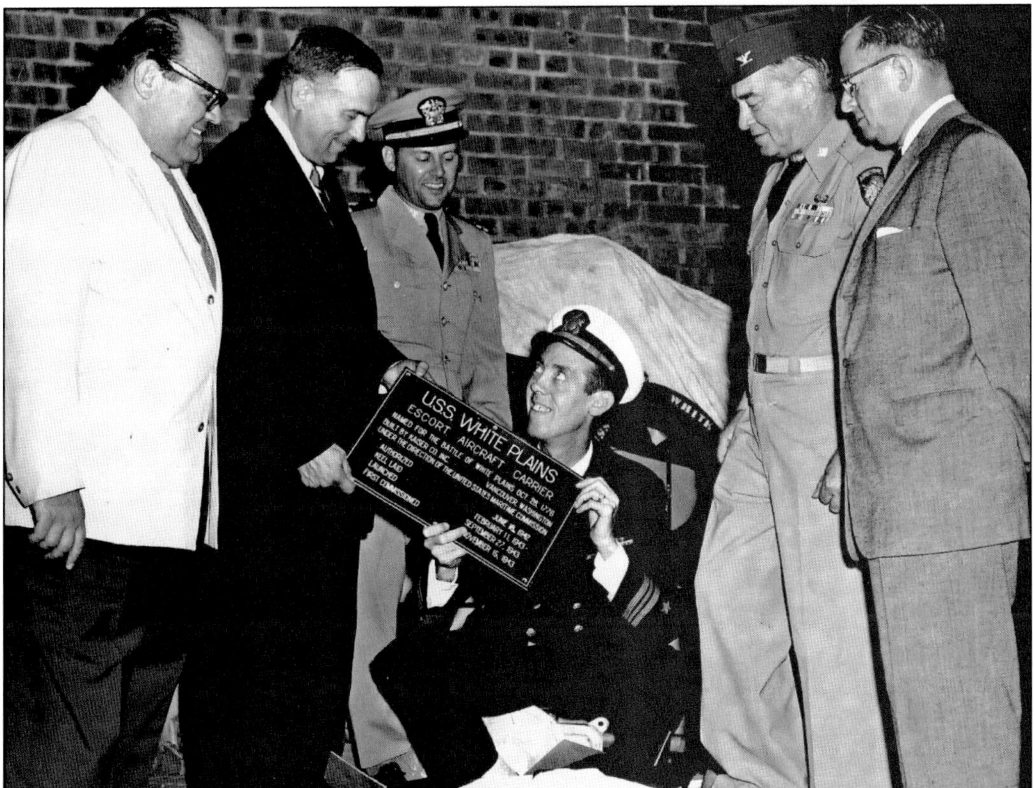

During World War II, the battleship USS *White Plains*, named after the Battle of White Plains during the Revolutionary War, served proudly in combat in the Pacific. When the ship was decommissioned in 1959, arrangements were made for the binnacle, bell, lanterns, and other artifacts from the ship to be given to the City of White Plains. Thousands came to White Plains for the parade in honor of the *White Plains*. Here, Mayor Richard Hendey (in the dark suit) receives an official plaque from Navy personnel. (WPCA.)

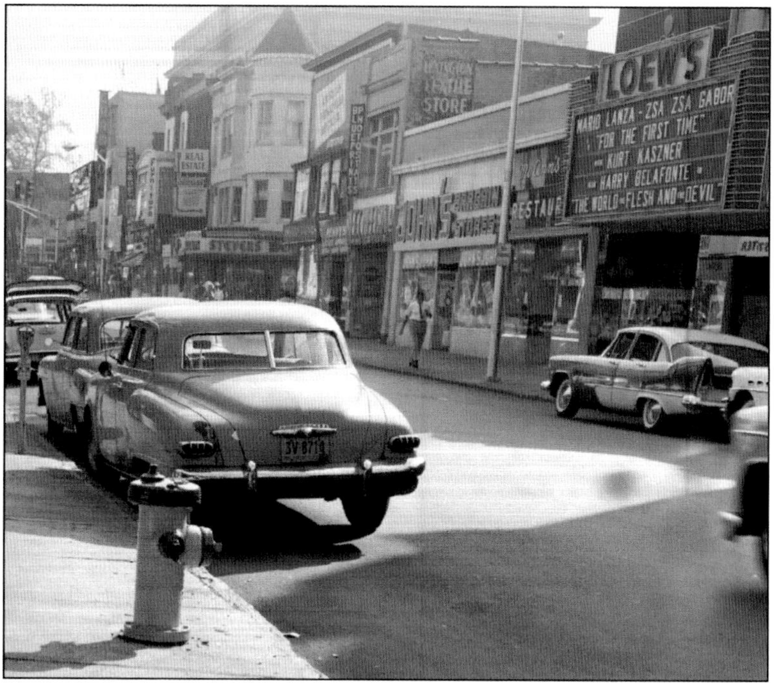

This shot of Main Street from September 23, 1959, shows the bustling, prosperous business district of White Plains's downtown just as it began its descent toward destruction and redevelopment. Loew's was one of five theaters in White Plains at the time. Other businesses visible include eateries (including a chop suey restaurant), bargain stores, real estate offices, and clothiers. (WPPL.)

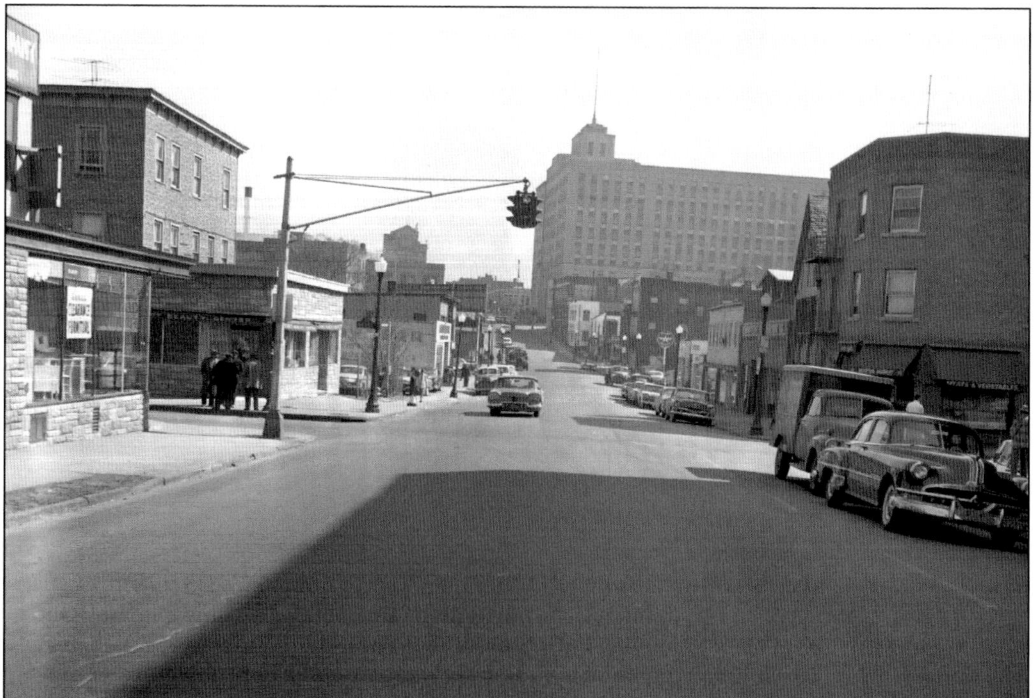

This is the intersection of Brookfield Street and Martine Avenue in 1959. Local businesses were located on each of the four corners of the intersection. From left to right are Fordham Lumber Company, the Peridot Beauty Center, Martine Market, and Isaac Leven & Son Furniture (not visible next to car on the right). The area is now dominated by the courthouse plaza, the library, and the Galleria. (WPPL.)

Seven

The 1960s

The 1960s began with a fire in older buildings on Main Street that made plain the need for redevelopment in downtown. Residents, business owners, and public officials debated the nature and course of that redevelopment for the next 20 years, while large parts of the downtown area were razed and huge, modern buildings were erected along ever-widening streets. The White Plains Beautification Foundation, established in 1965, worked to maintain some measure of organic life amidst the concrete expanses, planting oak trees along East Post Road and installing bench planters along Mamaroneck Avenue and Main Street.

Everyone has their own sense of the kind of city White Plains is, and that sense is heavily conditioned by one's personal experience of it. Ina Schlesinger and Michael D'Amore, two educators who worked in White Plains in the 1960s and the authors of *Children in the Balance*, described White Plains's black community as "a pocket of want in the midst of a truly affluent society." In 1964, the White Plains School Board, under the energetic leadership of Supt. Carroll Johnson, instituted a racial balance plan, which was meant to more evenly distribute black students throughout the elementary schools in White Plains and stabilize the conditions in all schools. While the full result of the racial balance plan had yet to be comprehended in 1968, black people in White Plains were still pushing for improvement and change. Students boycotting at White Plains High School in 1968 were influenced by all these people and schools of thought. Their demands reflected the progression of the international black freedom movement. They were not simply pushing for integration, with its merely physical connotations. They were pushing for recognition, inclusion, opportunity, and power. Concrete changes resulted from the students' actions. Enrollment in humanities and social studies courses were broadened to non-academic track students as well, and a social studies student curriculum advisory board was created.

The 1960s ended with White Plains on the cusp of enormous physical and economic changes. The area for structures like the White Plains Mall, the Galleria, and the county courthouse complex had been cleared, but the projects would not be completed until roughly 1980.

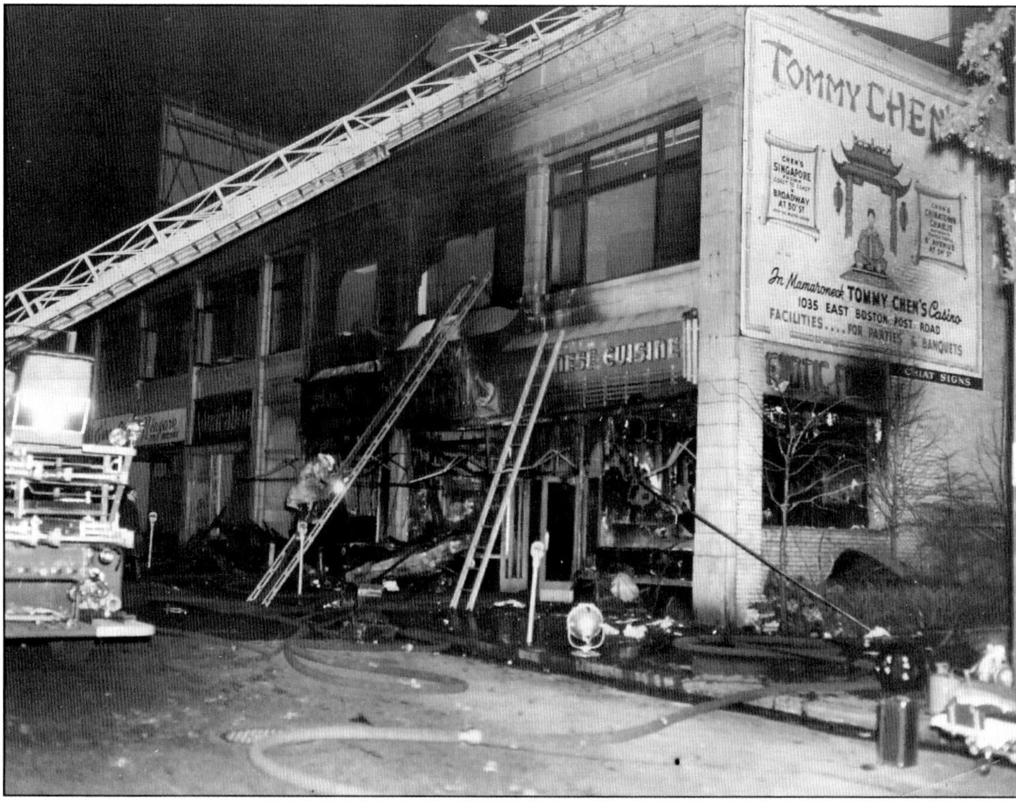

For two decades, a popular spot to dine on Main Street was Tommy Chen's Restaurant, situated across the street from the White Plains Municipal Building. In January 1960, a devastating fire struck the restaurant, causing over $100,000 in damages. (WPCA.)

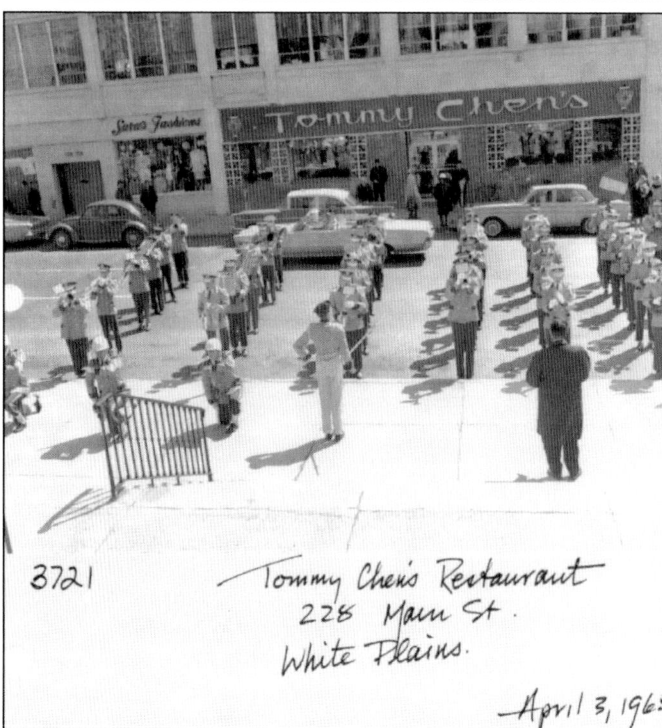

Eight months later, Thomas and Dolores Chen reopened for business, serving their loyal patrons for another 10 years until they lost their lease to a branch of Banker's Trust Company. (WPPL.)

The Italian American Club in Silver Lake held a benefit on June 10, 1961, and had Cab Calloway there to perform. Calloway was a Greenburgh resident and often appeared locally. The funds raised were used to give free swimming lessons to "underprivileged youngsters in the area," per the *Reporter Dispatch*. Along with Calloway, there was singing from John Benedetto of Port Chester, and Joe Stati and his Penthouse Serenaders. (Courtesy of the Westchester County Historical Society.)

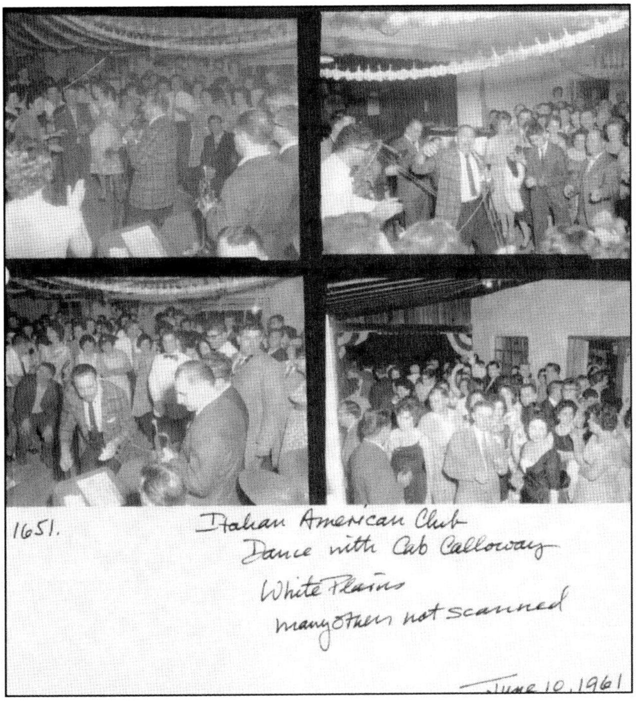

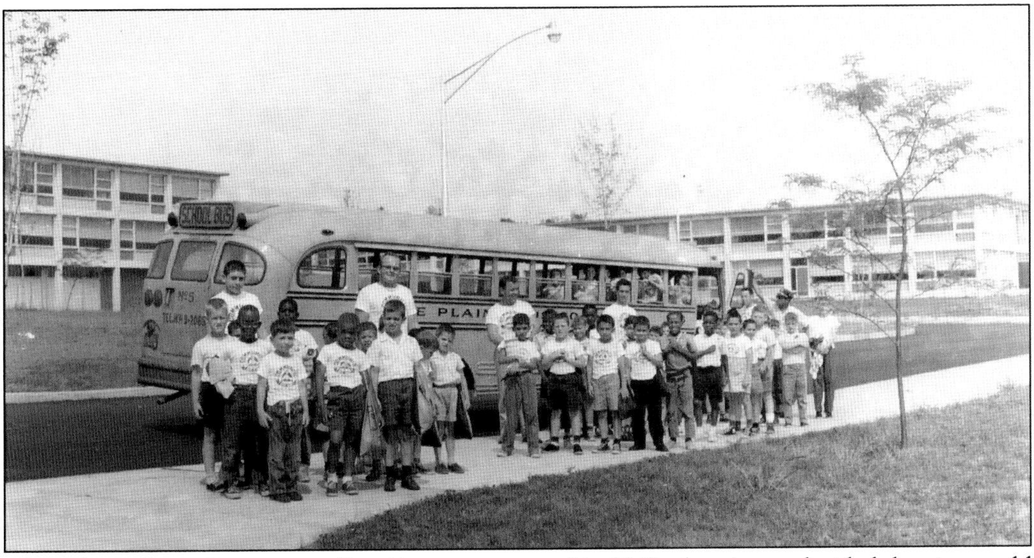

The White Plains Community Day Camp was started in 1949 when it was decided the city would establish some kind of day camp for children during the summer. The *Reporter Dispatch* had been raising money to send children to county and other summer camps up to this time. The new camp was funded through a mix of public and private money. On July 10, 1949, the first day of the White Plains Community Day Camp was held with mixed success—the children got along and had fun, but it rained. An early administrator of the camp, Blanche Hall, who was one of the "determined women" Mayor Ed Michaelian lauded for creating the camp, said the camp had been a great success and even promoted "inter-racial harmony" for the children and staff. Here are campers in the 1960s in front of White Plains High School. (Courtesy of the Westchester County Historical Society.)

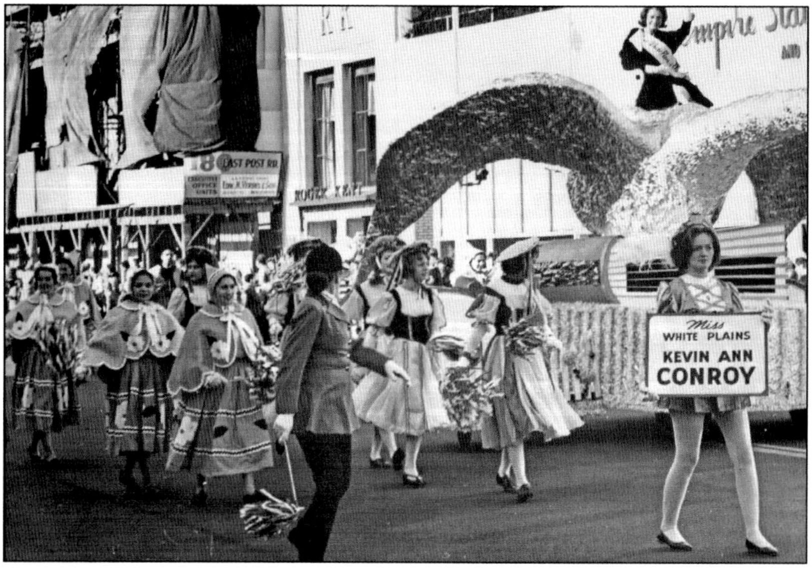

During the 1950s and 1960s, Macy's department store sponsored a Thanksgiving parade in White Plains that included floats of local interest, such as this one featuring Miss White Plains 1962, Kevin Ann Conroy. (WPCA.)

This 1962 photograph of women trying on hats at Genung's store on Mamaroneck Avenue is emblematic of a period that ended by the mid-1960s, when larger chain stores sapped business from over 970 local merchants, and the city's walkable downtown shopping district was being razed to create space for the ambitious plans of the urban renewal acolytes. A report by the state and local chambers of commerce in 1964 reported that White Plains was still second only to Yonkers for retail revenue that year, with apparel the second-largest share of the $250,000 reported in sales done by stores like Genung's. (WPPL.)

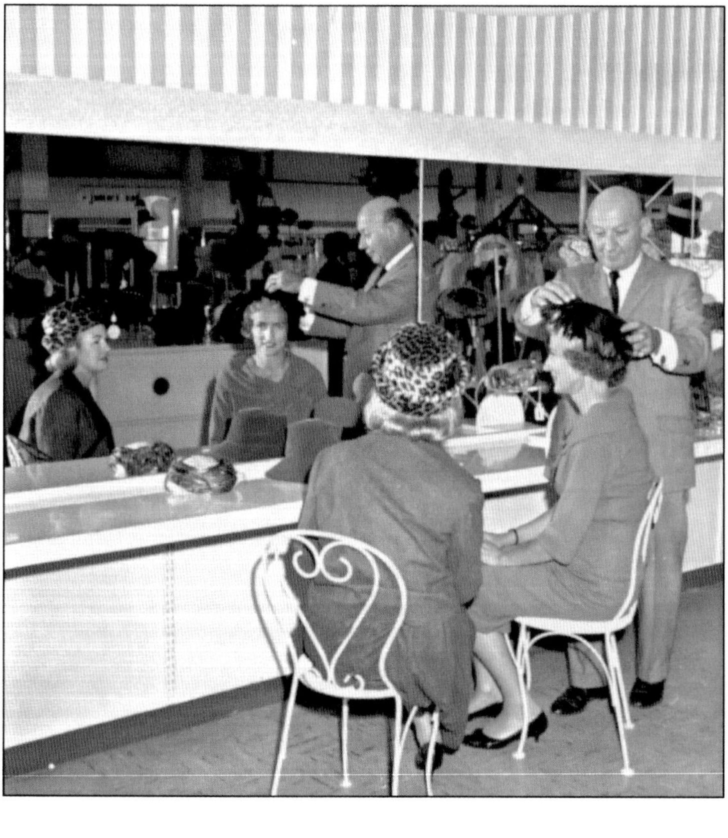

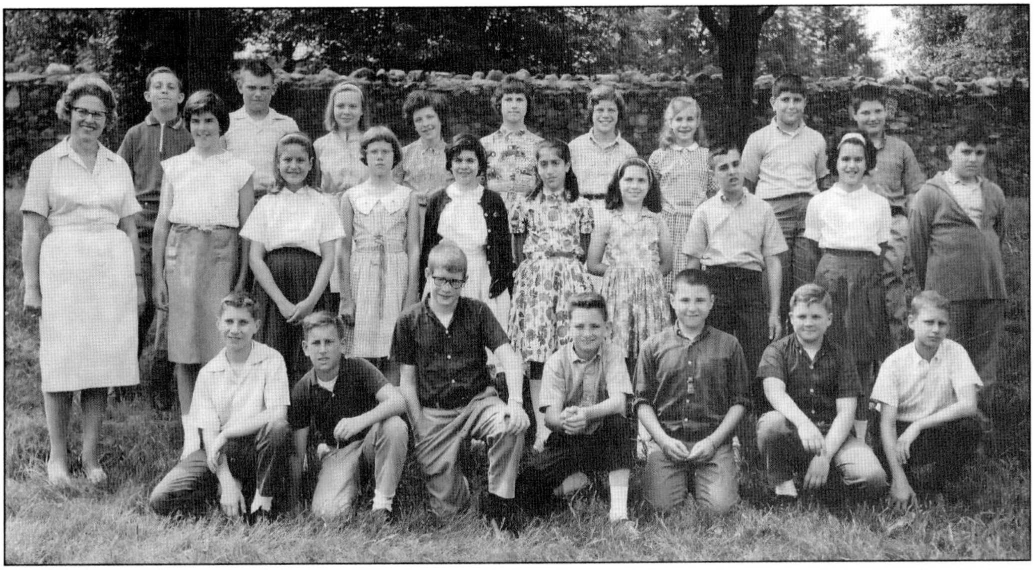

In June 1963, the sixth grade at Ridgeway School posed for a photograph in honor of their graduation. This is Grace Fingeroth's class, section 6-2. From left to right are (first row) Eddy Braily, Jimmy Ruben, Nicky Wolff, Barry Swerdlof, Marc Krause, Matthew Palmer, and Griff Trow; (second row) Mrs. Grace Fingeroth, Joan Barish, Melissa Rosen, Paula Jones, Barbara Weiner, Karen Leventhal, Barbara Damin, Billy Moses (Moe), Ellen London, and Johnny Sherman; (third row) Dave Weinkrantz, Wayne Brooks, Jan Piekos, Betsy Freeman, Betty Grayson, Marsha Levy, Emily Keonig, Scott Golden, and Bob Hemly. (Courtesy of Lee Palmer.)

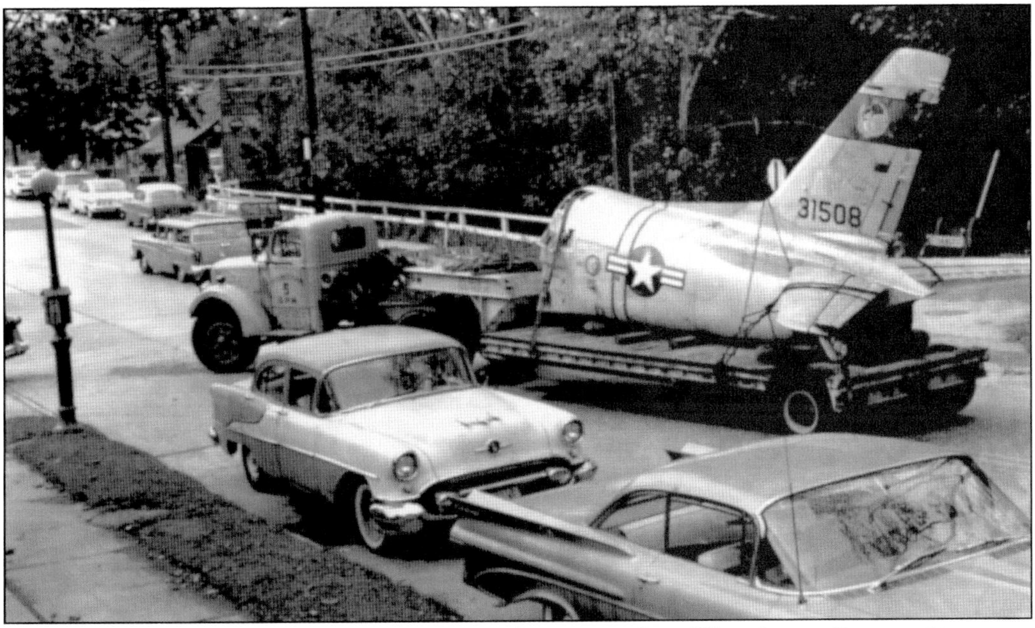

On September 26, 1962, an F-86 jet was moved in pieces from Westchester County Airport to Gedney Park. The airplane was left behind at the airport by the Air National Guard, and in June 1961, the city decided to acquire it and repurpose it for recreational purposes. The Department of Recreation and Public Works collaborated to transport the seven-ton machine in pieces from the airport to the park. The *Reporter Dispatch* described it as "a plaything worthy of the jet age." (WPPL.)

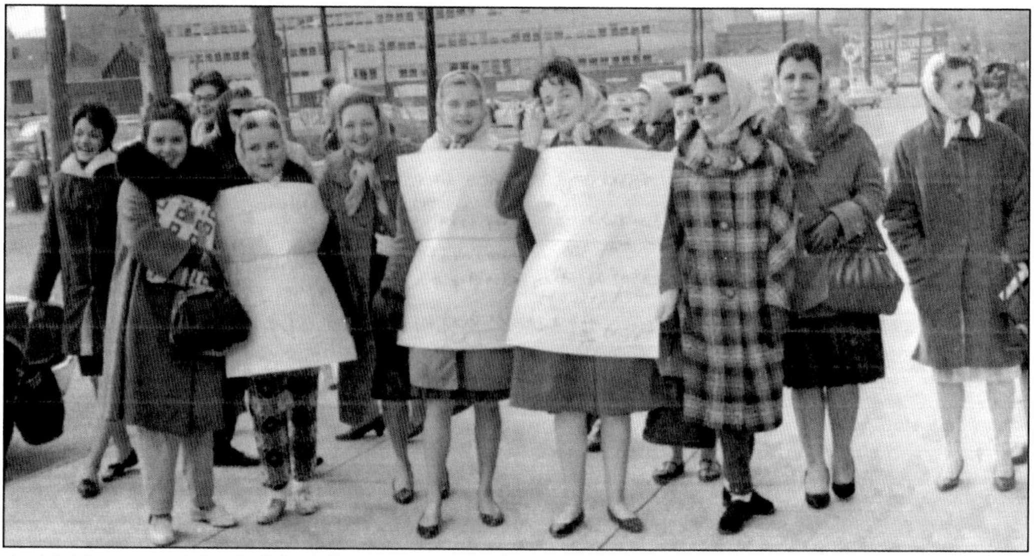

At 10:15 a.m. on March 26, 1963, over 100 employees walked out of AT&T on Hamilton Avenue to protest the use of split shifts. Nearly all the employees who walked out were women, and they were represented by the Communication Workers of America. Later in the year, a new contract was signed by the union and AT&T. The strike received coverage from newspapers since the White Plains location was responsible for handling international calls. Here, strikers are shown in front of the AT&T building on Hamilton Avenue. (Courtesy of the Westchester County Historical Society.)

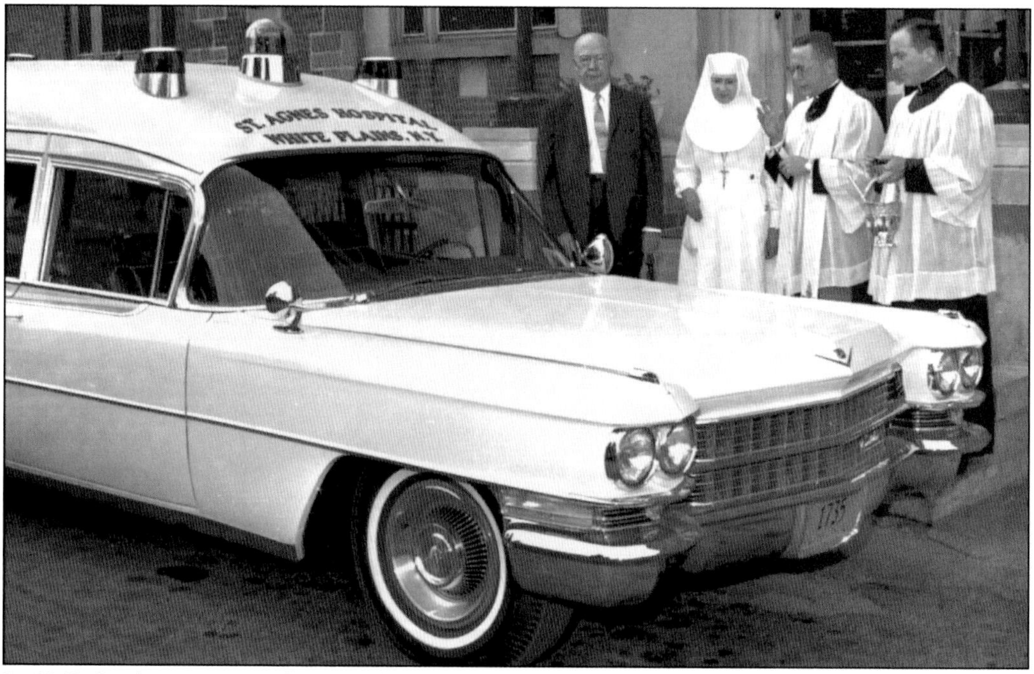

In 1963, St. Agnes Hospital acquired a new ambulance and had it blessed by priests. The hospital was founded in 1908 by Sisters of St. Francis for the care and treatment of "crippled children," as they were called then. Facilities grew through the 1930s and 1940s, and a full-service hospital was developed in addition to the largely free services offered to children with disabilities. The hospital closed in the early 2000s, and the Bristal, an assisted living facility, opened in 2012. (WPPL.)

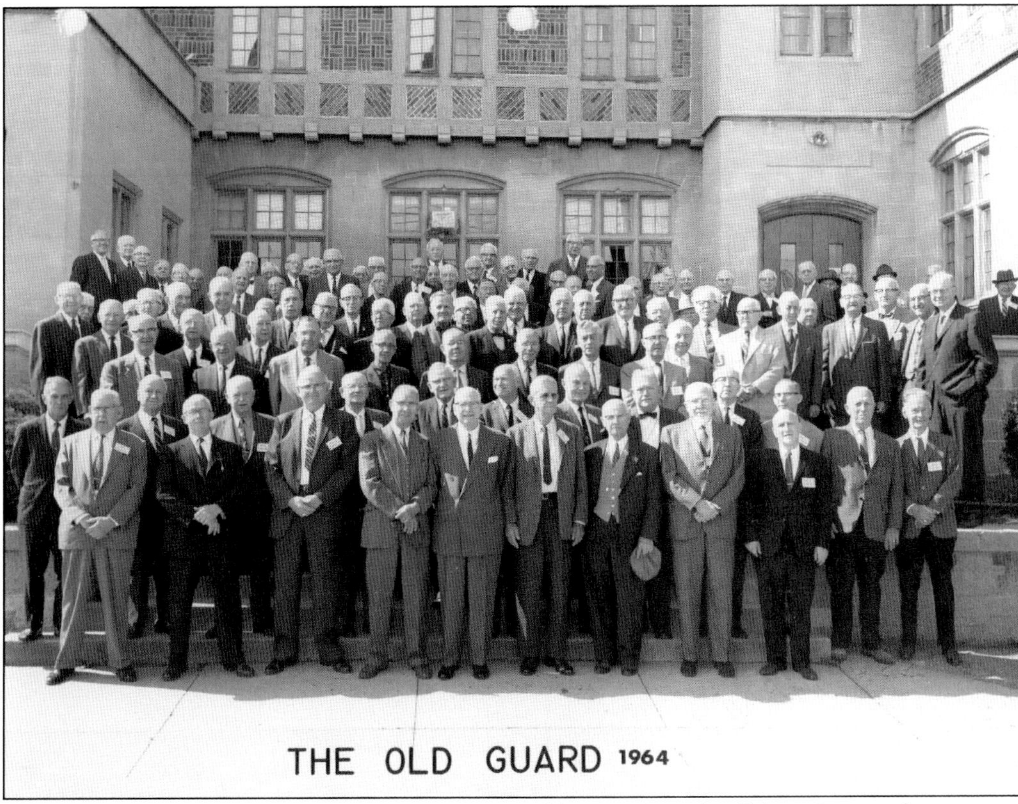

The Old Guard of White Plains began meeting weekly in 1954 and still does. It started as a project of the White Plains Council of Community Services intended to develop ways to help older people find friends, engage in creative activity, and be of service to others. The first meeting was held on September 14, 1954. Soon a constitution was adopted, and the group grew. The diverse professional and personal backgrounds of members made for "a wonderful spirit of contagious fellowship," according to the group's history. Pictured above is the Old Guard of 1964 commemorating its 10th anniversary in front of the YMCA on Mamaroneck Avenue. (WPPL.)

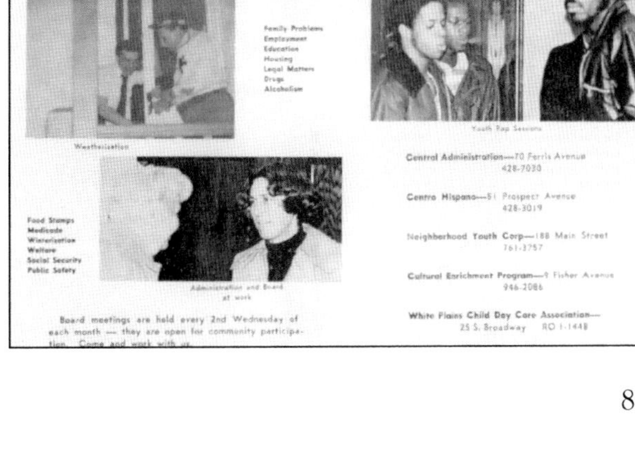

The White Plains Community Action Program (CAP) was started in 1965 in a storefront that had once been a bar on Ferris Avenue. Eugene Lowe, Sioux Taylor, Ellen Citino, Mary Taylor, Pecola Robinson, and Cora Stewart formed the nucleus of CAP at its outset. CAP provided recreation, education, food, health care, information, and financial assistance to some of White Plains's poorest residents. This image comes from one of CAP's annual reports. (WPPL.)

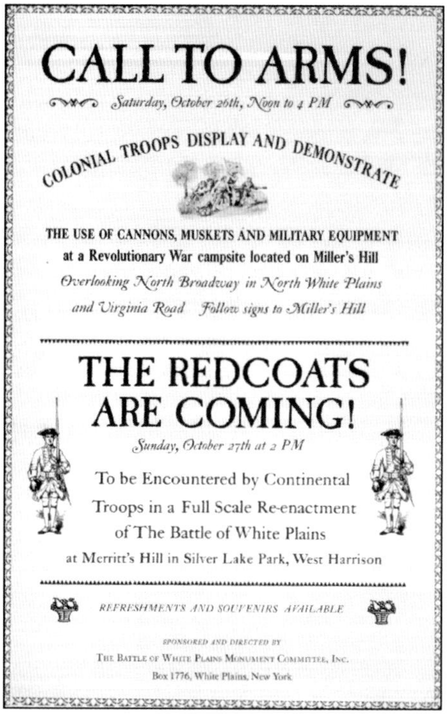

This "call to arms" was for a full weekend of reenactment activities at two different sites near White Plains. The battle reenactments were the inspiration of Al Cerak and became an annual event beginning in the early 1960s. Staged on Miller and Merritt Hills, the reenactments drew hundreds of participants from all over the Northeast. (WPCA.)

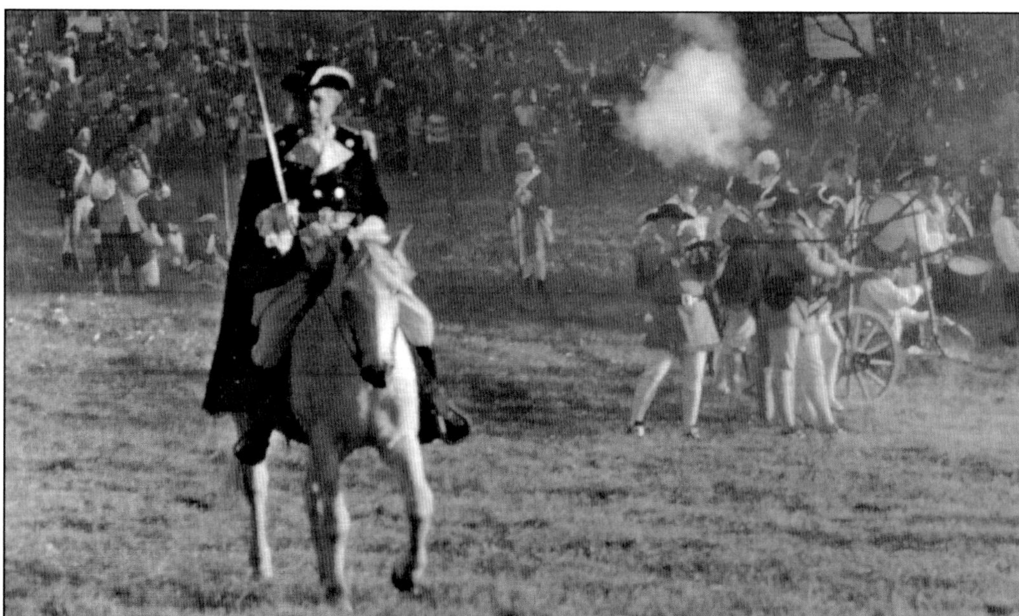

Beginning in 1965, Stephen Holden Jr. (1904–1998) portrayed Gen. George Washington in local celebrations, such as this battle reenactment, and he often rode a white horse. Holden was a White Plains attorney, a 12-year member of the White Plains Common Council, and served as president of the Battle of White Plains Monument Committee and of the White Plains Historical Society. His research helped establish the authenticity of the Jacob Purdy House as Washington's headquarters in 1776. (WPCA.)

This undated photograph shows Stephen Holden Jr. (left) and Albert Cerak (1909–1974) in costume. Cerak was the founder of the Battle of White Plains Monument Committee in 1959. A lifelong resident of Buckhout Road, Cerak was a well driller by profession. He had a passion for local history, especially the Revolutionary War, and remembered first suggesting the restoration of the Purdy house in 1928 when he was 18 years old. In 1970, Cerak was described as the "chief reason that White Plains is a city which remembers heritage." (Courtesy of the Westchester County Historical Society.)

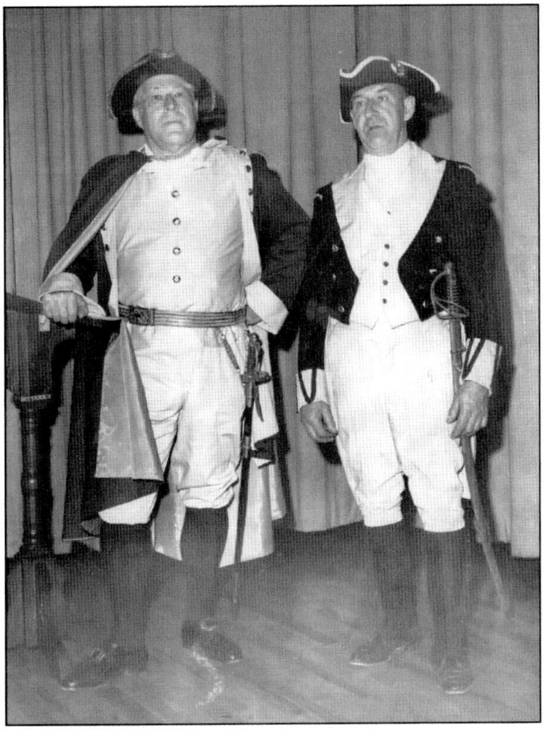

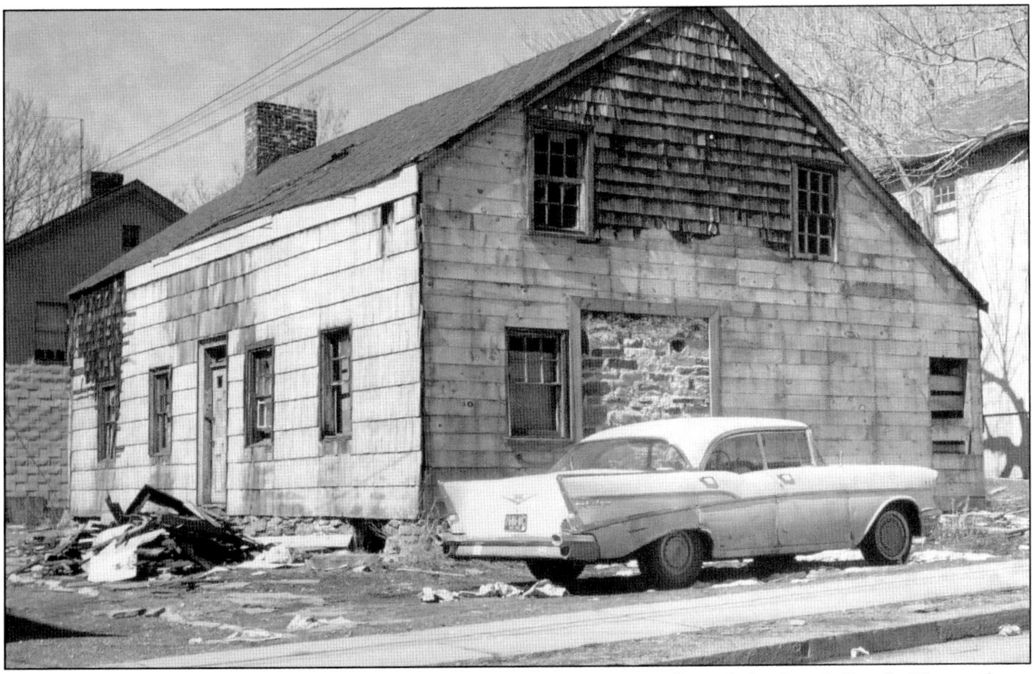

In 1963, the Battle of White Plains Monument Committee purchased the Jacob Purdy House from the Urban Renewal Agency. Shown here as it appeared in the 1960s, it had for several decades been used as a boardinghouse and reportedly a brothel. During the rest of the decade, Albert Cerak and Stephen Holden Jr. raised funds in preparation to move the Jacob Purdy House out of the urban renewal area. (WPCA.)

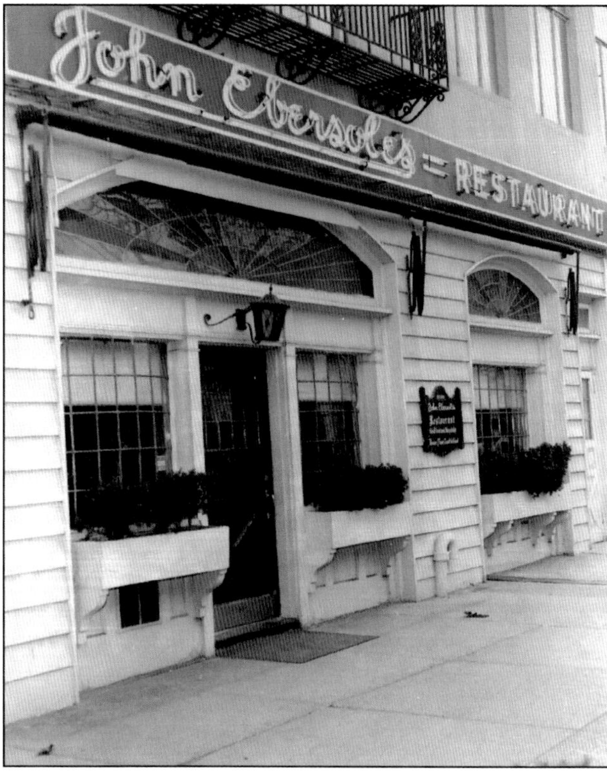

John Ebersole moved to White Plains from Iowa in 1920 and opened his Nut and Coffee Shop the following year. By 1934, he had established his family restaurant on Mamaroneck Avenue near Post Road. Beginning in 1950, he served on the White Plains Common Council and spent nine years on the Recreation Advisory Council. When Ebersole retired in 1960, the city's recreation department named the ice skating pavilion on Lake Street in his honor. (WPCA.)

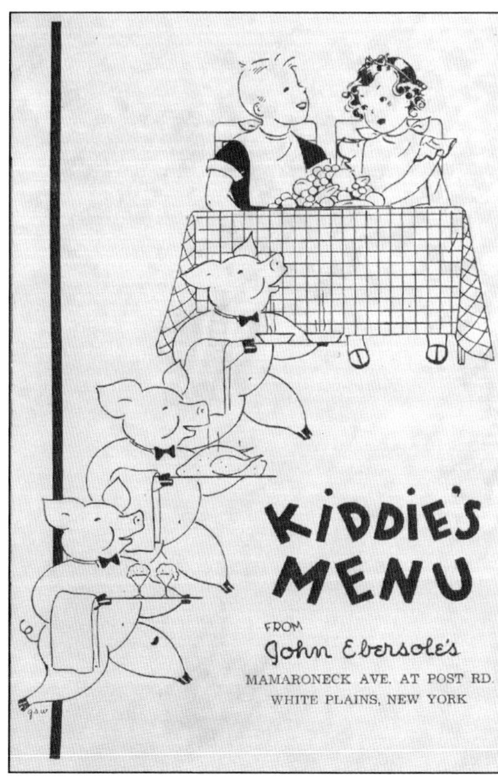

Ebersole's Restaurant, at 149 Mamaroneck Avenue, was a popular dining spot for families through the 1960s. Run by Ebersole's son-in-law Hugh Leslie for over 20 years, it never served alcoholic beverages. The kiddie menu announced, "Uncle John says if you eat all your vegetables, you may keep your menu." A fresh vegetable plate with a muffin, ice cream, and hot chocolate cost 45¢. (Courtesy of Lee Palmer.)

The ice skating pavilion was created in 1957 and later named Ebersole Ice Rink for the former city council member and restauranteur. The recreation park on Lake Street was created in 1932 on city land that had fallen into disrepair as a site for waste. Thousands of people visited each year after the rink opened, and it was the site of annual ice capades and countless teenage dates. (Courtesy of the Westchester County Historical Society.)

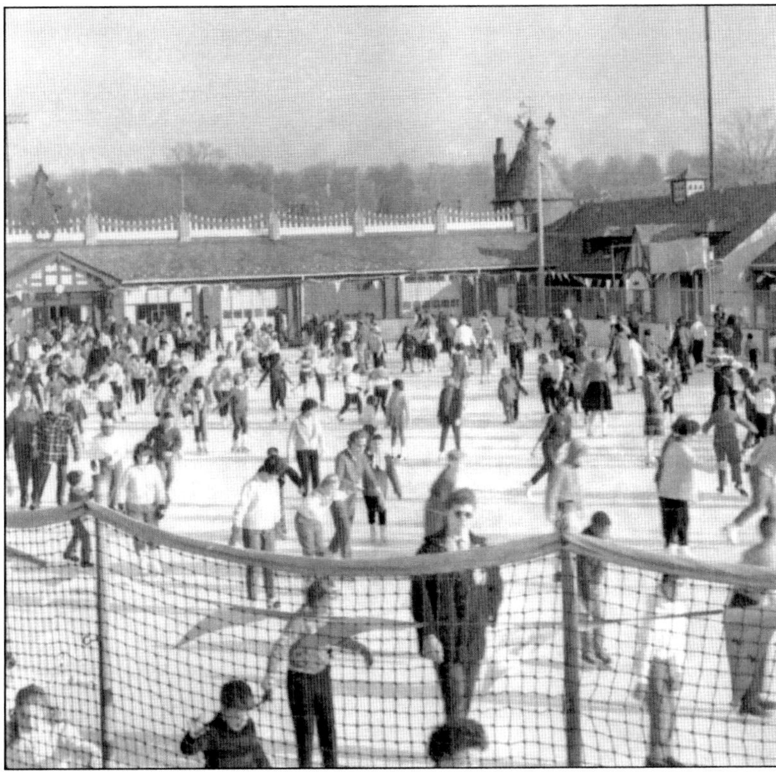

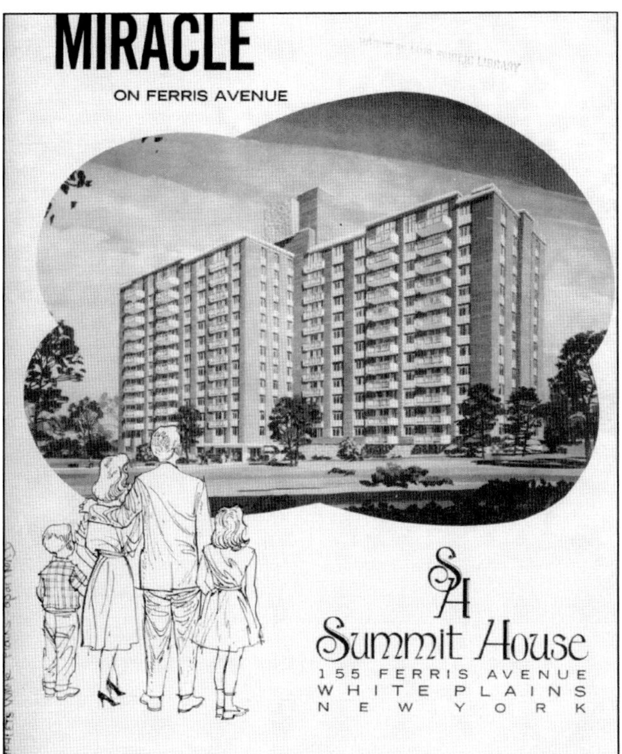

Summit House, the "Miracle on Ferris Avenue," was built in the mid-1960s and emblematizes the creation of large, modern apartment buildings that took place in the 1960s and 1970s. A percentage of Summit House apartments were set aside for lower income families, establishing a pattern that White Plains follows to this day. The Ferris Avenue neighborhood was one of the poorest areas of the city in the mid-1960s, and the Community Action Program (CAP) was founded there. CAP claimed the placement of four families in Summit House as one of its first major accomplishments. (WPPL.)

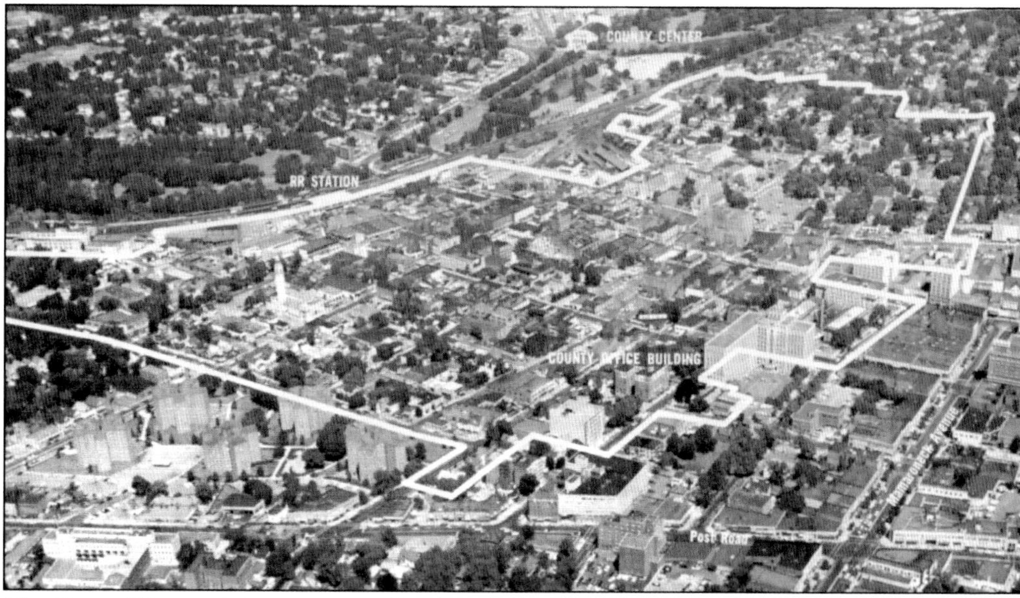

The Central Renewal Area was initially identified in the late 1950s, and by 1962, the White Plains Common Council commissioned Raymond & May Associates to present a plan for urban renewal. Raymond & May call the area outlined in white "a conspicuous exception to the spectacular growth experienced by downtown White Plains" during the 1950s. They wanted to eliminate the mix of building types and uses in favor of large-scale, architecturally modern private office buildings and public spaces. (WPPL.)

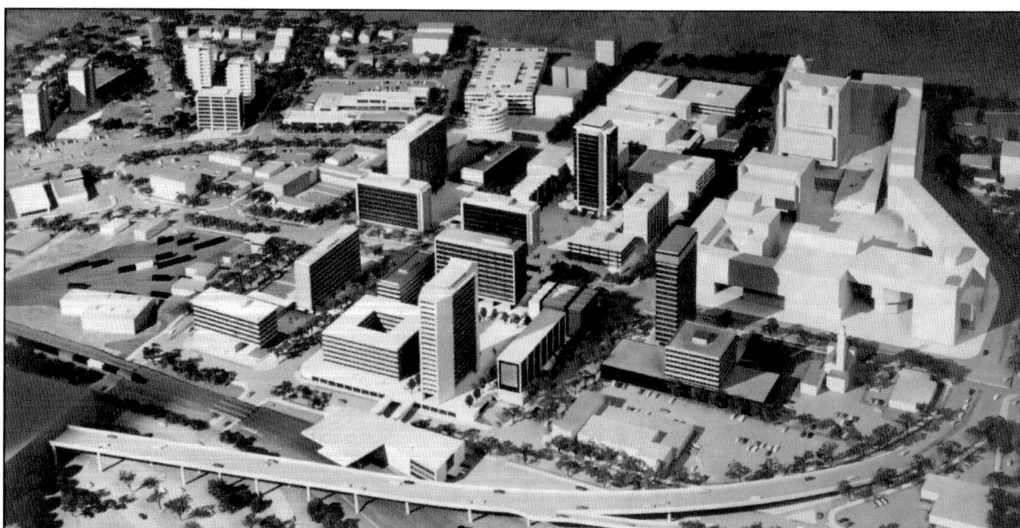

Like many other urban renewal project planners, Raymond & May created ambitious, expansive proposals that promised a bright, progressive future. The organic, complex development of urban spaces was eliminated in favor of massive, hyper-planned projects that focused on commuters, businesses, and large-scale modernist architecture. Note the proposed "Feeder Route" that would lead from I-287 in Greenburgh directly into the downtown building complex. The plan, which would have created soaring overpasses and eliminated much street-level life, never came to fruition as planned, defeated by a mix of community organizing and budgetary restrictions. (WPPL.)

Clarence's Shoe Shine Parlor, shown here at 129 Brookfield Street, was in the heart of a neighborhood that included the majority of black-owned businesses in White Plains in the mid-20th century. Street-level life, with its mix of local residents, visiting shoppers, and business owners, was basically obliterated by the central renewal project, which favored large, empty, architecturally modern spaces. Recent development has sought to revive street-level community spaces in the city, with more attention to walkability and approachable architecture. (WPCA.)

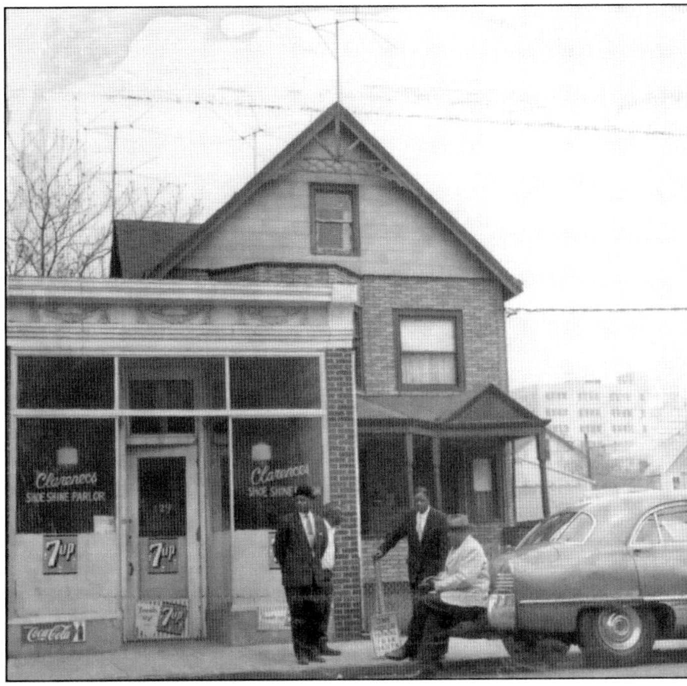

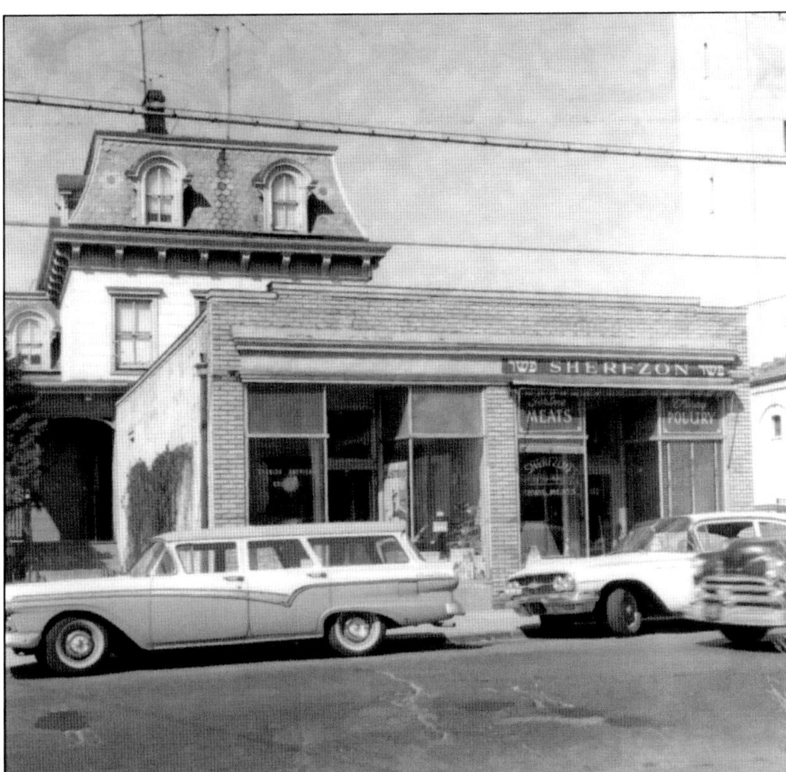

Sherfzon Jewish Meats was a kosher market located at 100–102 South Lexington Avenue. This photograph is from a series showing properties formerly within the central renewal project in White Plains, which included most of the downtown area. To the left of the market is the Spanish American Club, which was a gathering place for Spanish-speaking residents, including Cubans who fled prerevolutionary Cuba. (WPPL.)

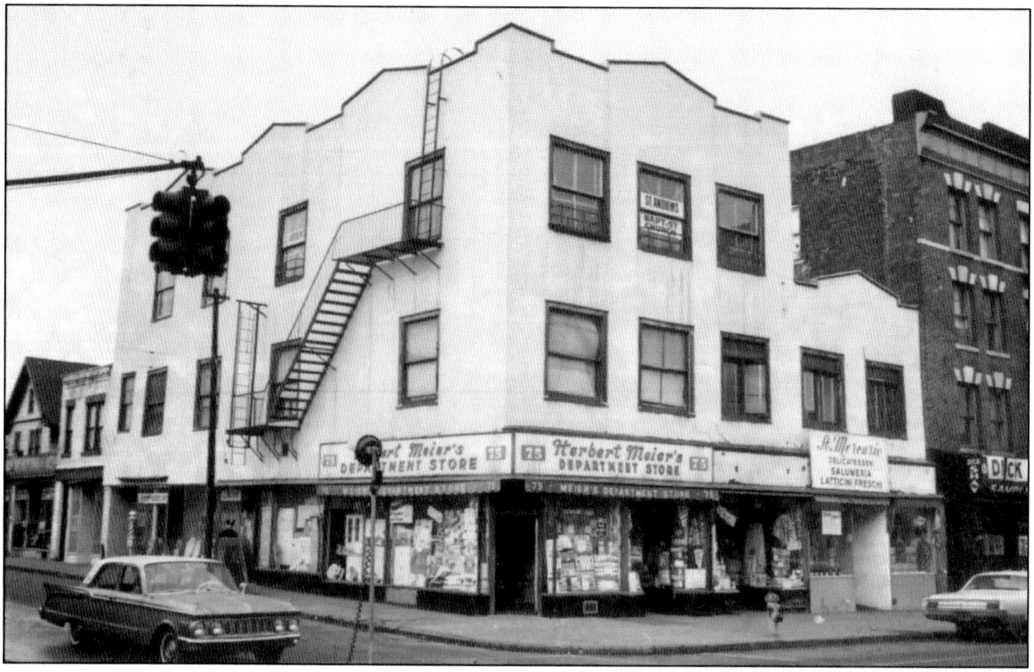

This picture of Herbert Meier's Department Store exemplifies that character of downtown White Plains before urban renewal—a hodgepodge of buildings from various eras in different styles; a mix of residential and commercial spaces; and a human-scale, pedestrian-friendly environment. Within this one stretch, there is a barbershop, an old-fashioned department store, an Italian deli selling meat and fresh cheese, a Baptist church, and numerous apartments. (WPPL.)

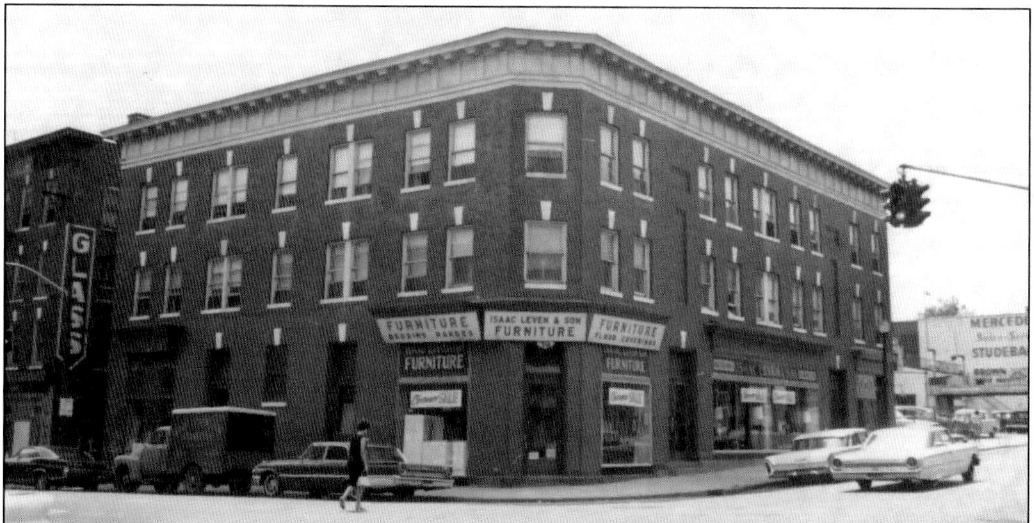

Isaac Leven & Sons, a furniture store located at the 76 Martine Avenue where Brookfield Street intersected it, was a fixture of downtown pre–urban renewal. One of the city's earliest Jewish congregations met in the store before building a synagogue on Fisher Avenue. This intersection no longer exists, replaced by the large government plaza that was the heart of the central renewal project. The White Plains Public Library now stands roughly where Isaac Leven & Sons once did. (WPPL.)

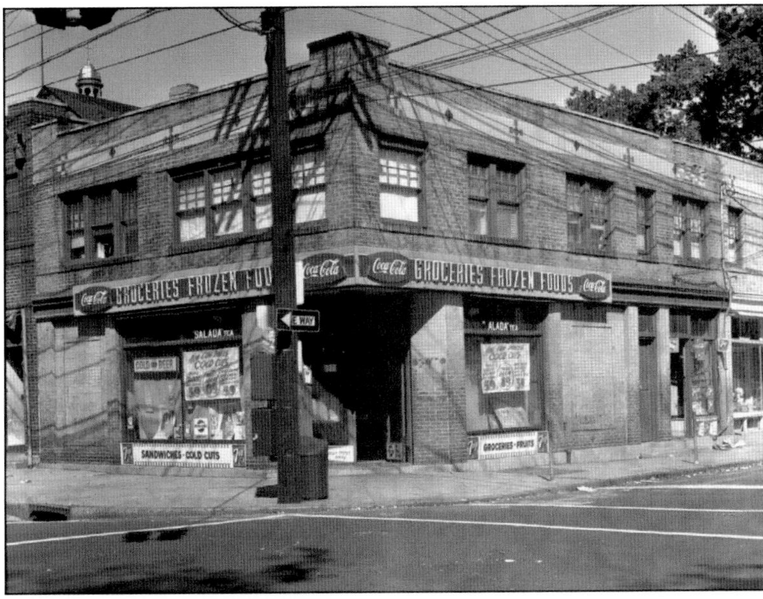

This grocery store, at 24 Fisher Avenue, is typical of the buildings targeted for demolition during urban renewal. Such places were considered an undesirable mix of commercial and residential spaces by the government officials and private developers who pushed urban renewal forward. (WPPL.)

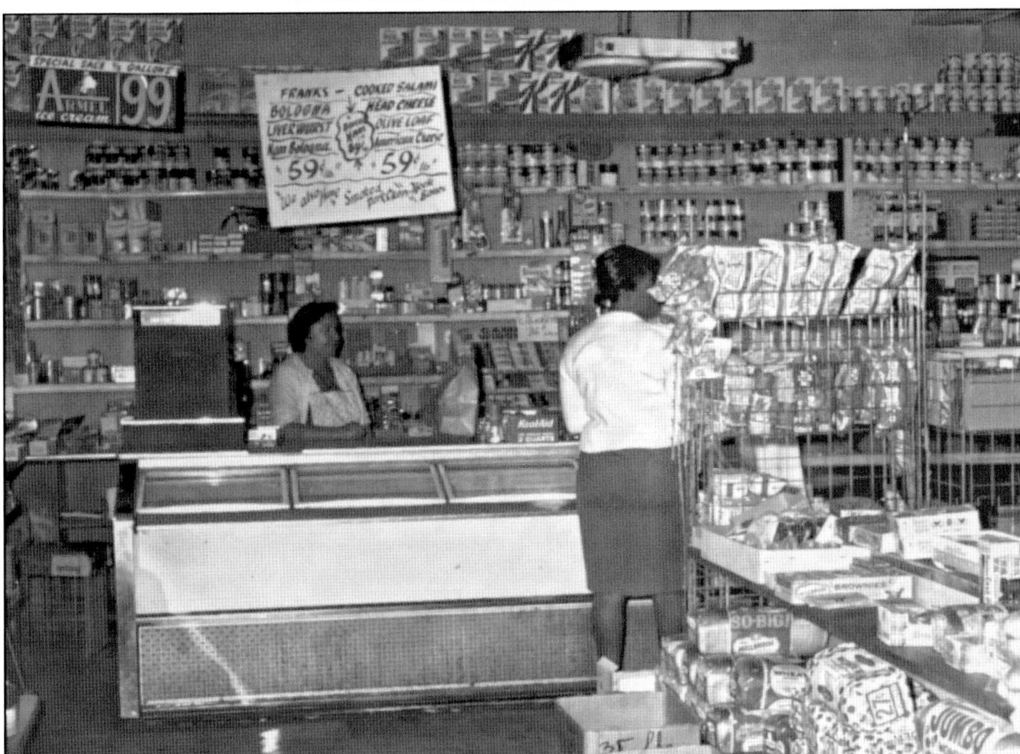

While the condition of many buildings marked for demolition was dire, they were nonetheless home to the mix of people and businesses that hold neighborhoods together. The reigning ideology of the time asserted that small-scale shops mixed in with apartments and even single-family homes was outmoded, and new developments strictly segregated residential and commercial spaces. Additionally, the downtown of White Plains was reshaped to fit the interests of commuters in automobiles rather than pedestrians. (WPPL.)

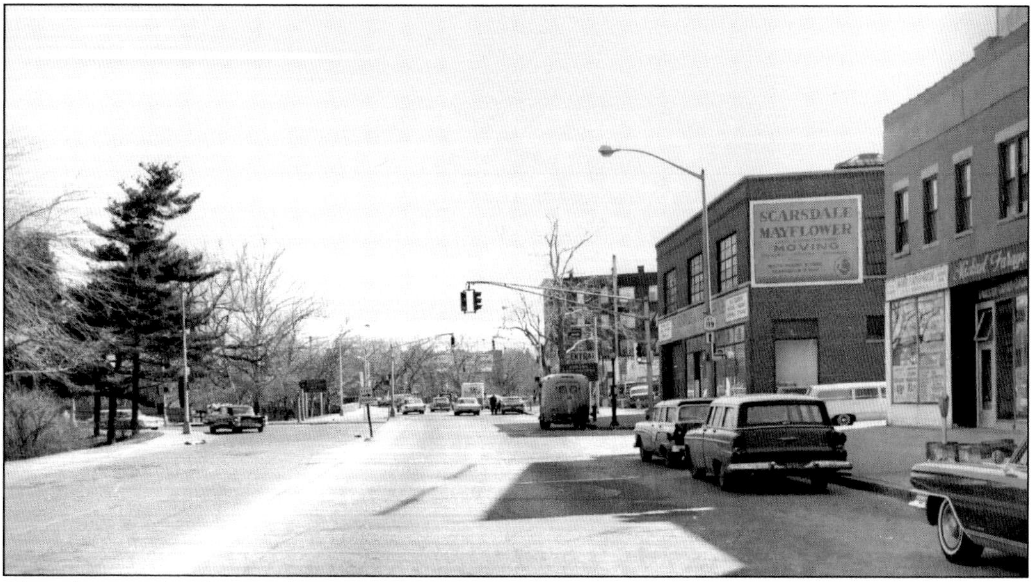

This photograph of Central Avenue or Tarrytown Road shows the mix of businesses and housing that used to line the street on the way into White Plains. Along with a moving company on the corner of School Street on the right, there was a barbershop, luncheonette, laundromat, car dealership, and apartment building on the blocks before the street crossed the Bronx River Parkway. This area, now a mix of empty space and parking lots, was the subject of an ambitious urban renewal plan that never happened. (Courtesy of the Westchester County Historical Society.)

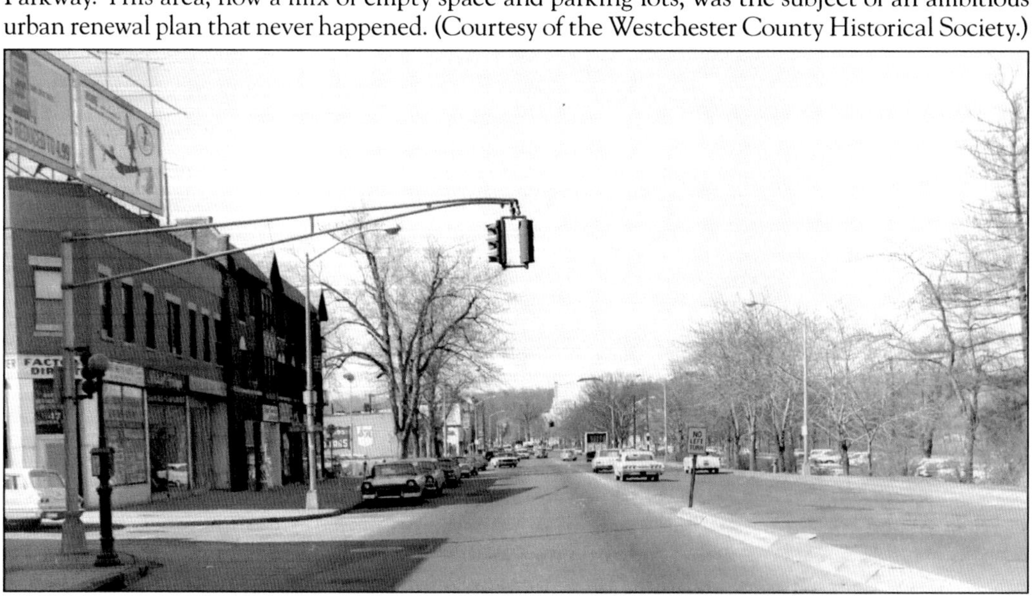

Looking toward the Westchester County Center on the same stretch of Central Avenue or Tarrytown Road in 1964, one can see the types of mixed-use buildings that were once common in White Plains. In 1970, an enormous 1,000-unit housing complex that would have included recreation spaces and some commercial enterprises was proposed for this area of Battle Hill. Over the next five years, at a cost of nearly $1 million, the project failed to overcome planning issues, organized resistance by neighborhood residents, and bureaucratic mismanagement. The area was eventually used to accommodate the wider version of Tarrytown Road that exists today. (Courtesy of the Westchester County Historical Society.)

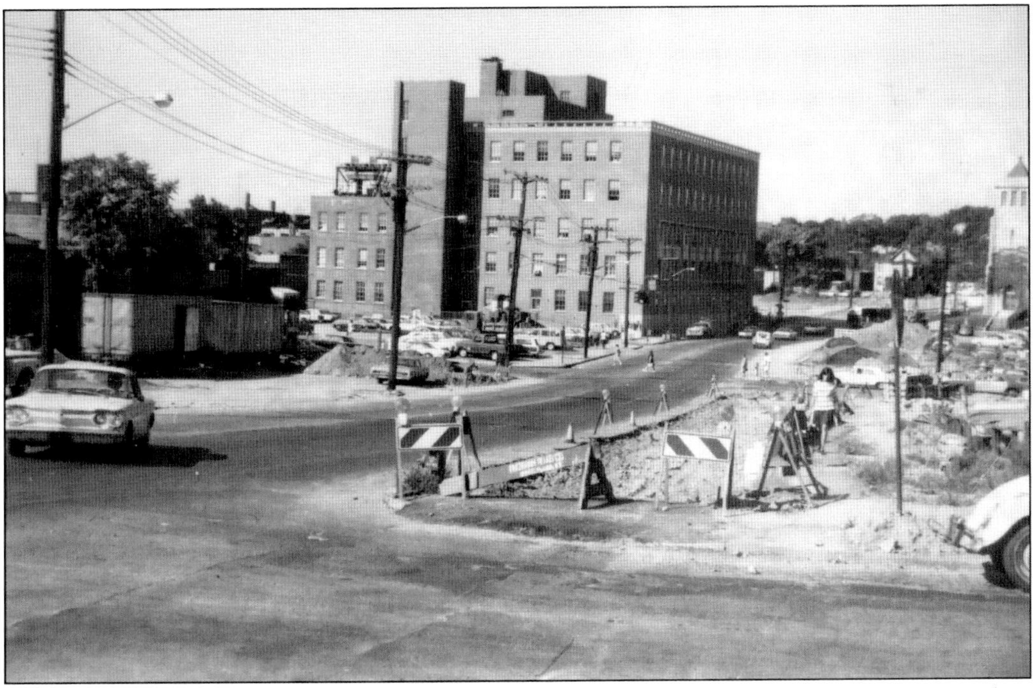

This photograph shows the widening and flattening of Hamilton Avenue in 1968. It was taken from Hamilton Avenue and Cottage Place, looking west. St. John's Church is visible at far right, and the AT&T building is at center. Soon, it would become the nucleus of a much larger building. (WPCA.)

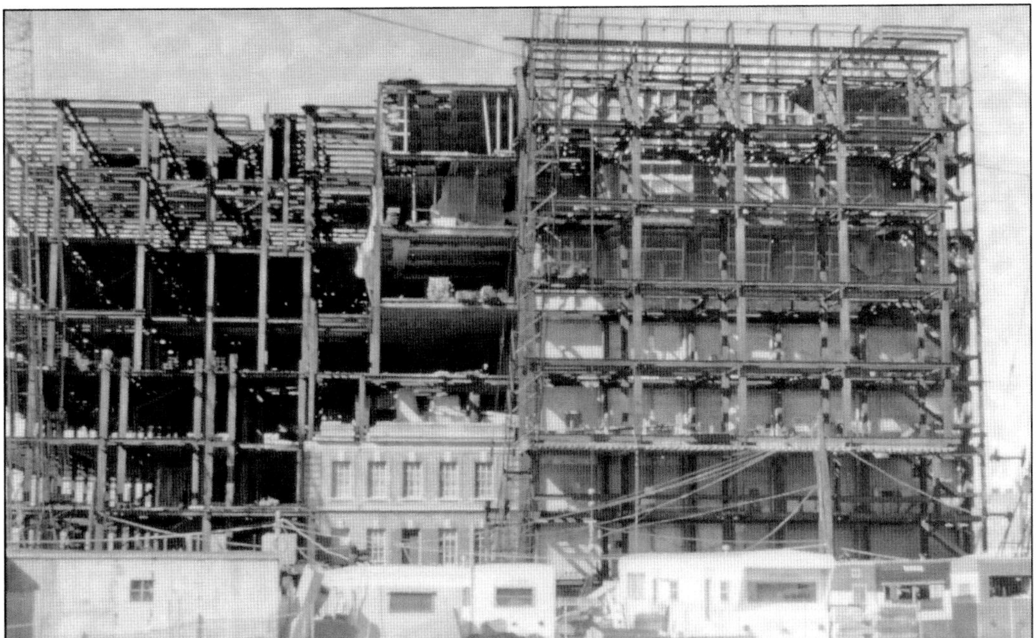

Part of the older AT&T building was still visible as it was encased inside of a jumbo structure, which still exists today. It occupies much of a block between Main Street and Hamilton Avenue. (WPCA.)

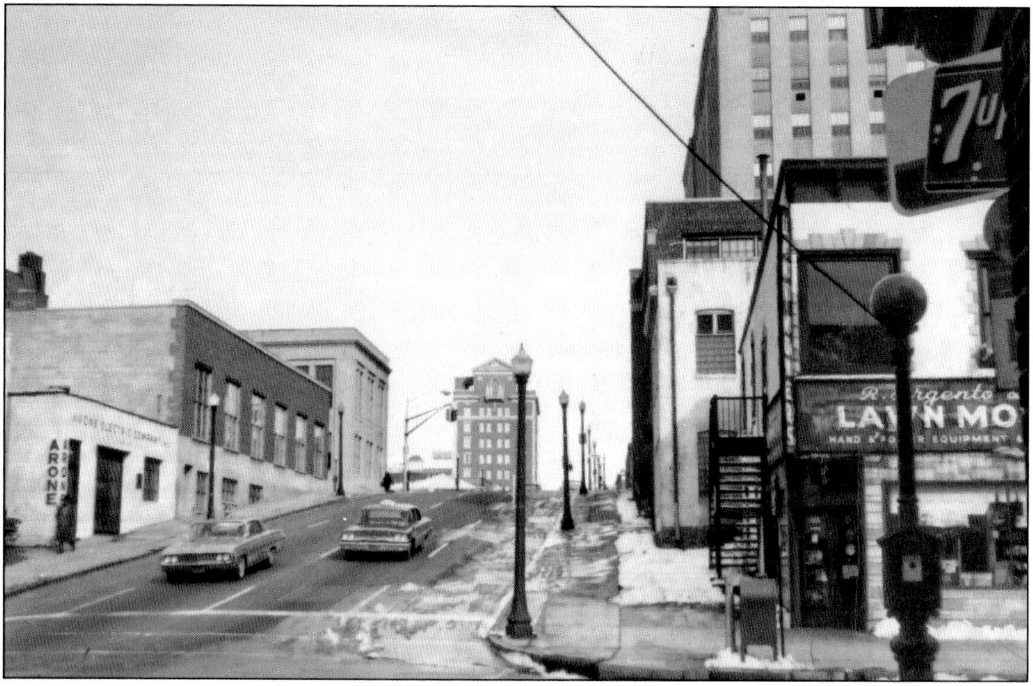

This view of Martine Avenue looking toward Mamaroneck Avenue gives a sense of how dramatically the landscape in the area was altered by the central renewal project. Visible at right is Argento & Son Inc., a lawn and garden equipment business started in 1919 that is still in business today. This part of Martine Avenue was raised to eliminate the hill. (WPCA.)

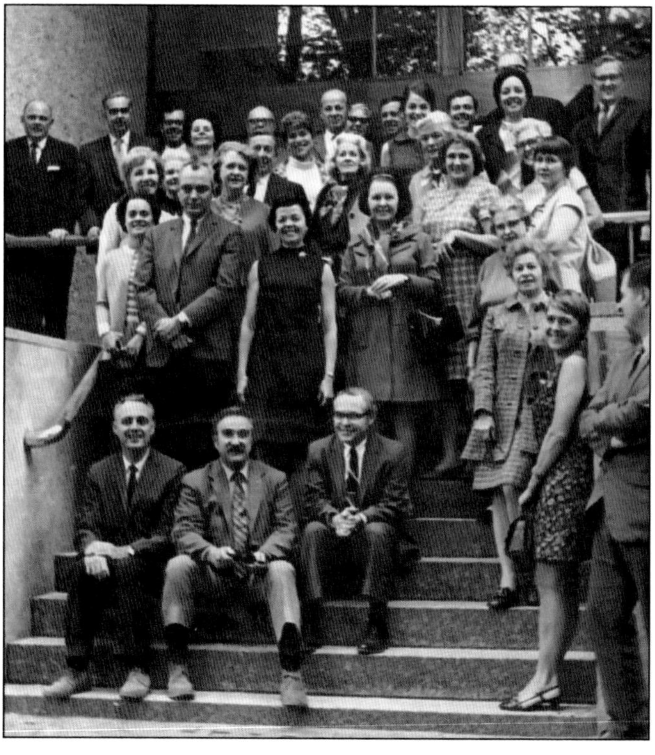

In 1969, as urban renewal was about to change the face of White Plains dramatically, 32 members of the White Plains Beautification Foundation traveled to eight cities in five countries in Europe. Their goal was to gather ideas that could be related to White Plains and affect the look of the city in the future. In Amsterdam, the group heard the bells playing from the Royal Palace and decided that would be a wonderful way to beautify White Plains. This resulted in their donation of the carillon, which still rings out from atop the county courthouse. (WPCA.)

Eight

THE 1970S

During the 1970s, people in the city of White Plains saw plans started in the early 1960s come to fruition. The Central Renewal Area was completely transformed, with whole neighborhoods and streets entirely removed and replaced with the huge county courthouse complex, the White Plains Public Library, and a new AT&T building. A large strip of downtown between Main Street and Martine Avenue, from Lexington Avenue to Court Street, was left empty for years while plans for the Galleria were finalized. Mike Coffey, a city council member, made creative use of the huge, barren area to initiate community gardens.

More corporations opened up home offices in White Plains in the 1970s. Nationwide Insurance, IBM, Union Carbide, Sage Instruments, Burns International Security Services, and AT&T all set up shop in the city. While modest growth of residences for low- and middle-income folks continued, the decade saw the advent of the "luxury" apartment condo buildings that have since become a fixture of downtown's residential market.

Culturally, the 1970s were rich with bars and clubs hosting bands regularly—some of whom were regional acts on their way to greater fame. In 1975, the Westchester Council for the Arts was designated as the regional arts council and started to fund exhibits and artists throughout the county. John H. Harmon Jr. established the Afro-American Cultural Foundation and was instrumental in creating the Panorama, an annual celebration "to present the facts of the contributions of the Black Community to the nation and also to discover the hidden talents which never had the opportunity of expression." The first Panorama was held in 1968 in Mount Vernon. By the 1980s, it had grown to include numerous programs and performances in many different parts of Westchester throughout the entire month of February. Today, the African American Advisory Board works on the county level to preserve and share black history.

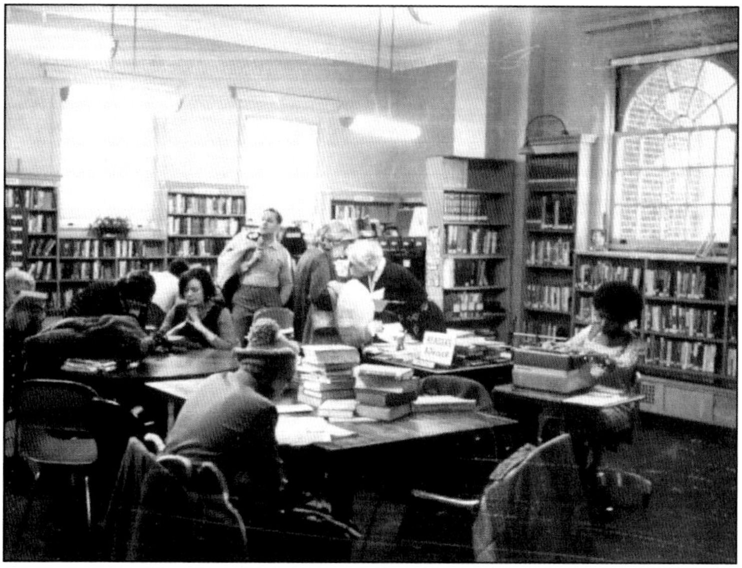

This shot was taken by Dr. May Virginia Valencik, library director, on January 2, 1970, at 4:00 p.m. in the afternoon. While the people in it may have been posing, the scene is typical of the old Grand Street library, where conditions became ever more cramped during the early 1970s. (WPPL.)

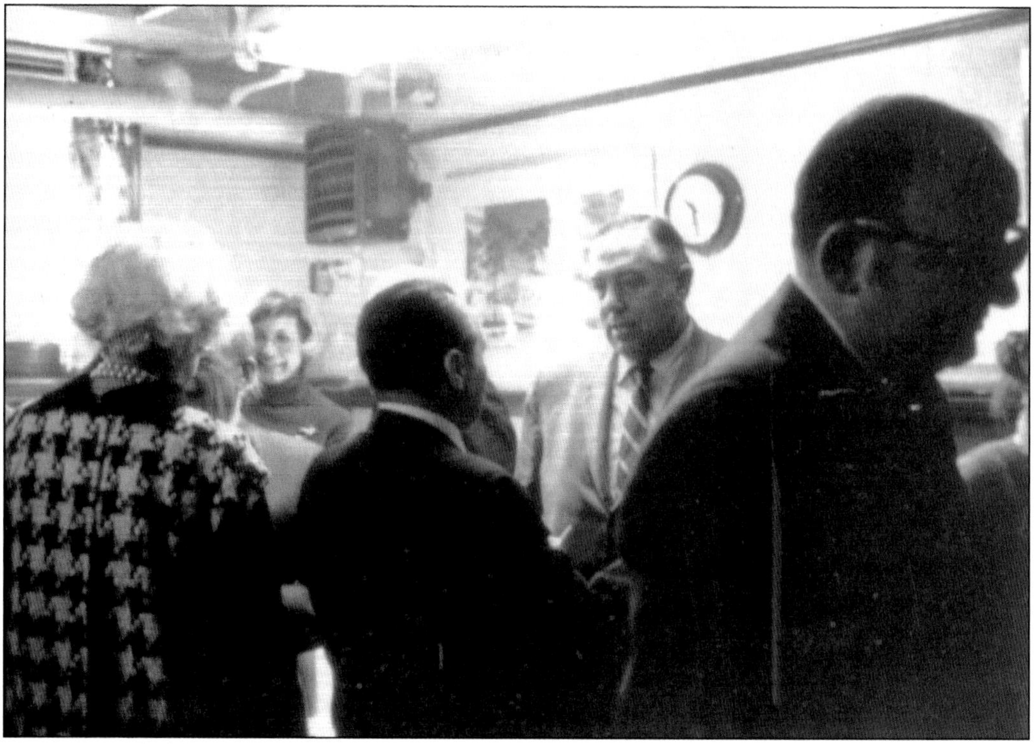

A party was held in the basement of the Grand Street Library prior to its demolition in 1974. The figure underneath the clock is Mayor Richard S. Hendey, who oversaw the central renewal project that moved the library to its current location at the corner of Martine Avenue and Martin Luther King Jr. Boulevard. Hendey was also a strong proponent of a downtown library that would be accessible by public transportation. In the late 1950s, there was a campaign to move the library out to the intersection of Bryant and Mamaroneck Avenues to meet the need for a new building, rather than waiting to have a new library constructed with the rest of the central renewal project. (WPPL.)

This 1974 shot of the library on Grand Street prior to demolition shows the condition of the area while the central renewal project was being completed. The library, now demolished, was built with funding from Andrew Carnegie. (WPCA.)

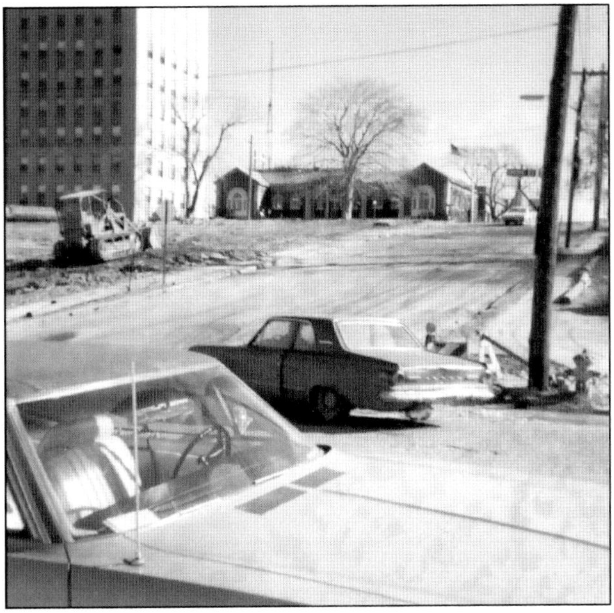

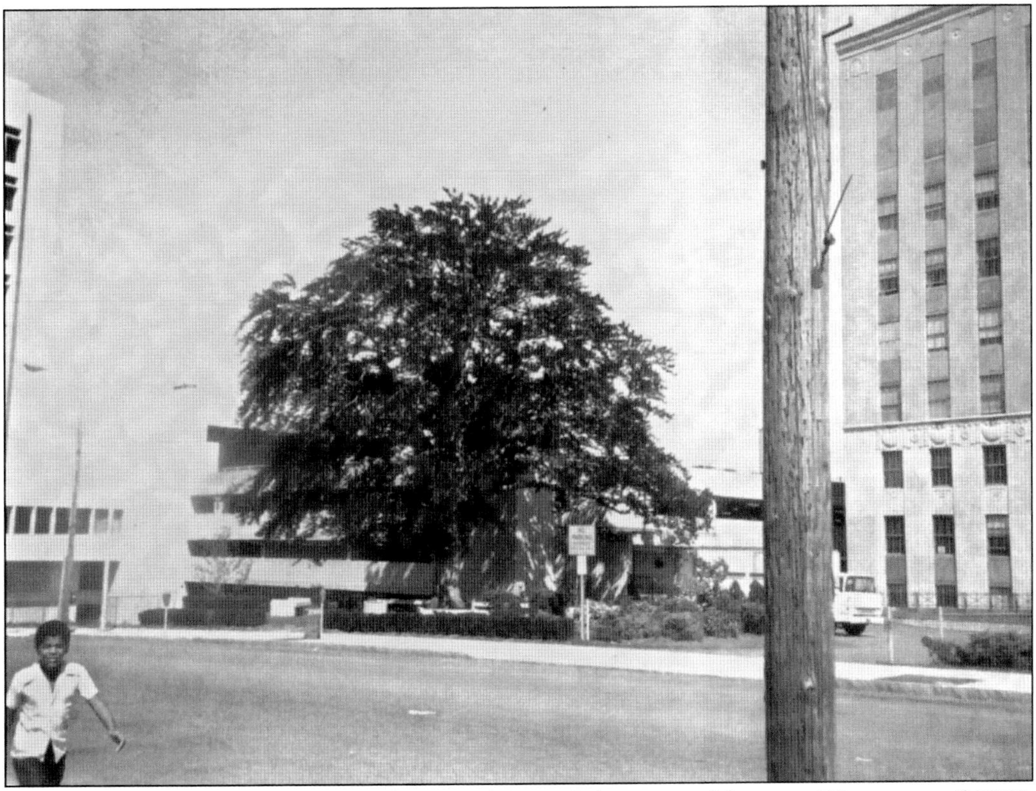

The Copper Beech tree in front of the Grand Street Library stood for over 100 years until 2008, when it succumbed under a combination of fungus and aphids. The White Plains Beautification Foundation was responsible for saving the tree from the fate of the Grand Street Library, and the county offices were built around it even after the library was gone. It thrived there in spite of a complete change in its surroundings. (WPPL.)

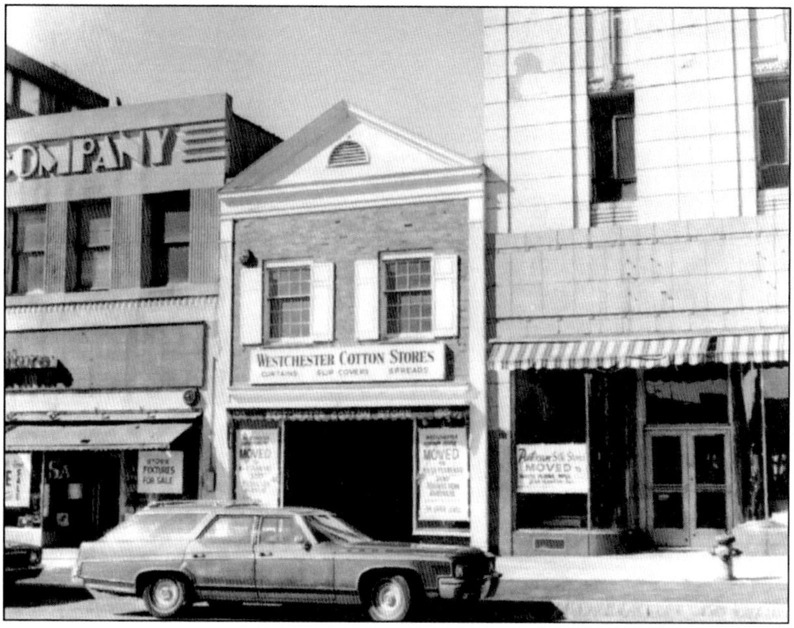

Signs in the windows of shops along Main Street announce the move to the White Plains Mall on Hamilton Avenue. Business owners and city officials clashed at times over the relocation, with concern from the merchants about losing customers and fair compensation for moving. (Courtesy of the Westchester County Historical Society.)

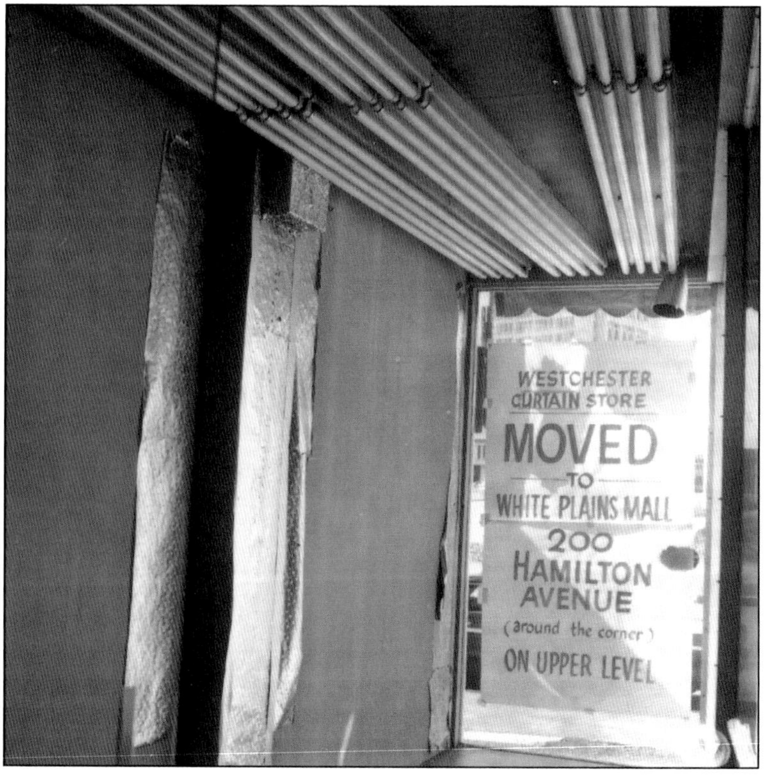

This picture, taken from inside the Westchester Cotton Store, at 155 Main Street, documents the process of moving the business from its original location to 200 Hamilton Avenue, the White Plains Mall. A group of business owners began organizing in the mid-1960s to secure spots for their shops in the new Hamilton Avenue space. (Courtesy of the Westchester County Historical Society.)

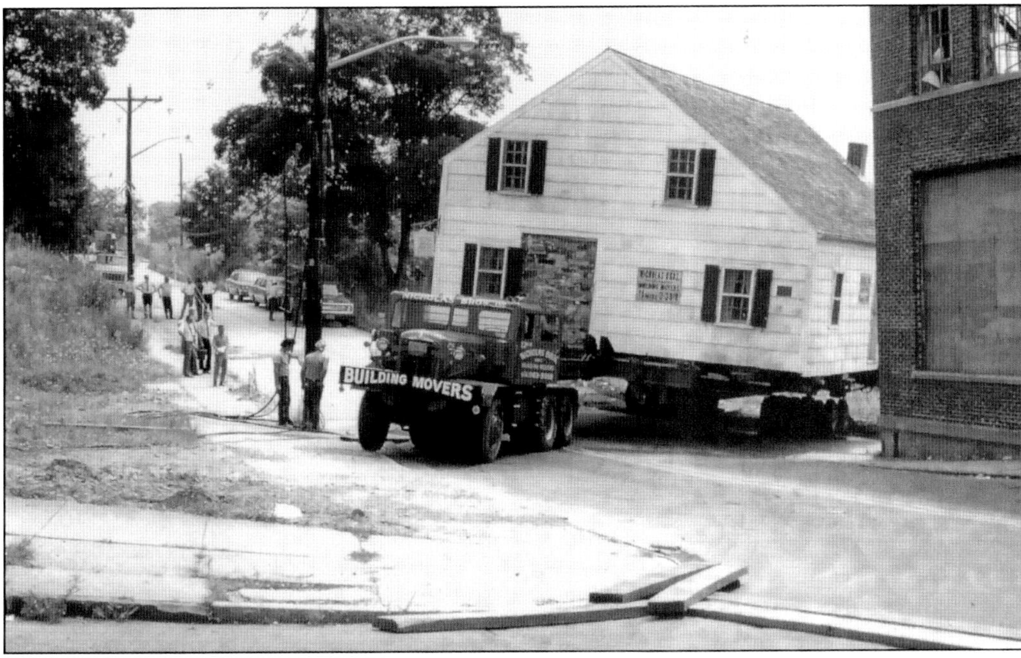

It was a tight squeeze negotiating this turn at John and Ridge Streets as the Jacob Purdy House was moved from Spring Street to its new home up the hill at 60 Park Avenue. After years of planning, the move was finally accomplished on August 9, 1973. In April 1979, the Purdy House was added to the National Register of Historic Places. (WPCA.)

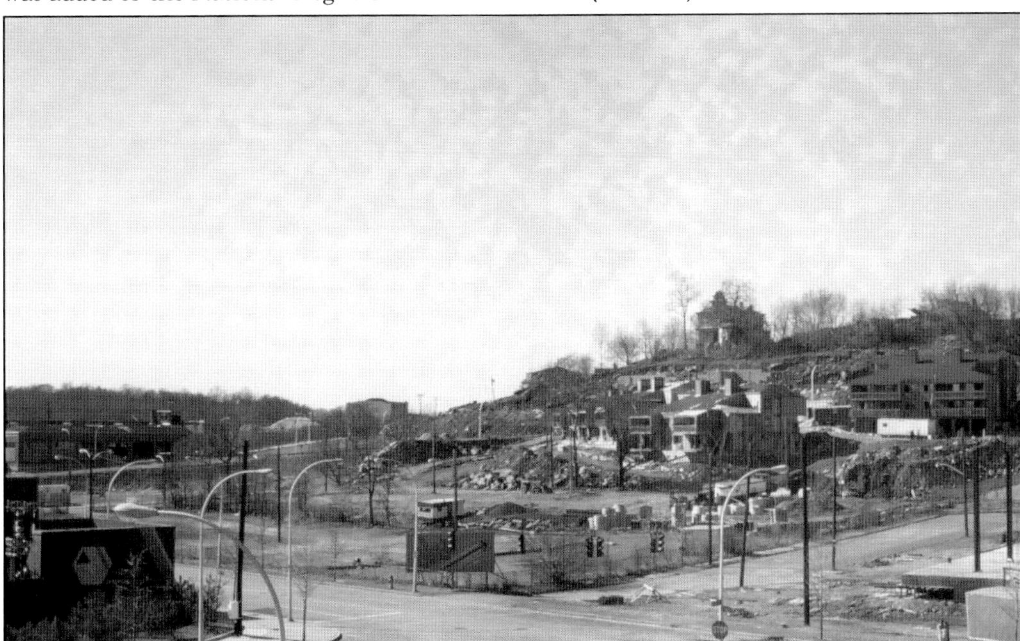

This view of Dusenbury Hill shows the Carpenter House, which still exists at the top of the hill overlooking the Bronx River Valley. Under construction are the Hillside Village Condominiums, which opened in 1977 as the first condominium development built in an urban renewal area in New York State. Seen in the distance is the Westchester County Center. (WPCA.)

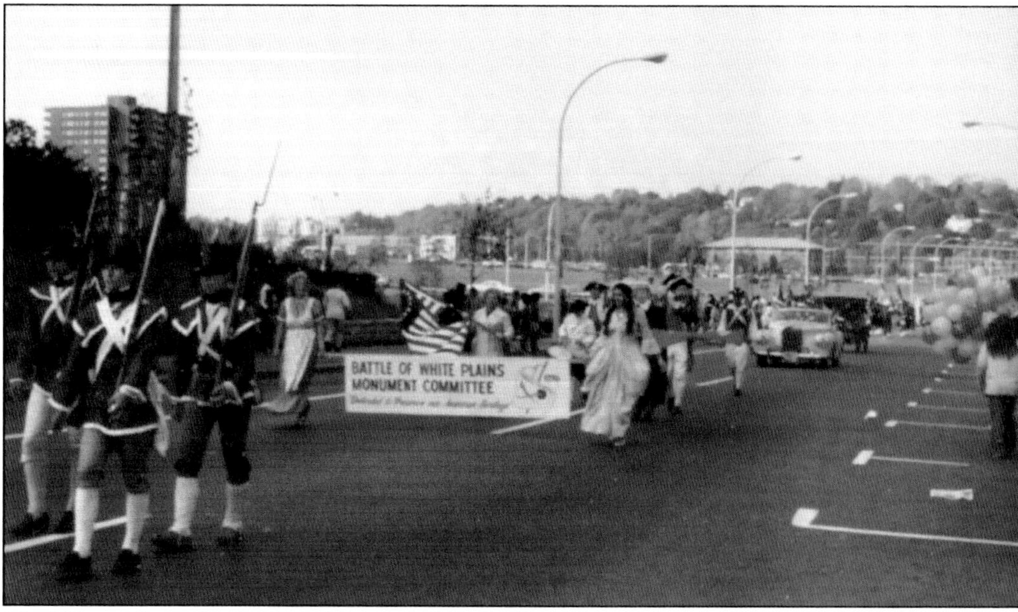

The White Plains Bicentennial Committee met for several years under the leadership of chairman Robert Ruger. It organized events throughout the year, including a kite festival, youth baseball jamboree, a public Common Council meeting in costume, musical events, art exhibits, readings of the Declaration of Independence, Battle of White Plains reenactments, and parades. Shown here is the Battle of White Plains Monument Committee marching up Main Streets on July 11, 1976. (WPCA.)

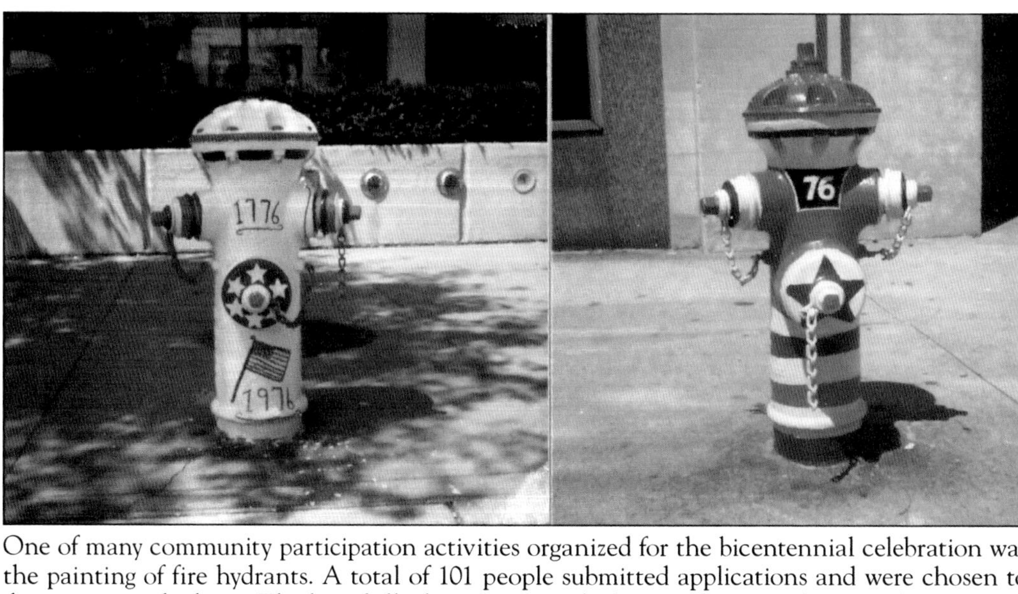

One of many community participation activities organized for the bicentennial celebration was the painting of fire hydrants. A total of 101 people submitted applications and were chosen to decorate a city hydrant. The list of all who participated, along with many photographs, is part of the White Plains City Archives. (WPCA.)

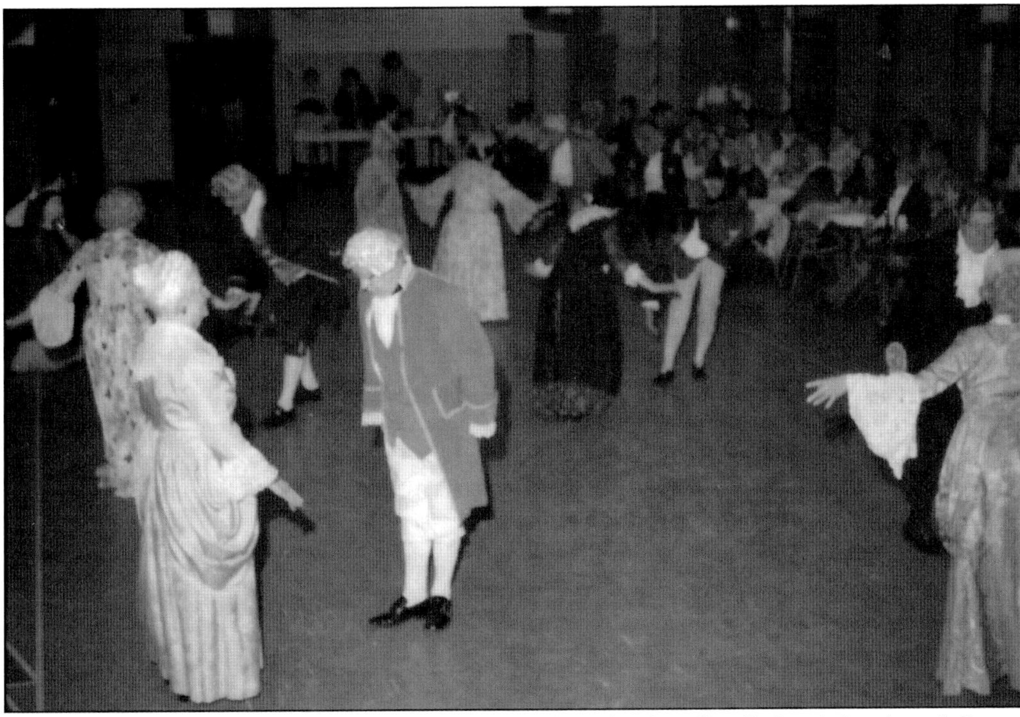

Mildred and Frank Diefenbach (at left), Sandra and Michael Coffey (behind them), and George and Martha Washington (played by Stephen Holden Jr. and Renoda Hoffman, at right) are pictured here enjoying one of the Colonial dances during the bicentennial celebration. Hoffman, the city historian, volunteered to teach classes in the gavotte, the minuet, and other Colonial dances and did so for many years at the Westchester County Theatre. (WPCA.)

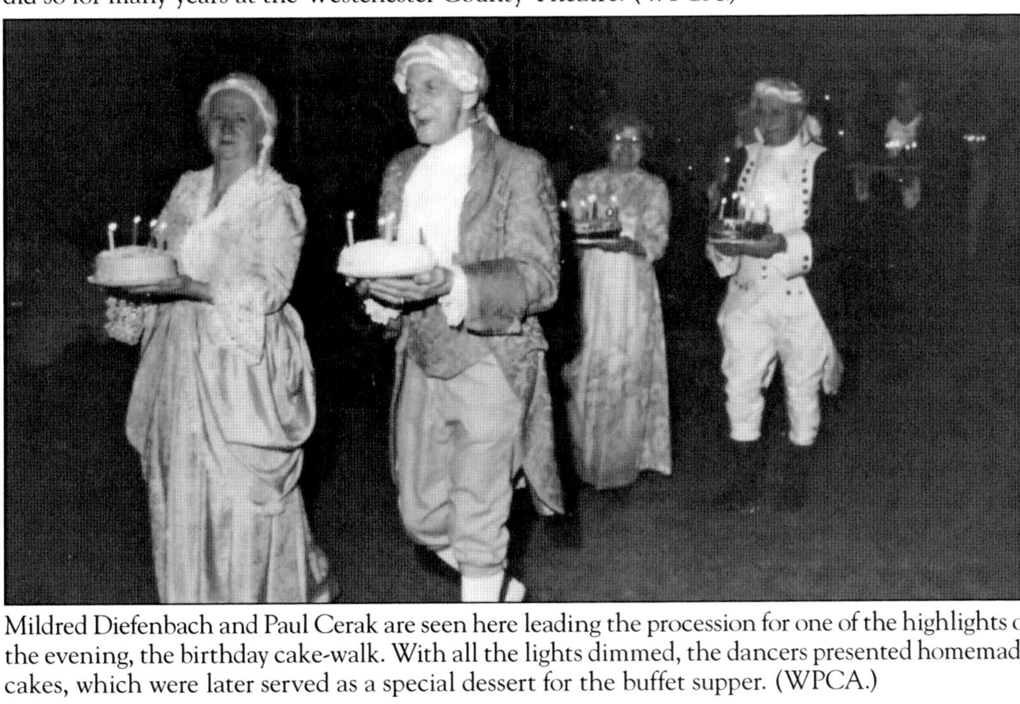

Mildred Diefenbach and Paul Cerak are seen here leading the procession for one of the highlights of the evening, the birthday cake-walk. With all the lights dimmed, the dancers presented homemade cakes, which were later served as a special dessert for the buffet supper. (WPCA.)

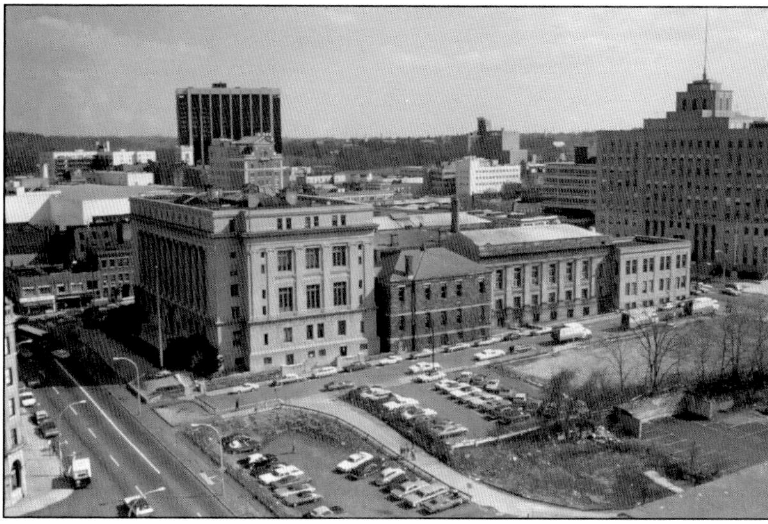

This May 1977 photograph shows the court complex just prior to the beginning of demolition and replacement by the Galleria Mall. Across Martine Avenue is the nine-story County Office Building at right. (WPCA.)

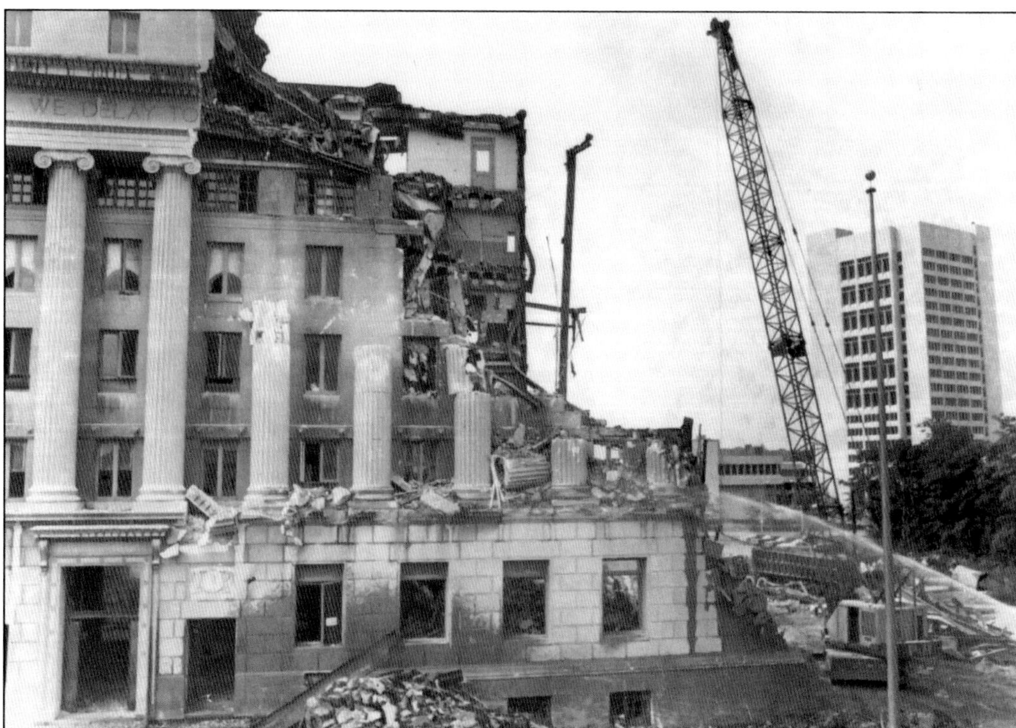

Community reaction to the impending destruction of the courthouse was mixed. A group dedicated to preserving the structure for architectural and historic reasons was formed, the Save the Courthouse Committee. It succeeded in having the courthouse placed on the National Register of Historic Places in January 1975. This delayed the demolition but only temporarily. The demolition, which was completed in July 1977, is pictured here with the new county courthouse in the background. (WPCA.)

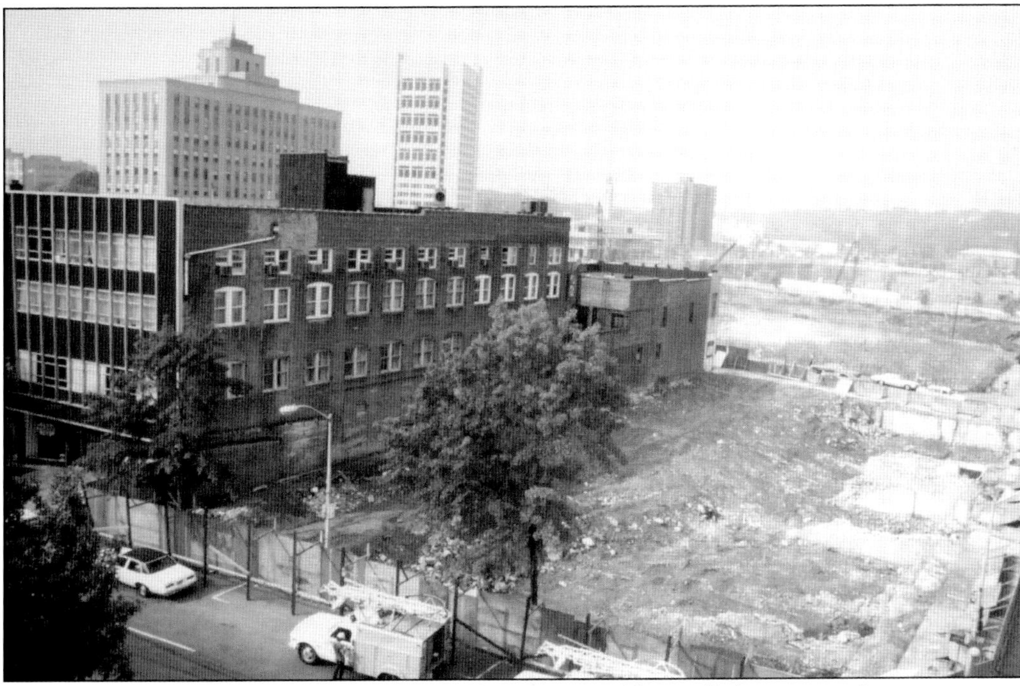

After the courthouse complex was demolished, one could see all the way to the train station from this vantage point on Mamaroneck Avenue. This empty lot is at the corner of Mamaroneck Avenue and Main Street and became the site of a circular fountain and later a musical fountain with "dancing waters." (WPCA.)

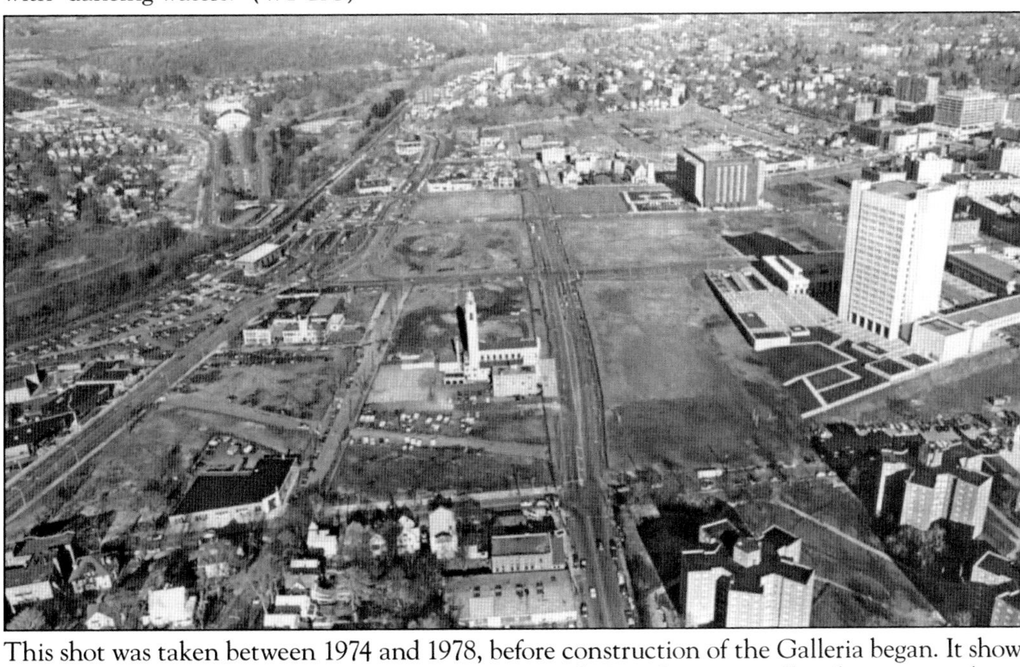

This shot was taken between 1974 and 1978, before construction of the Galleria began. It shows the completely razed areas along Lexington Avenue and Main Street, as well as the new courthouse complex and the completed White Plains Mall on Hamilton Avenue. Compare this with the aerial photograph of the Central Renewal Area in the 1960s to see the scale of the change. (WPPL.)

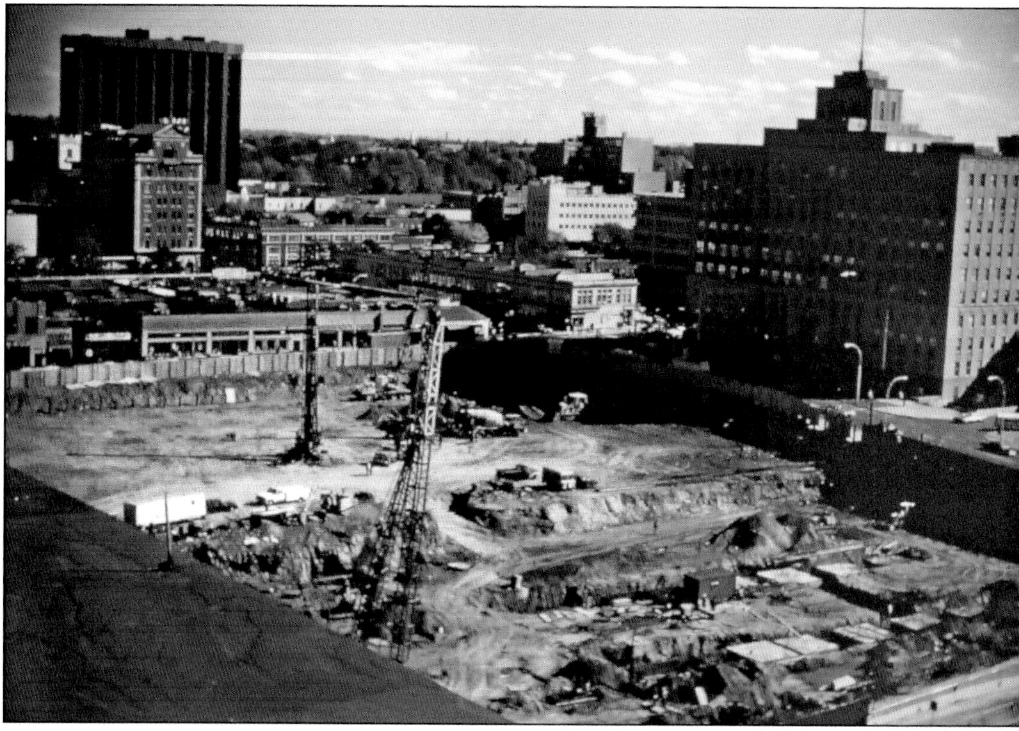

Taken from atop the nearby AT&T building, this January 1979 photograph shows the size of the Galleria Mall's footprint in downtown White Plains. (WPCA.)

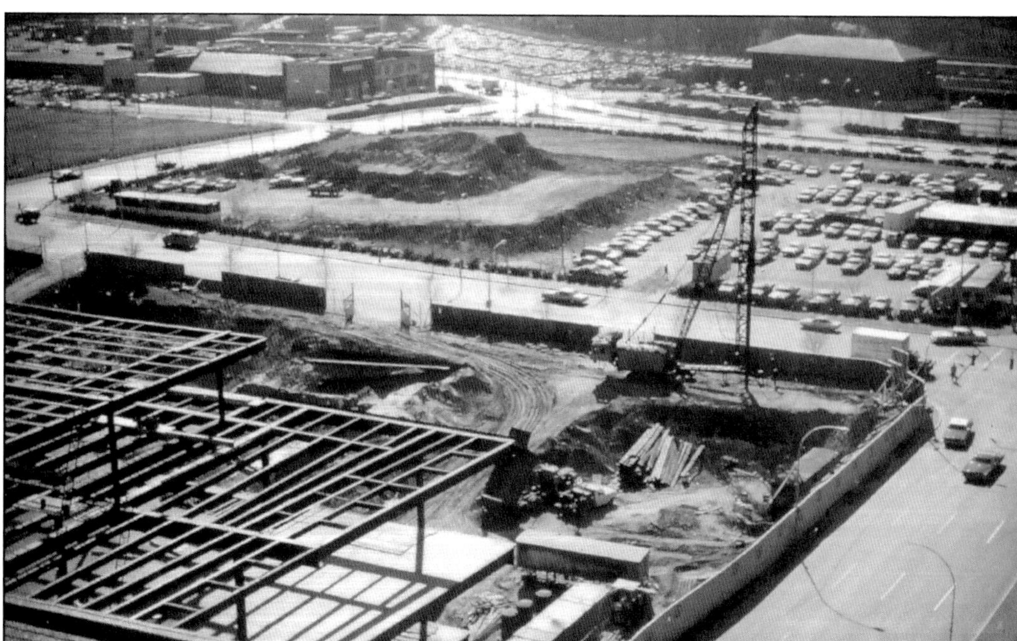

In March 1979, the Galleria construction was moving along, as shown in this view. The train station and Depot Plaza are seen in the distance. (WPCA.)

Nine

THE 1980s

During the 1980s, twenty years after the process of urban renewal started in earnest, the city had a completely reshaped downtown and a stable group of suburban neighborhoods. The Galleria opened in 1980, drawing folks from all over Westchester to a new (at the time) style of shopping. The "Platinum Mile" was, at its height, drawing an international group of businesses to the office parks along I-287 between White Plains and Rye. The city suffered without a movie theater, and a bit of the decay that urban renewal was supposed to eliminate crept back in as the forces of white flight from downtown areas and a reduction in social spending carried out by the Reagan Administration created a negative national narrative about the problems of cities.

A large redevelopment of the White Plains Metro-North Station was the major construction project of the 1980s in downtown White Plains. After the old station was razed in late 1983, a temporary station was used until the new transit center opened in 1987. Mayor Alfred Del Vecchio, whose tenure spanned the 1980s, was proud of the fact that the trestles that carry trains over Main Street and Hamilton Avenue were able to be updated without any interruption of traffic along either street.

Through all of these changes, the people of White Plains continued to organize themselves into various types of community-based organizations, from the White Plains Council of Neighborhood Associations to the Concerned Citizens for Open Space.

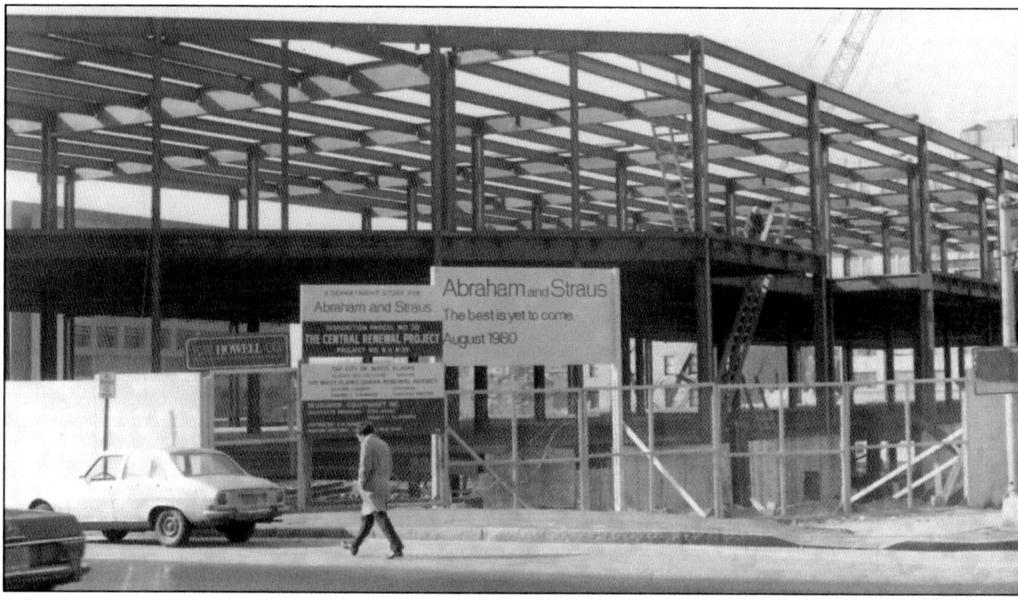

Abraham and Straus was a department store that traced its roots to 19th-century Brooklyn. The Galleria was anchored by an Abraham and Straus, seen here under construction in 1980. Macy's absorbed Abraham and Straus in the 1990s and is located in the spot now. (WPPL.)

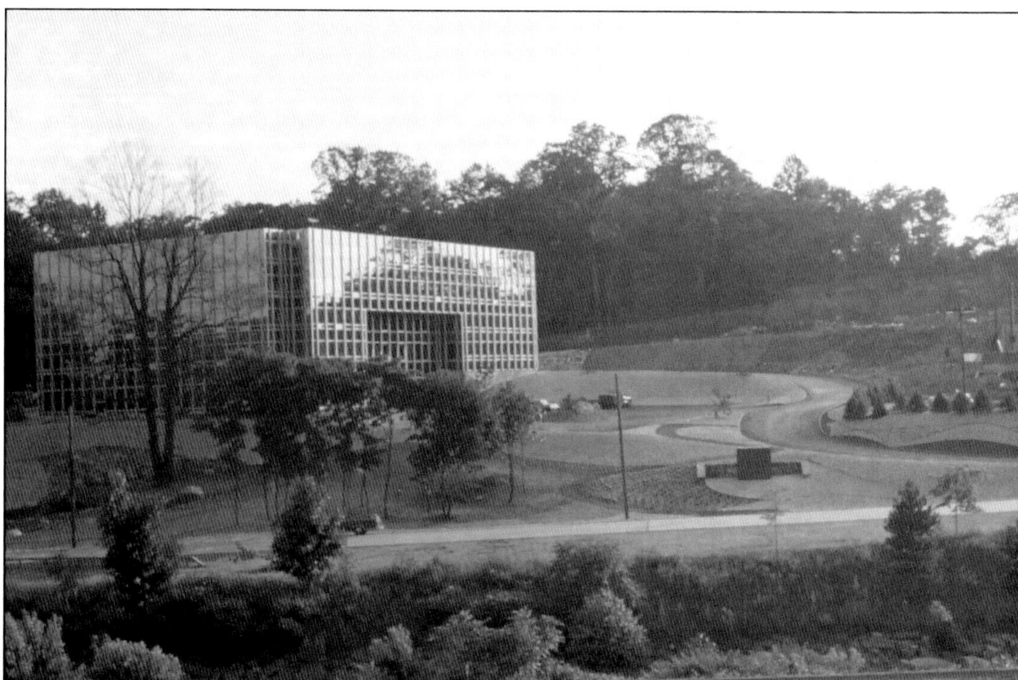

The "Platinum Mile" was the name given to the stretch of Westchester Avenue that paralleled Route I-287 from White Plains to Rye where many large corporations built offices (and even headquarters) between the 1960s and 1980s. Since then, some of the original and largest companies have left, replaced by smaller ones and repurposed buildings. (WPCA.)

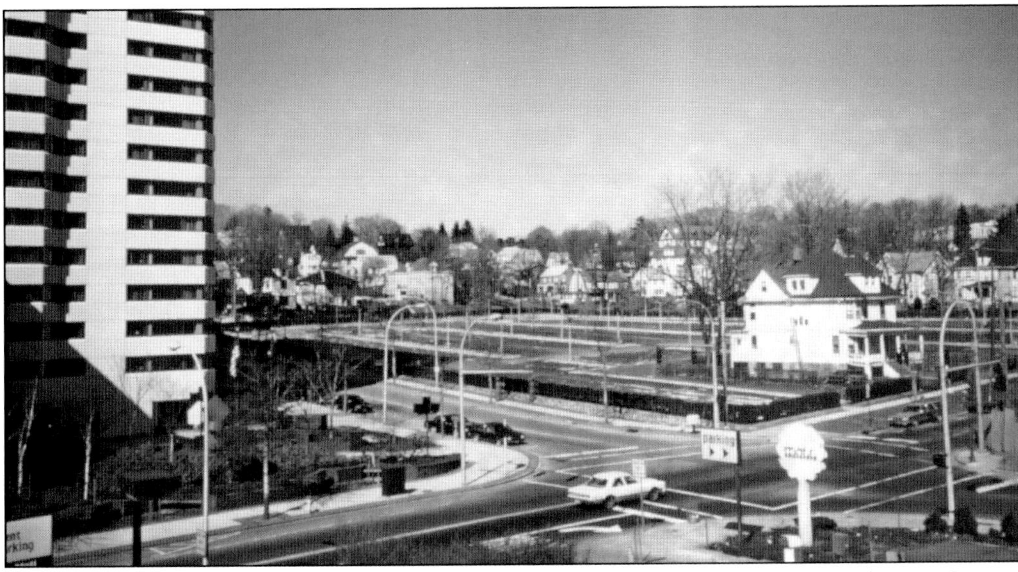

This is a 1984 view of the last holdout on the block, 21 Barker Avenue. At left is La Reserve Hotel, now the Residence Inn by Marriott, and out of sight at the bottom is the Hamilton Avenue Mall. (WPCA.)

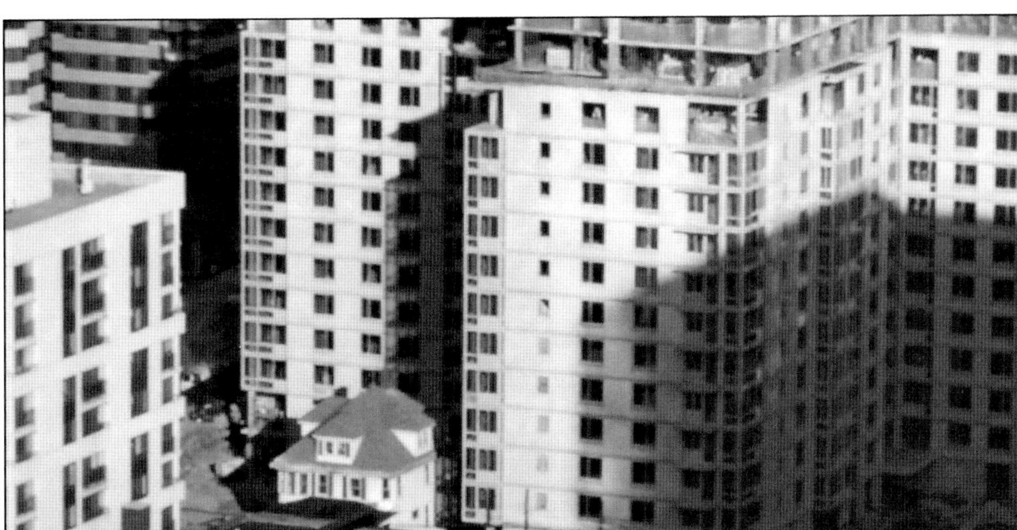

This photograph tells the rest of the story. The owners of 21 Barker Avenue held on to the house as long as they could, but eventually the Avalon Apartments were built around it. On March 13, 2008, the long cherished home at 21 Barker Avenue was demolished. (Courtesy of Larry Auerbach.)

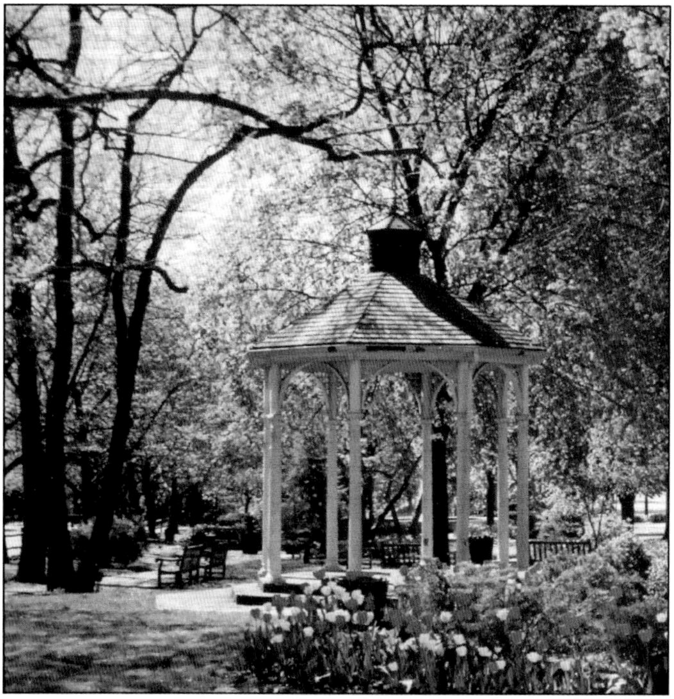

This Victorian-style gazebo in Tibbits Park, dedicated on October 14, 1984, is 18 feet wide at the base and 12 feet high. Erected by the White Plains Beautification Foundation, it was named in honor of Edwin G. Michaelian, who served as mayor of White Plains from 1950 to 1957 and as Westchester County executive from 1958 to 1973. Joyce Michaelian noted in her remarks at the dedication ceremony, that the gazebo is just a few blocks from Michaelian's boyhood home on Cottage Place. (WPCA.)

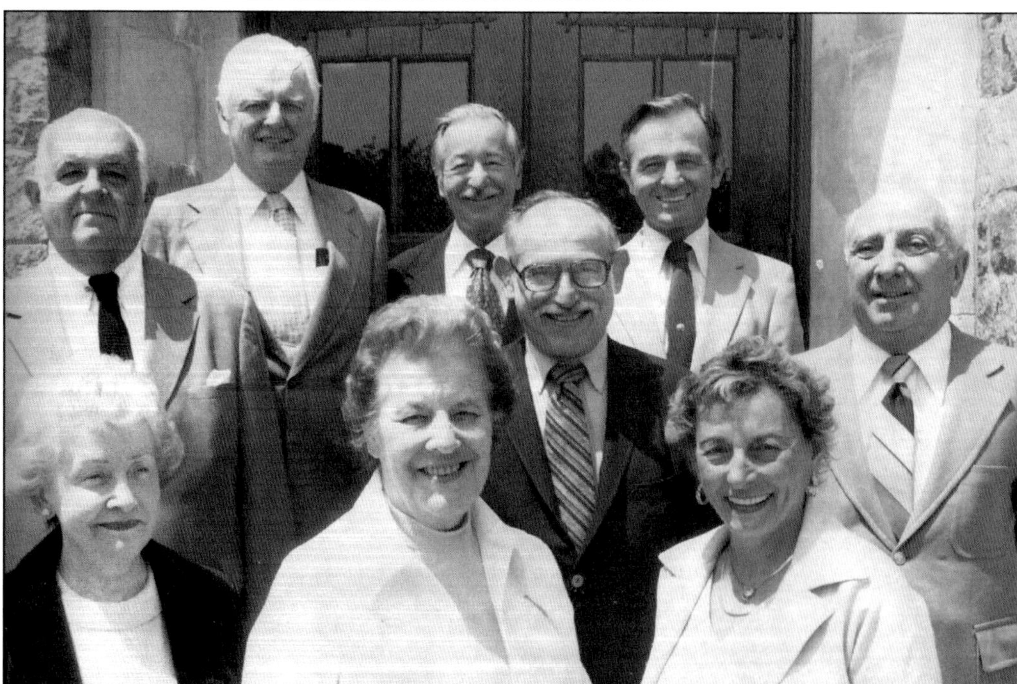

For the members of the White Plains High School class of 1933, their 50th reunion was an important event. Pictured here is the committee who organized the June celebration. From left to right are (first row) Ruth Wood, Laurel McGuire Holzer, and Anne Schleicher Rosen; (second row) Frank McMahon, Jim Mulhall, Mike Casarella, David Schwarz, Dr. Sal DeCarlo, and Mike Savanella. (WPCA.)

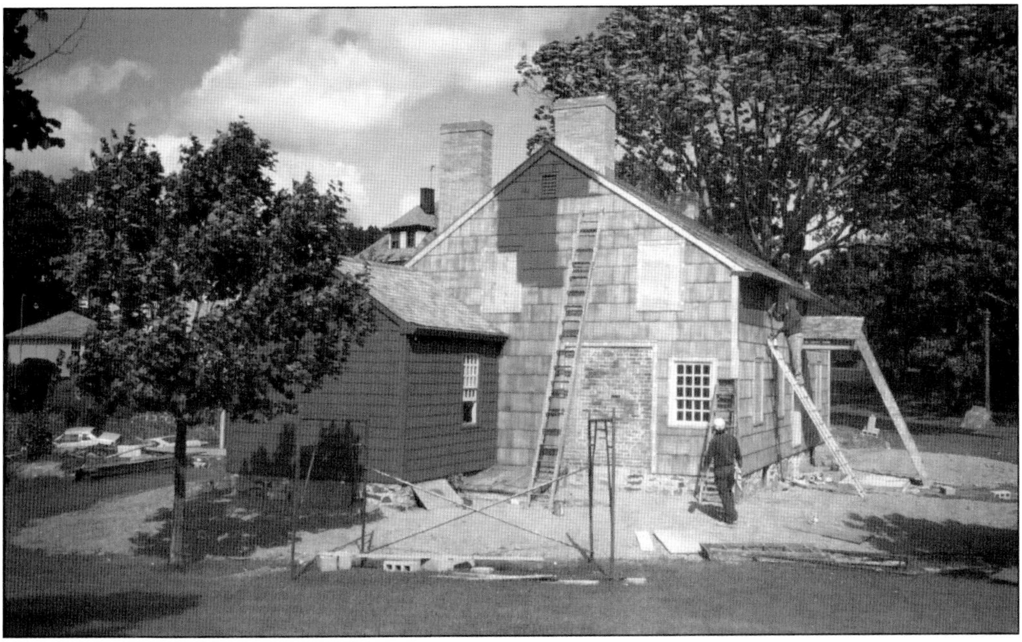

During the 1980s, efforts were made to rehabilitate the interior and exterior of the Jacob Purdy House. Donations were solicited from local businesses, and the White Plains Historical Society, which succeeded the Battle of White Plains Monument Committee, oversaw projects by dozens of volunteers. (WPCA.)

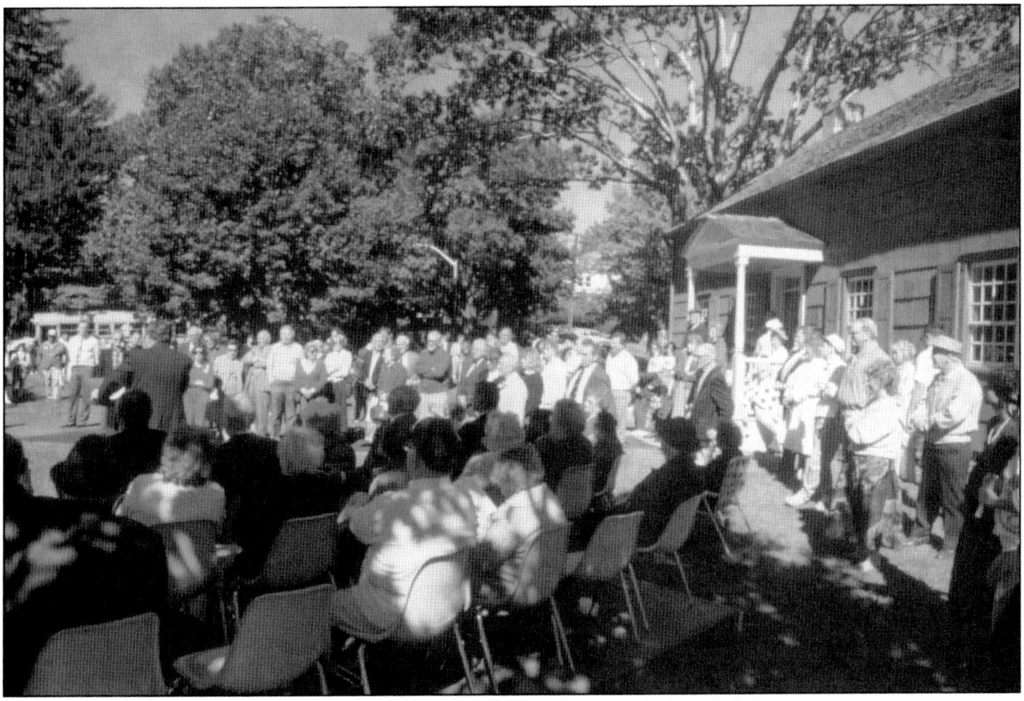

As the 1980s came to a close, the Jacob Purdy House was dedicated as a Colonial museum on September 24, 1989. A large crowd gathered for the celebration, which included speeches, musical entertainment, and tours of the house. (WPCA.)

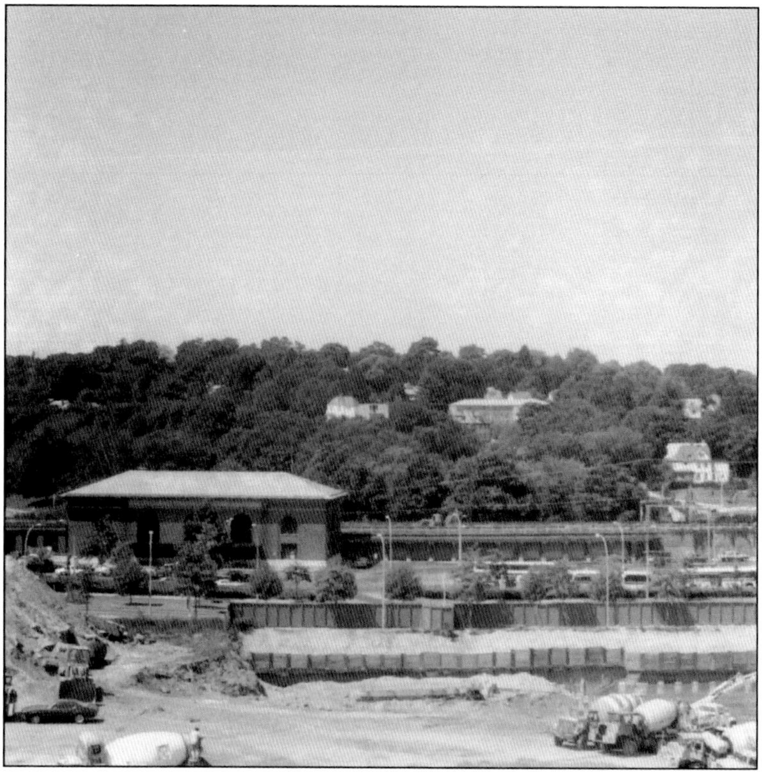

The train station stood alone facing acres of cleared land in this 1983 photograph. The politicians clashed over what type of temporary station to provide in the estimated three-year interval before the new station would be ready for use. (WPPL.)

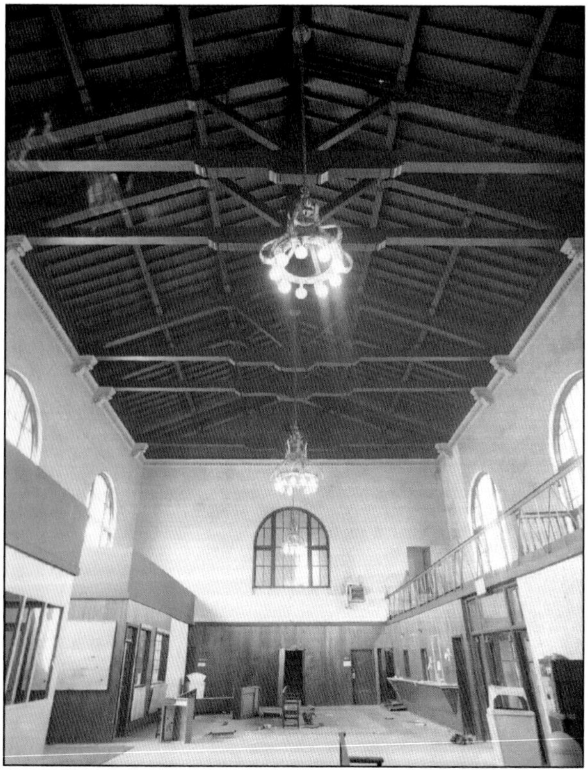

In September 1983, after months of planning and debating by commuters and public officials, the railroad station was dismantled. The stately interior is seen here as demolition work started. (WPPL.)

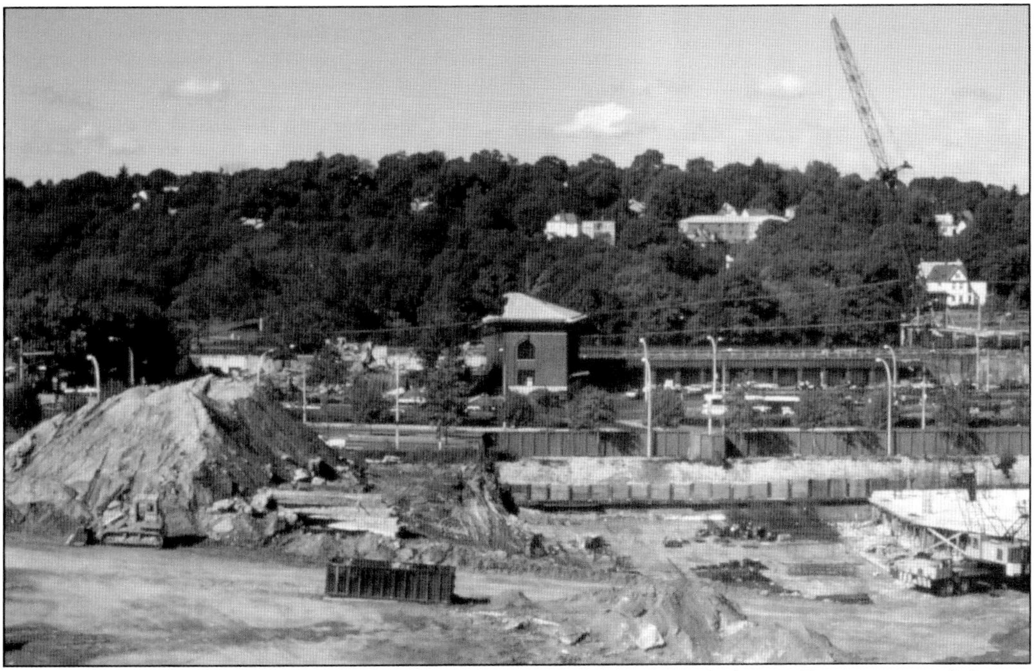

The decision about where to locate the temporary station was made but still controversial. It was located north of Main Street and consisted of attached prefabricated units housing a ticket office, a newsstand, restrooms, and a snack bar. This October 1983 photograph captured the last vestige of the 1914 station. (WPCA.)

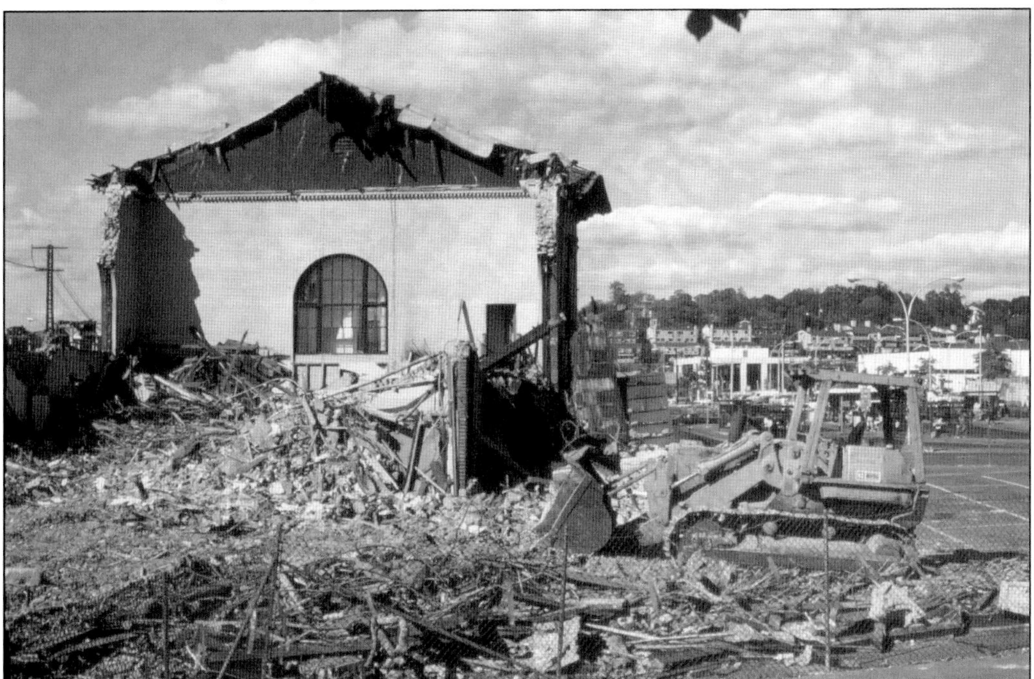

Demolition revealed the familiar interior of the doomed station. The new train station was built one block north of the old one. (WPCA.)

Westchester County... The Golden Apple

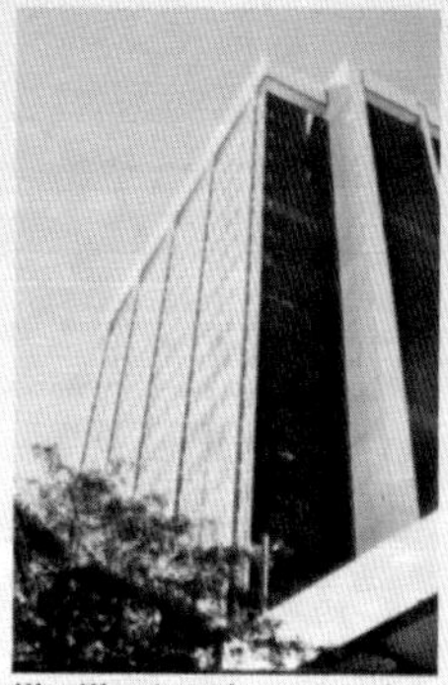

Welcome to a look at one of the unique suburban areas in the United States — Westchester County. "The Golden Apple" is a great place to call home for your business or your family — or both. This publication is an introduction and guide to one of America's most prestigious counties, and it also serves as a directory to some of our important business firms.

The Golden Apple is growing because it is unique. To homeowners, Westchester means excellent schools, plenty of cultural opportunities, and acres of golf and other recreation. It can be identified also by its green, rolling hills and fine suburban homes. For business people, Westchester means convenience because it borders on New York City and because a growing number of banks, brokerage houses, and other financial institutions are transforming it into a major financial center.

No doubt about it . . . The Golden Apple has a lot to offer. We hope you'll come see for yourself.

A Bit of History

Westchester's past is as illustrious as its future promises to be. In 1642, Jonas Bronck was the first settler to move north from Manhattan, when he purchased 500 acres from the Indians along the Bronx River. Other European settlers came to southern Westchester over the next 100 years, including the French Huguenots, the Dutch (Yonkers was originally called "Jonkheer's Land"), the English, and the Quakers. Farming was predominant, and large tracts of land were carved out by wealthy gentlemen.

The Revolutionary War era was one of the most significant in county history. The Battle of White Plains on October 28, 1776, is perhaps the best known of early Revolutionary battles. This skirmish led only to minor casualties but was very important from a strategic point of view, allowing Washington's Army to survive and withdraw to New Jersey.

The Battle of White Plains is only one example of Westchester's significant colonial history. In Mount Vernon, American freedom of the press was born during John Peter Zenger's trial at what is now a national historic site, St. Paul's Church. And in 1776, the State of New York was born at the White Plains courthouse.

Following the Revolutionary War, Westchester's commercial development was rapid. Stagecoaches were followed by railroads in the 1840s. Some of the earliest businesses were manufacturing concerns — Otis Elevator in Yonkers, a carpet mill in Yonkers, and the Port Chester Bolt and Nut Company. The corporations would arrive later.

With the use of railroads and "newfangled" automobiles, Westchester quickly became known as a "commuter" bedroom suburb. That characterization has undergone steady change since World War II and especially since the 1960s, when dozens of large corporations and financial institutions began moving in. As population and business development increased, beautiful homes followed. Today, more people work and live in Westchester than ever before.

There are many historical symbols that remain. Tours are currently offered at restored estates such as Philipsburg Manor in North Tarrytown and Washington Irving's Sunnyside in Irvington. Washington's headquarters is located on Virginia Road in North White Plains, and the restored Lyndhurst, a Gothic architectural masterpiece, is in Tarrytown.

The Golden Apple Today

Ask any Westchesterite why he likes his home county. Chances are one of the reasons will be proximity to New York City. Both residents and business people enjoy the convenience of being minutes away from midtown Manhattan — the commercial center of the world, as well as the home of many fine museums, Broadway shows, nightclubs, ballet, and opera. All are within easy reach by car or train.

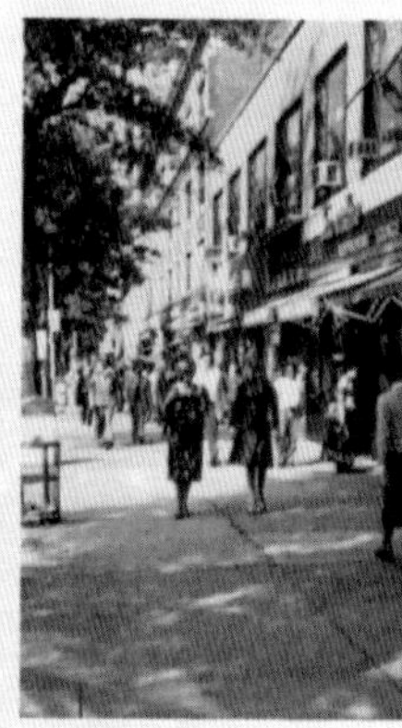

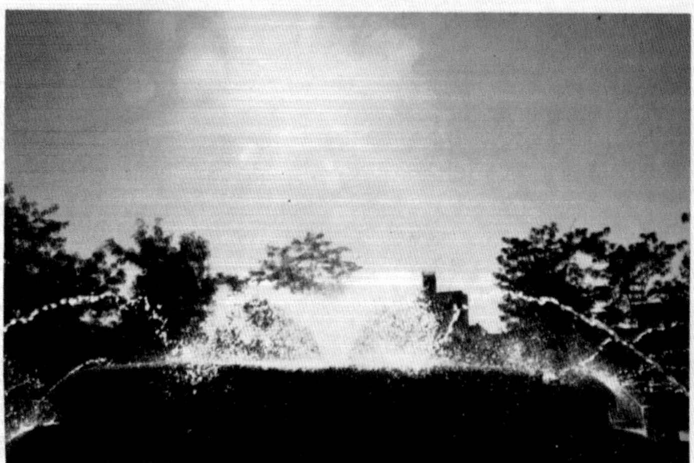

Top: Westchester One towers over the city

Left: The fountain in front of Bergdorf Goodman is a refreshing sight on a warm summer day

Above: Bustling downtown shopping district

Opposite page: An aerial view of White Plains looking eastward

6

The Golden Apple was a marketing scheme by the White Plains Chamber of Commerce to give Westchester County an identity to rival New York City, the Big Apple. The materials it released were superlative in every respect—the best businesses, best schools, best neighborhoods, best recreational opportunities, and best location! (WPPL.)

Ten

The 1990s

As the 20th century drew to a close, White Plains was at something of a low point in development activity, though there was no corresponding loss of civic pride or engagement. The effects of corporate downsizing, mergers, and restructurings created the conditions for companies like Nestle (which had come in 1952) to close their offices in White Plains.

While new development and another reshaping of the downtown area would not happen until the early 2000s when construction of City Centre began, the 1990s abound with examples of the civic engagement and local organizing White Plains is known for. The White Plains Historical Society conducted its annual events, the White Plains City Archives and library became primary sites for community memory, and organizations like the Slater Center and El Centro Hispano contributed to the vitality of the community.

Even with the ever-taller buildings and usual attempts at rebranding, White Plains remains a city full of historical buildings, places, and characters.

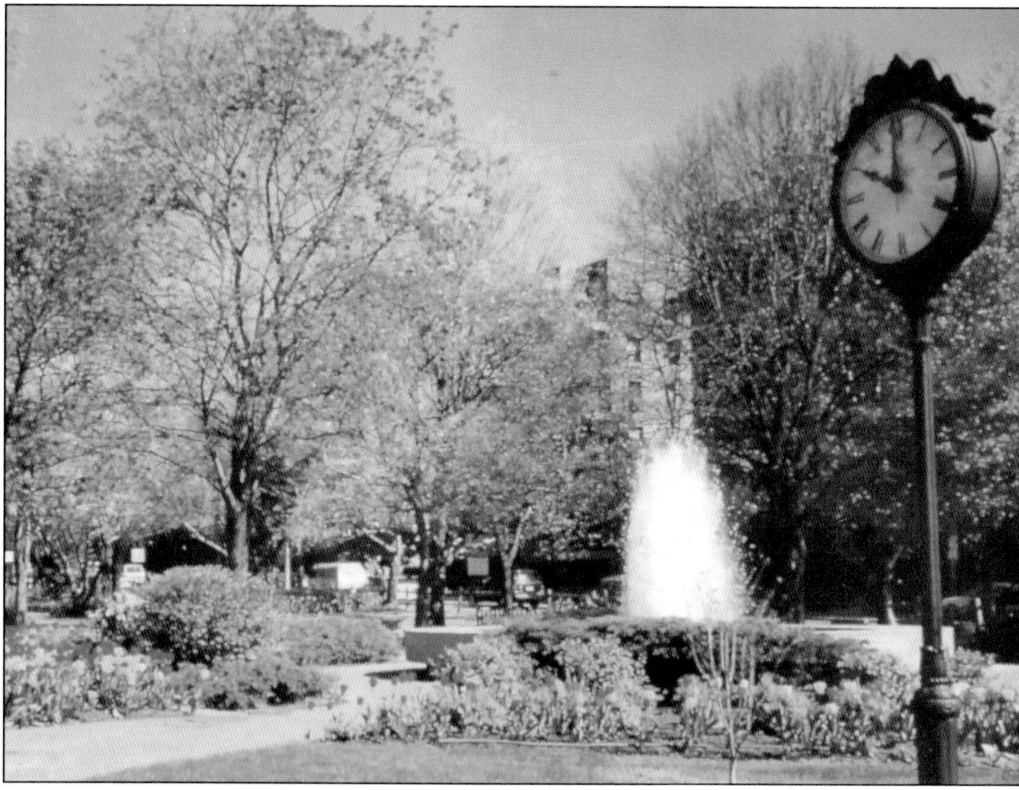

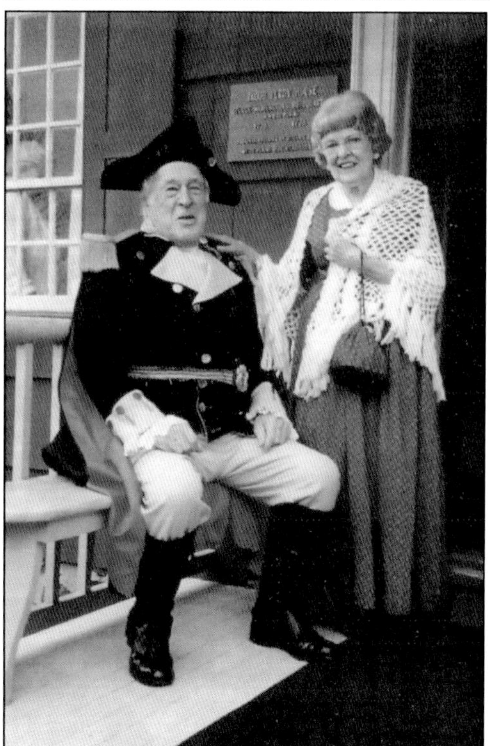

Renoda Hoffman (1909–2005), author and longtime White Plains city historian, was also very involved with the White Plains Beautification Foundation. In 1991, the foundation surprised her by donating a clock to the city in her honor. It stands in Tibbits Park, at the corner of Main Street and North Broadway. The Victorian-inspired design is over 13 feet tall and is accompanied by a bronze plaque that pays homage to Hoffman and recognizes the 25th anniversary of the White Plains Beautification Foundation. (WPCA.)

Stephen Holden Jr. and city historian Renoda Hoffman are seen here in their familiar roles as George and Martha Washington at a Jacob Purdy House event in February 1992. Sponsored by the White Plains Historical Society, the celebration was in honor of George Washington's 260th birthday. (WPCA.)

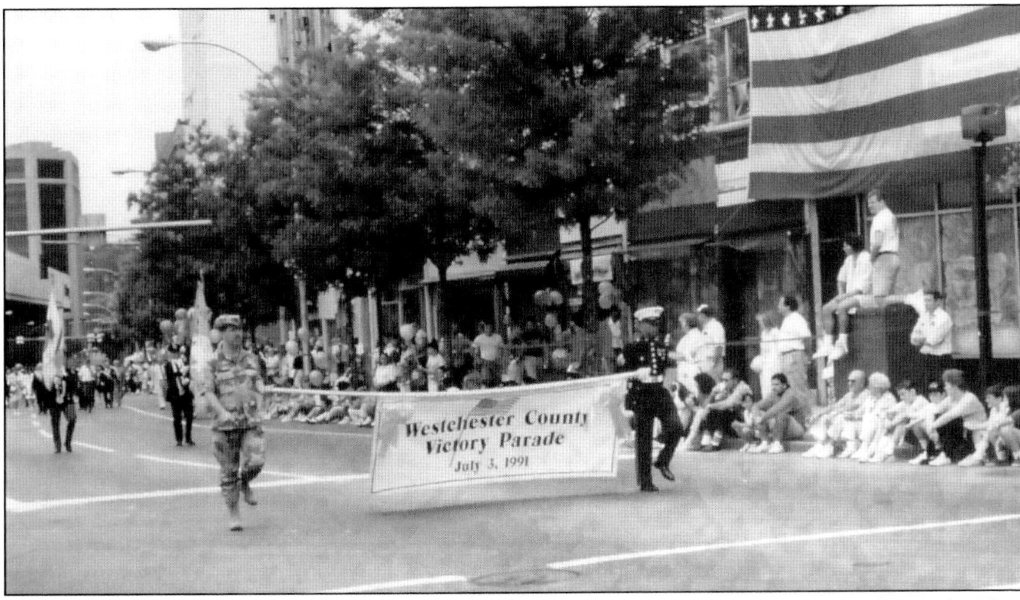

Organized by the City of White Plains and Westchester County, a victory parade was held on July 3, 1991, as a "hometown" salute to those who served their country during the Persian Gulf War. Police estimated attendance to be 137,000 at the midweek parade in downtown White Plains. The parade included floats, fire apparatus, and military vehicles. (WPCA.)

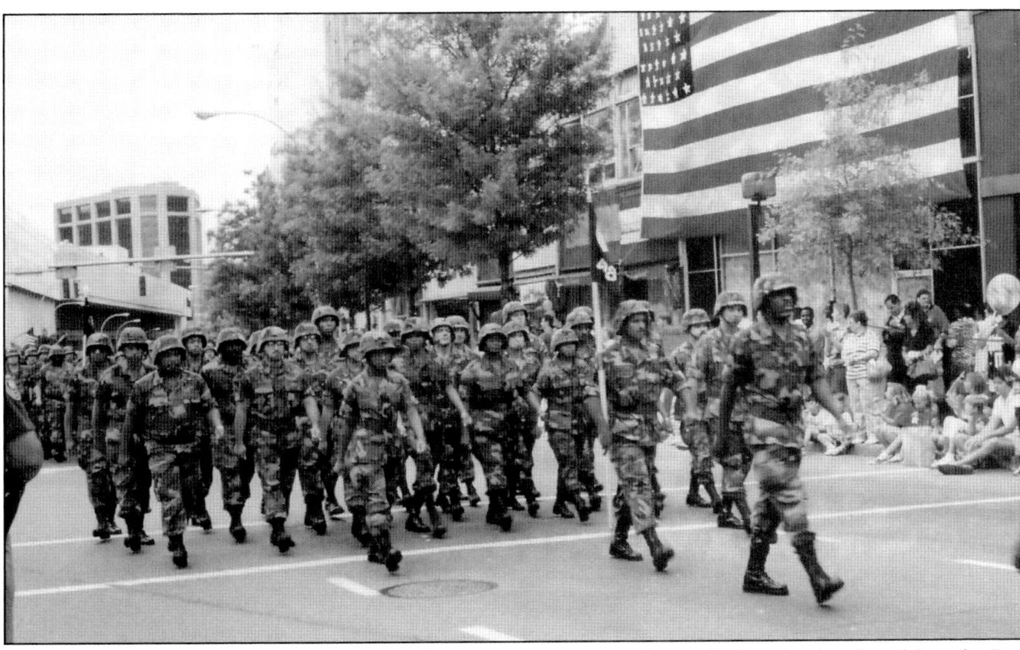

A total of 10,000 marchers participated in the victory parade, including high school bands, Boy and Girl Scout troops, and public officials. A total of 2,000 troops from the Greater New York City metropolitan area marched, 737 of them from Westchester County. During the reception at the Westchester County Center after the parade, those who served overseas received medals inscribed "Operation Desert Storm, 1990–1991." (WPCA.)

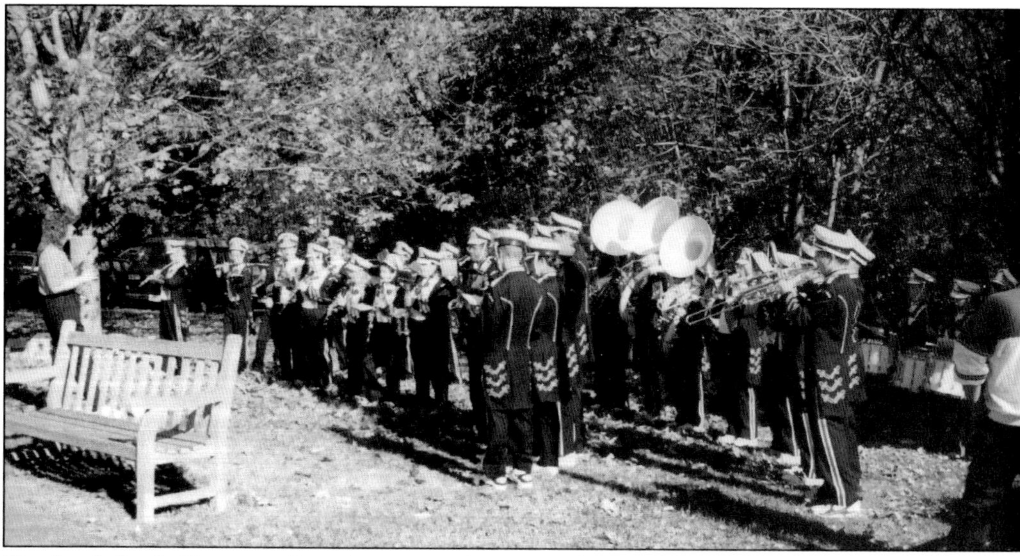

The Jacob Purdy House, on Park Avenue, is the setting for annual events to celebrate Washington's birthday in February and the anniversary of the Battle of White Plains in October. Shown here, the White Plains High School marching band, under the direction of Lesley Tompkins, plays patriotic music for an October event. (WPCA.)

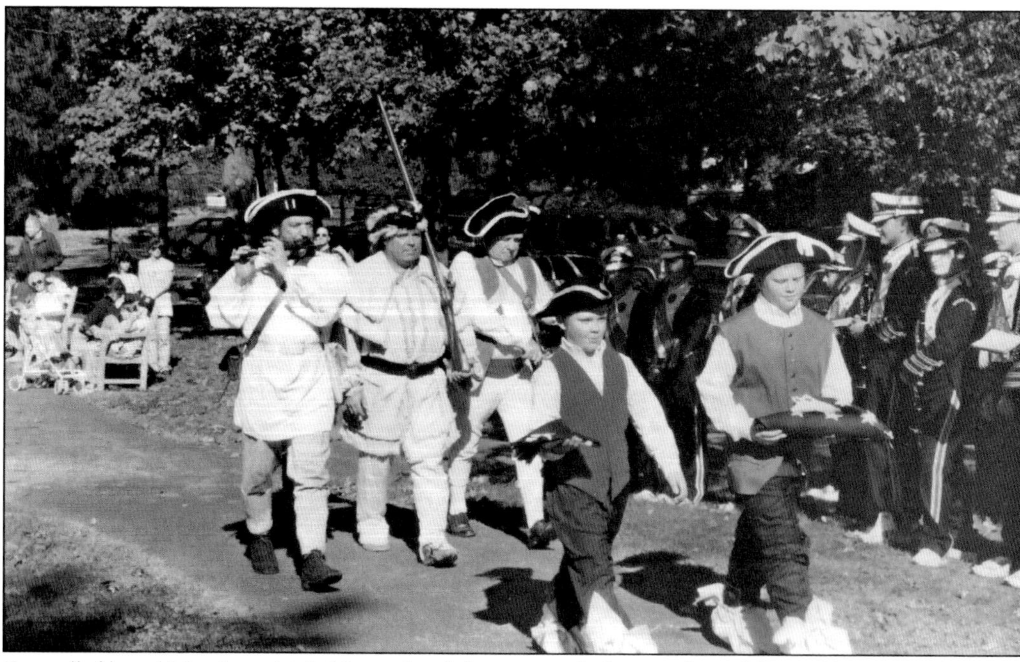

Scott (left) and Matthew (right) Jones lead the way with flags and are followed by an unidentified man; their father, Denis Jones (center); and drummer Ray White (right) at one of the celebrations at the Jacob Purdy House. The White Plains Historical Society is the caretaker for the Jacob Purdy House and sponsors the programs held there. (WPCA.)

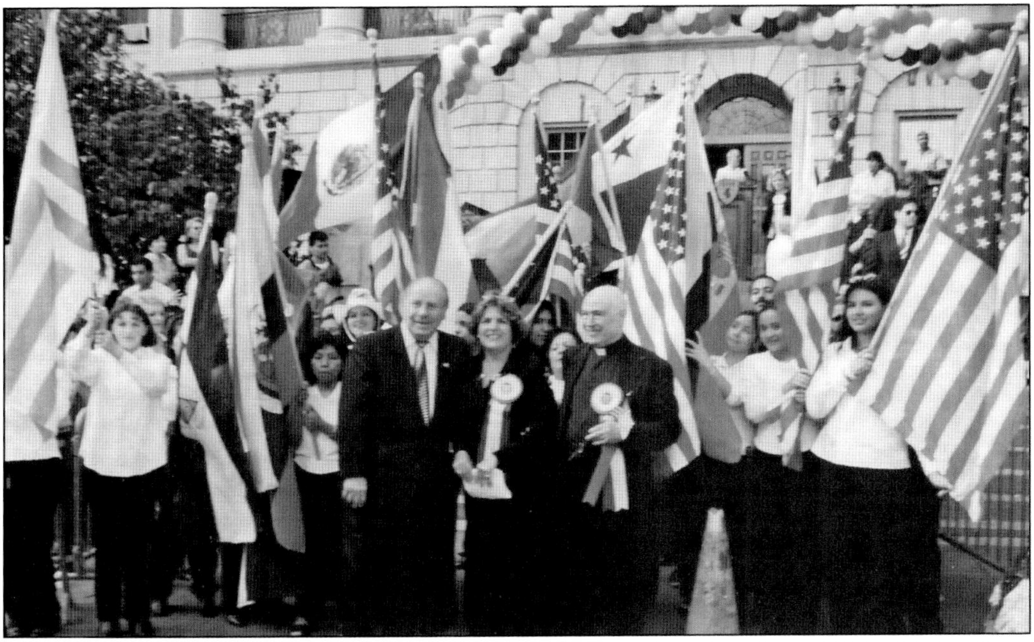

El Centro Hispano was a cosponsor of the first Hispanic Day Parade in White Plains. This picture shows Mayor Joseph Delfino; Isabel E. Villar, founding executive director of El Centro Hispano; and Rev. Jose Vilaplana, assistant pastor at St. Bernard's Church. Founded in 1974, El Centro Hispano sponsors programs in education and technology, support services, cultural events, outreach, mentoring, and scholarships. (Courtesy of El Centro Hispano.)

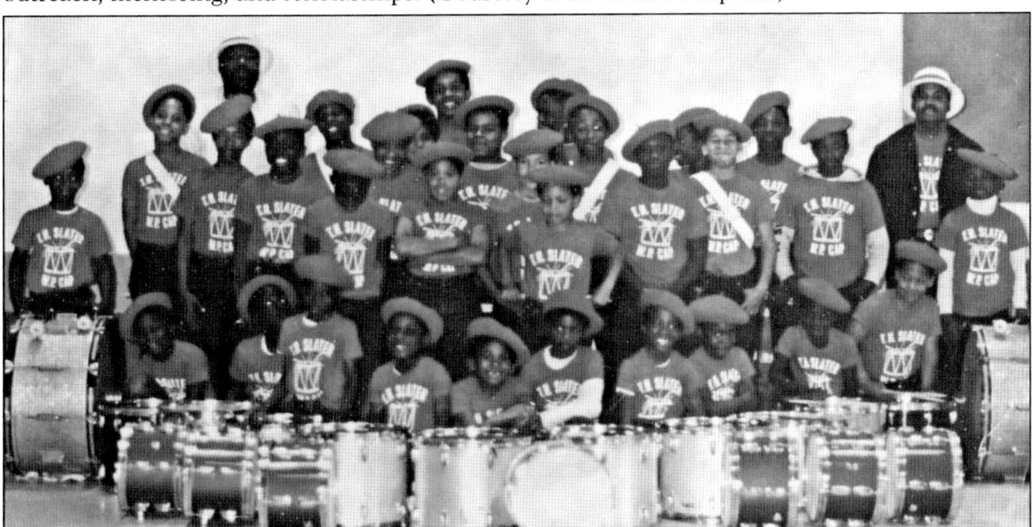

Shown here is the Thomas H. Slater Center Drum Corps shortly after it was established in the mid-1980s. The corps director, Jerome "Bump" Robinson, is in the back row at left, and Charlie C. Booth, first executive director of the Thomas H. Slater Center, is at right. The Slater Center was opened in 1979 and named for Rev. Thomas H. Slater, late pastor of the nearby Bethel Baptist Church. The drum corps was a popular group in local and county parades and was renamed the Jerome "Bump" Robinson Drum Corps after Robinson's death in 2004. (Courtesy of the Thomas H. Slater Community Center, Inc.)

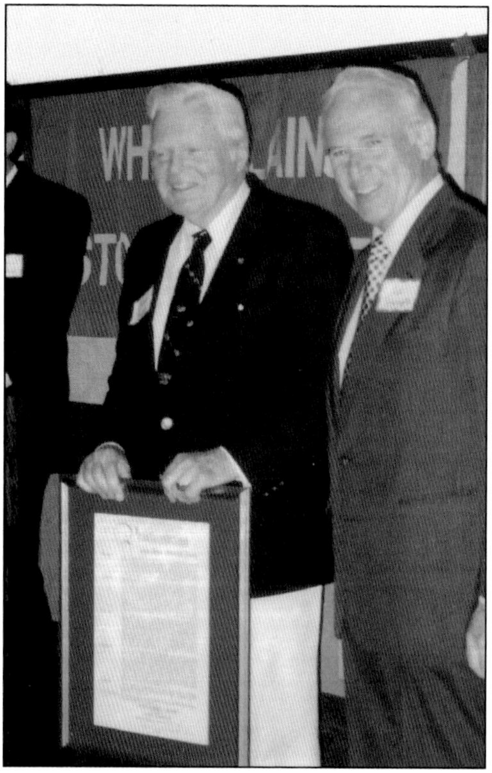

Shown here with White Plains Historical Society president Jack Harrington (right) is the man known as "Mr. White Plains," Robert F. Ruger (1912–2010). After decades of government and community service, he was honored in 1994 as a "Citizen Extraordinaire" by the White Plains Historical Society. Ruger, a lifelong White Plains resident, was a leader and volunteer and served White Plains in many ways, including 12 years on the Common Council. Among numerous awards he received was a Silver Star after World War II for raising over $25 million in war bonds. (WPCA.)

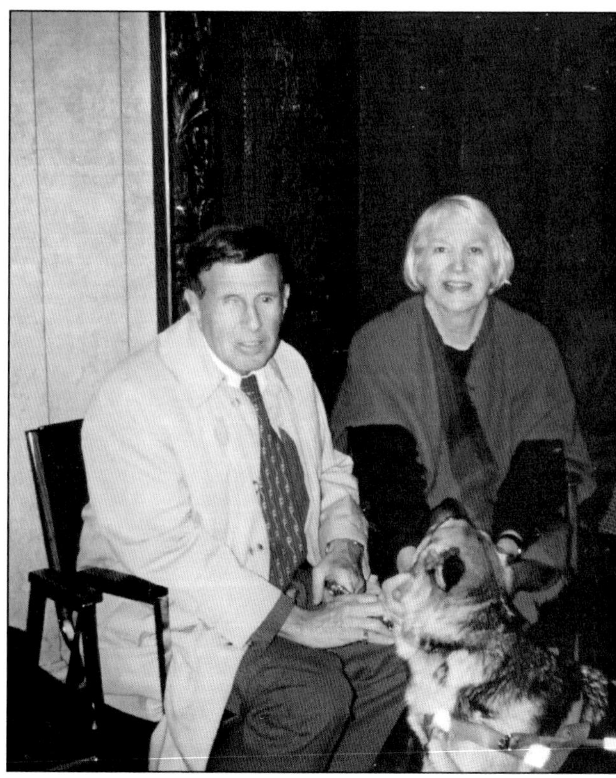

The White Plains Beautification Foundation began as a small committee within the chamber of commerce in 1952, the inspiration of city resident Brian Wallach. Wallach was the group's first president and continues to serve the foundation, along with his wife, Beth, who was president from 1987 to 1990. Beth also hosted a popular cable show called *This Blooming City* for 22 years. The Wallachs were honored as "Citizens Extraordinaire" in 1998 and are seen here with Brian's service dog Fritz in 1999. (WPCA.)

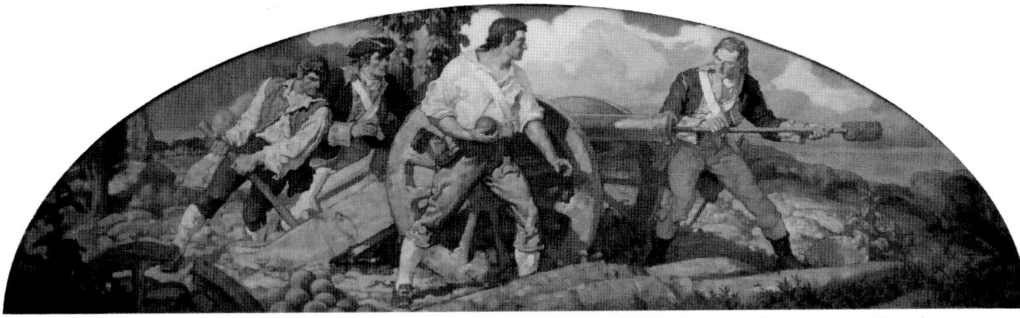

This crescent-shaped 1932 painting on canvas, by Edmund Ward, once hung over the doorway to the postmaster's office on Grand Street. Inspired by Ward's design for the postage stamp in 1926, it has commonly been called "Hamilton at the Cannon." However, Ward, in a 1983 interview, said he did not paint Hamilton. He said the painting depicts "a humble gun crew." After the post office building was sold, Ward, fearing his mural would be lost to demolition, arranged for it to be restored and transferred to the White Plains Public Library, where it still hangs today. (WPPL.)

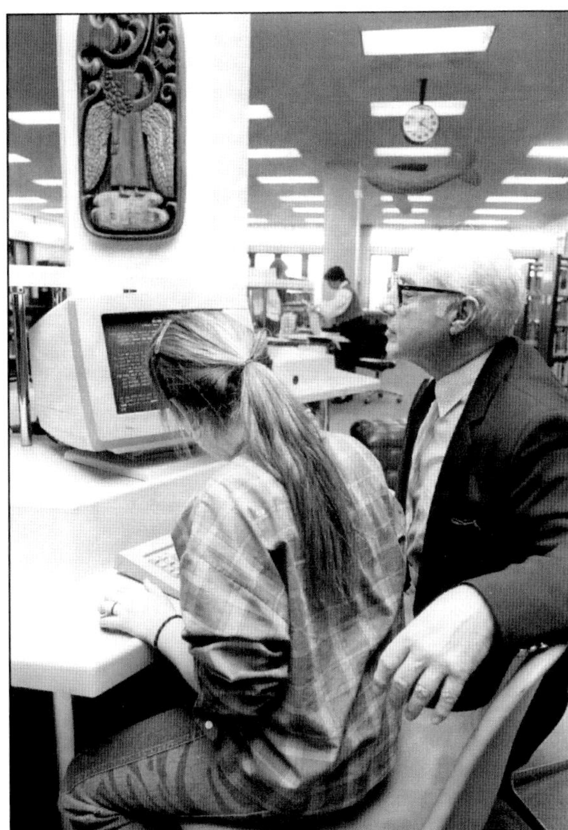

Mayor Alfred Del Vecchio is shown how to use LUIS, the public library's online public access catalog, in the early 1990s. Del Vecchio served as mayor from 1976 to 1993, a time of continued development for the city that included the opening of the Galleria and the Westchester Financial Center. (WPPL.)

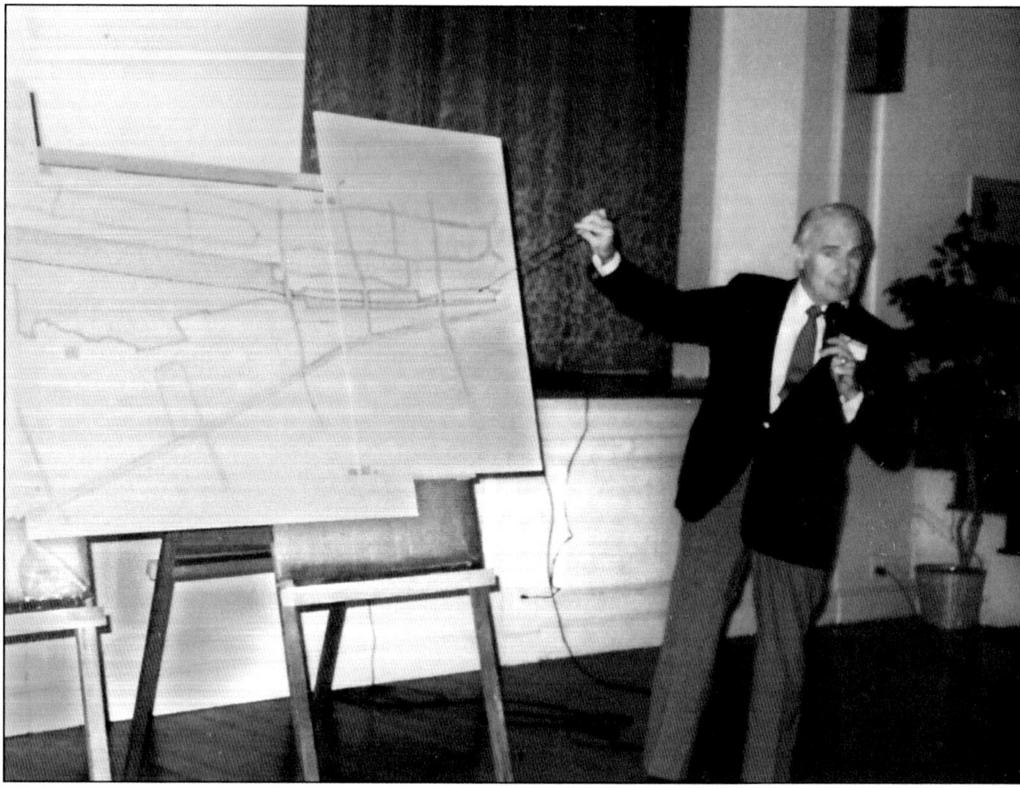

John W. "Jack" Harrington (1919–2017) was passionately dedicated to preserving the history of White Plains. He was president of the White Plains Historical Society from 1988 to 2003 and, in concert with his wife, Peg, who served as secretary, spearheaded many projects for the society. Jack was keenly interested in conservation issues, serving for 12 years on the city's Conservation Board. He is shown here in 1993 making a presentation during his successful campaign to create a walking trail out of the abandoned roadbed of the New York, Westchester & Boston Railway. The trail was later named in his honor. (WPCA.)

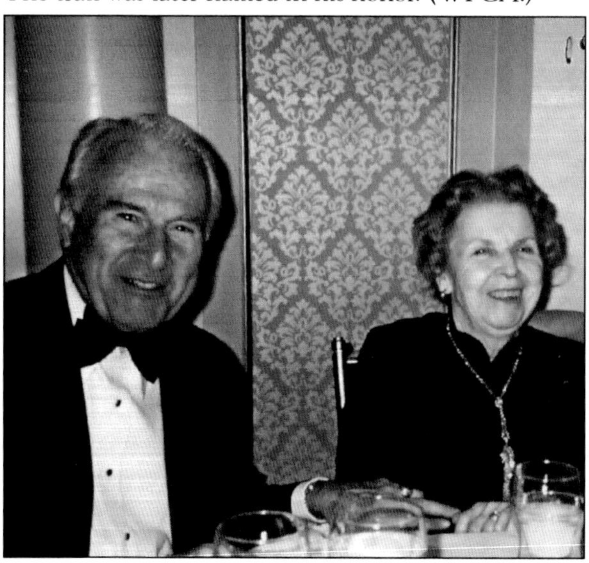

Peg and Jack Harrington are seen here celebrating at a testimonial dinner in April 1998. They worked tirelessly as a team to direct and support historical society functions and Purdy House maintenance. Jack's obituary in 2017 noted, "He reminded us over and over again that the best way to weave a diverse community together [is] through a shared 'sense of place.' " (WPCA.)

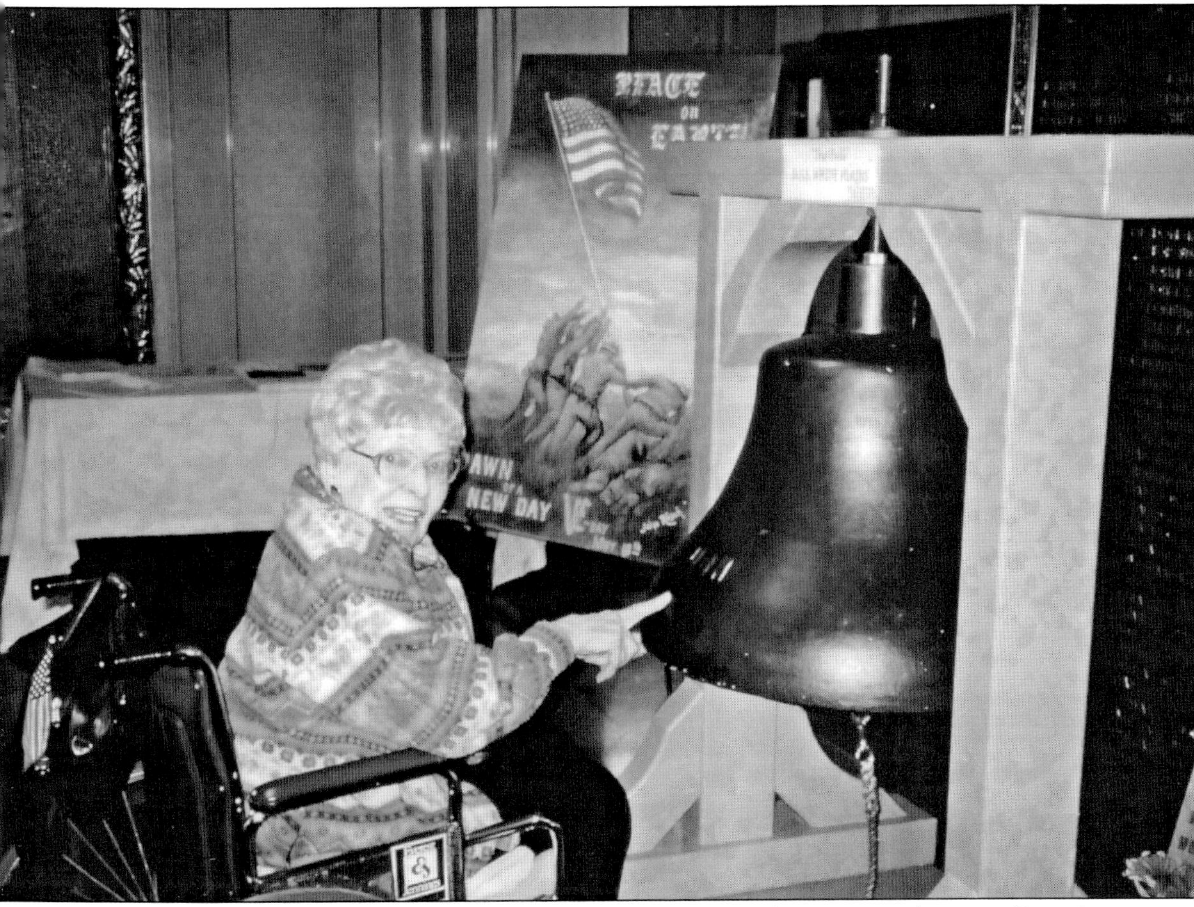

On October 5, 1999, the City Clerk's Office sponsored a tribute to longtime city historian Renoda Hoffman on the occasion of her 90th birthday. An exhibit featured examples of Hoffman's works as a writer, editor, artist, photographer, and historian and noted that "her vision inspired the creation of our City Archives." Hoffman is shown here at the birthday reception with the original bell from the first USS *White Plains*. Mayor Joseph DelFino announced that the White Plains City Archives would be named the Renoda Hoffman Room. (WPCA.)